Business Barometers

used in the

Management of Business

and

Investment of Money

*A Text Book on Applied Economics
for Merchants, Bankers
and Investors*

By

Roger W. Babson

83055

(TWENTY-SIXTH EDITION)
Issued 1937

Published by
BABSON'S REPORTS INCORPORATED
Babson Park, Mass., U. S. A.

First Edition Copyrighted 1909
Second Edition Copyrighted 1910
Third Edition Copyrighted 1910
Fourth Edition Copyrighted 1911
Fifth Edition Copyrighted 1912
Sixth Edition Copyrighted 1913
Seventh Edition Copyrighted 1914
Eighth Edition Copyrighted 1915
Ninth Edition Copyrighted 1916
Tenth Edition Copyrighted 1917
Eleventh Edition Copyrighted 1918
Twelfth Edition Copyrighted 1919
Thirteenth Edition Copyrighted 1920
Fourteenth Edition Copyrighted 1920
Fifteenth Edition Copyrighted 1921
Sixteenth Edition Copyrighted 1923
Seventeenth Edition Copyrighted 1925
Eighteenth Edition Copyrighted 1926
Nineteenth Edition Copyrighted 1928
Twentieth Edition Copyrighted 1929
Twenty-first Edition Copyrighted 1929
Twenty-second Edition Copyrighted 1931
Twenty-third Edition Copyrighted 1933
Twenty-fourth Edition Copyrighted 1935
Twenty-fifth Edition Copyrighted 1936
Twenty-sixth Edition Copyrighted 1937

by

Roger W. Babson

Printed in the United States of America

" People will endeavor to forecast the future and make
agreements according to their prophecy. Speculation of this
kind by competent men is self-adjustment of society to the
probability." — *Judge Holmes in a United States Supreme
Court decision.*

TABLE OF CONTENTS

FOREWORD

"*A study of past disturbances leads to the conviction that no business change has occurred which was not preceded by loud warnings. These warnings ought not to pass unheeded, and in order to recognize them promptly it is necessary that accurate statistics be furnished. Much improvement has been accomplished in the last few years, though it is to be regretted that so much of our statistical information is fragmentary or inaccurate. Official and private publications furnish much valuable information. They include voluminous figures of deposits and loans of banks, movement of specie, exports and imports, railway earnings, wholesale prices, and the condition and probable yield of crops. A vital defect in many of them is the omission to give, for purposes of comparison, similar figures for previous months and years. Another defect is the absence of uniformity in the methods and classification employed. These comparative statistics would afford a means of determining the trend of events, and give warning when prices are unnaturally high or any branch of business is overdone. It is also noteworthy that we do not sufficiently consider statistics relating to the course of affairs in foreign countries, the influence of which upon our own condition is of the utmost importance, by reason of the enlargement of our trade and the closer international relations of modern commerce. Other statistics, which are inadequate or lacking and which would be of great value, are those pertaining to the employment of labor, capital invested in new enterprises, amounts expended in new construction, volume of production in the various kinds of manufactures, and statistics of state banks and savings institutions similar to those pertaining to national banks. After making due allowance for the insufficiency of statistics, it must be said that the failure to pay sufficient attention to those already available is equally to be regretted."*

The above was written in 1902 by the late Hon. Theodore E. Burton, U. S. Senator from Ohio, and is very interesting as a matter of prophecy. The "vital defects" mentioned have, however, now largely been overcome, and the office of the author of this book has obtained and is now able to furnish regularly figures which Senator Burton then so much desired.

PREFACE

(Fundamental Principles which readers of this book should
always keep in mind.)

NEITHER this book nor any other can aid a
banker, merchant, or investor to reach his
goal *within a short time*. Nobody knows
nor *can know* what conditions or prices are to exist
within a few weeks, or even months, and 95% of
the men who endeavor to take advantage of these
monthly movements — or even who worry about
them — never make much headway.

Success is the result of ignoring these monthly
fluctuations in commodity and security prices,
and of striving to anticipate and profit by the
major movements coming every few years. *These
major movements can be foretold* if one will spend
the necessary time and money in studying fundamental conditions. *Therefore a fortune is within
the grasp of every reader of this book who has and
uses the necessary figures.* There are, however,
two requisites:

1. One must develop self-control, both to refrain
from attempting to profit by the monthly fluctuations, which 95% of the people endeavor to follow,
and to act quickly and take advantage of the major
movements, which 95% of the people fail to profit
by, either because they are infatuated with prosperity or scared by panic or depression.

2. One must develop patience, and remember
that it takes years to build up success in this way;

that it is an especially slow process at first, so that what we spend for obtaining the data the first few years may seem large during these early years. The expense, however, is infinitesimal compared with the value. In truth, it is due to the fact that most people ignore these figures, that 90% of our business men are said to " fail."

Some ask: " Are not students of fundamental conditions working to their own disadvantage in urging others to unite in this work? " My answer is *"Theoretically* — yes." On the other hand, every honest preacher, physician, lawyer, teacher, judge, and soldier who is truly serving his function in the community must strive to eliminate the trouble, upon the existence of which he is dependent for a livelihood. But, until the world no longer needs preachers, physicians, lawyers, judges, soldiers, there will be periods of overexpansion and depression when commodities and securities will rise and decline in price. *We who study fundamental conditions and act in accordance with what they teach,* will both perform a distinct service to our country and slowly but surely create for our institutions and ourselves huge fortunes.

The writer of this book wishes to acknowledge the aid which he has received from many friends in this country and abroad. He wishes also to thank his efficient corps of assistants who have aided greatly in the compilation, and commends the various books, papers, and periodicals which he has quoted from or used in other ways.

He also wishes again to thank his many friends in the various stock exchange firms, bond houses, and banks who have been patient during the experimental and formulative stages of this work. These friends have not only recognized the difficulties under which the work has been performed, but have always aided greatly by criticisms and suggestions. May the writer never abuse this friendship!

R. W. B.

BABSON PARK, MASS., January, 1937

CHAPTER I

STATISTICS are divided into two classes, viz.: Comparative Statistics and Fundamental Statistics; and the following gives a short description of these two classes:

(1) Comparative Statistics

So far as the merchant is concerned, comparative statistics relate to the weight, quality, age, and method of manufacture of the merchandise in which he deals, together with such " trade figures " as are published in the trade journals.

From the investor's point of view, comparative statistics include all particulars concerning the bonded debt, the earnings, and the general physical and financial condition of properties. Such statistics are very necessary to bankers and investors for comparing similar securities of different companies, or different securities of the same company. If such data are always up to date, such comparative statistics are very valuable for enabling one to select safe securities, either for permanent investment or for buying and selling again. As the largest and most successful stock exchange brokers, bond houses, and mercantile firms are already well supplied with comparative statistics, and, so far as they are useful, are obtaining excellent results from

them, we shall not here discuss details concerning
this class.   It should be clearly understood, however, that such statistics are worthless for determining the *general course* of the entire market.

Comparative statistics determine only actual
values, enabling one to select safe securities or good
merchandise, or to select the better of two or more
companies' securities or grades of merchandise.
With the general market conditions remaining
fixed, comparative statistics might be used for
forecasting a rise or a decline; but the general
market is so seldom stable, that comparative statistics cannot be depended upon to serve this
purpose.   It is this fact, that they are inadequate
for analyzing general conditions, that has brought
comparative statistics into ill repute.   The *market*
value of securities or merchandise may continually
decline, and the *intrinsic* value of the same increase, or vice versa.

Whoever bases either purchases or sales upon
earnings, physical conditions, or other comparative
statistics alone *with the idea of selling at a profit*,
usually loses money.   Note the phrase, " With the
idea of selling at a profit."   Such statistics may be
used for selecting a *safe* investment or *good* merchandise, such as one may desire to hold perma-
nently or for a very long while; but they are
absolutely worthless for the " turns."   It is because
this fact is not being recognized by many firms,
content with accumulating only comparative statistics, that even with their elaborate statistical
departments they are often on the losing side.   In

short, comparative statistics treat only of surface conditions.

(2) Fundamental Statistics

Fundamental statistics relate to *underlying* conditions of the country and make it possible to analyze demand, supply, money conditions, etc. Fundamental statistics, although now used by only the most careful investors and merchants, are by far the most necessary and profitable.

It is the purpose of this book to show the importance of considering underlying and fundamental conditions before buying or selling securities or merchandise.

The idea that we *must* have periods of over-expansion and depression every few years is entirely untrue. In this sense there is no such thing as a business " cycle."

There is no circle of events through which business absolutely must pass. The trend of business depends upon what people do. When the majority try to get more than they give, over-expansion results, and this in turn demands contraction and readjustment. If there had been no over-expansion there would have been no need of readjustment. The way to prevent business depressions is to keep business at an average rate of prosperity — in other words, prevent the inflation and over-expansion which make depressions necessary.

The welfare of any nation depends upon the development of its resources and the efficiency of distribution. As these two factors are increased the people of that country can have more prosperity,—that is, they can have more of the comforts they desire. This is the only way in which the real welfare of any people can be improved,—by producing more goods and distributing them with less waste. When you look back over our business history, you see a continuous series of fluctuations. We have had periods of intense activity, high prices, speculation and borrowing, followed by periods of depression, falling prices, and failures. The first we called "boom times"; the latter "hard times." In reality, however, the "boom times" were only an effort to borrow from the future — to have more luxuries than the development of our resources warranted. The "hard times" were the natural reaction, during which we paid up for our excesses.

Consequently past financial history has consisted of distinct movements, and, although of different durations, each movement has usually consisted of four periods, namely:

1. A Period of Over-expansion
2. A Period of Decline
3. A Period of Depression
4. A Period of Improvement

Sometimes as in the 1890's for example an area may temporarily be interrupted and develop in two or more parts.

The idea that reckless over-expansion can ever become permanent and will not be followed by a business depression is false. The idea that there can be an unlimited period of depression without succeeding general activity and high market prices, is likewise a mistaken notion.

It, however, should be remembered that there are *major* swings of about twenty years' duration, and also minor movements of about three to five years' duration.

Theoretically, there should be a state where everybody is prosperous and nobody overtrades, where the cost of living is reasonable, and the wage-earner has a margin to save for old age or establish a higher standard of comfort. Yet it is true that we have never so far seen a condition so equable.

The record of crises and booms can be carried back beyond the history of this country. We can start from the opening years of the eighteenth century, when William of Orange was on the English throne. We can trace therefrom a complete rotation once in five to twenty years, and we can carry it into the last century with conditions exactly reflected on this side of the Atlantic. A condition of equilibrium is apparently the most difficult of all for the world's trade to maintain.

" Business may be quietly good, but that ambition to which we probably owe also the greater part of the world's progress insists upon forcing it beyond reasonable capacity. The result is always the same. The result of years of saving is over-confidence, inflation, waste, conversion of floating wealth into fixed wealth, and, finally, collapse and panic. Here is the plain evidence of two hundred years, and it may be assumed at no risk that it is the evidence of all commercial systems. Joseph with his seven fat years and his seven lean years expressed nothing more.

" What is not so readily realized is that a panic is followed by rapid recovery in stock prices, and one slower but still relatively quick in general business. This again is followed by an arrest in business, where, contrary to assumptions just as hasty and ill balanced as those which caused the bear attitude on the panic break, boom conditions are not immediately restored, nor does anything of the kind develop within a year or so after the crisis. The first recovery runs too far and has always run too far. What follows is not collapse, but dullness. It becomes imperative to make real savings in order to build up for the next boom in business."

A list of subjects about which merchants and investors systematically collect, analyze, and index statistics, is given on the following page, and for convenience they are combined under twelve headings, which headings are herewith described in full. In the later Chapters IV, V, and VI many of these important subjects are discussed in detail. These are the subjects studied by the oldest, richest, and most conservative financial and mercantile houses of the world for determining which of the above-mentioned periods the country is experiencing or is about to enter *at any given time*. The use of fundamental statistics eliminates much guessing and uncertainty concerning mercantile or stock market movements.

The only requirement is to collect, tabulate, and study the weekly and monthly figures as they are received. These plainly show whether the general tendency of any market is upward or downward, and whether it is the time to buy or sell, or to do neither.

As above stated, these fundamental statistics are even more important than comparative statistics. Not only are the latter of little value, unless supplemented by these fundamental statistics, but experience has shown that such investors as have confined their operations to standard securities, and such merchants as have bought standard goods, have made fortunes for themselves and their customers by a study of these fundamental statistics exclusively.

Some of the subjects generally used are:

Building and Real Estate: Including all New Building, Fire Losses, and records of the number of real estate sales.

Bank Clearings and Check Transactions: Clearings and Check Transactions excluding New York.

Business Failures: Failures, by number, liabilities, and percentage failing.

Labor Conditions: Employment and pay-rolls in certain industries, strikes and wage trends, living costs, trade union developments.

Money Conditions: Money in Circulation; Comptroller's Reports; Loans; Deposits and Surplus Reserve of Banks; Federal Reserve Statements.

Foreign Trade: Imports; Exports; Balance of Trade.

Gold Movements: Gold Exports and Imports; Domestic and Foreign Exchange, Money Rates.

Commodity Prices: Foreign and Domestic Commodity Prices; Production of Gold and other monetary influences.

Investment Market: Stock Exchange Transactions and Security Prices; New Securities; New Corporations formed.

Condition of Crops: Crop Conditions and Acreage.

Railroad Traffic: Gross and Net Earnings, Car Loadings, Tonnage and Number of Idle Cars.

Social and Religious Conditions: Labor Troubles and Church Membership Statistics, Political Factors.

These subjects may be briefly described as follows:

The number of miles of *new roads constructed,* and especially figures on *Building Statistics,* give a clue to what new construction work is going on throughout the country. The exactness with which business conditions could have been foretold in the past by such figures is truly marvelous. It may also be stated that iron is one of the first commodities to fall in price and one of the first to rise; therefore all merchants watch the price of iron.

Bank Clearings and Check Transactions are extremely good barometers of present conditions and are watched with keen interest by all successful merchants and manufacturers. Many large corporations each week compare the changes in their total sales with the changes in the total bank clearings or check transactions. If they find that these figures continually show an increase, while their sales remain fixed, they immediately endeavor to ascertain the reason therefor. Moreover, some firms divide the country into sections and compare by sections their sales with the bank clearings for said sections, thus having a check on the work of each individual sales office.

Failures both in number and liabilities are especially good barometers of the conditions of trade. By ascertaining each month the average number of concerns in active business and the number that have failed, the percentage of failures may be readily determined. Contrary to the ordinary impression, it is too few failures which foretell disaster and panic.

The statistics of *employment* and *pay-rolls* by the Department of Labor and by certain states are extremely valuable, even though they do not represent the whole country.

Union wage trends and *number of strikes* coupled with the trend of living costs reflect the fluctuations in general business. Trade union developments are having increasing effect on business conditions. Fluctuations of membership point to changing tides in business.

Before the enactment of the Johnson Act in 1924 restricting immigration to a definite and relatively small quota basis, manufacturers and those in the construction business studied data on immigration and emigration as indicative of the conditions of the labor market. It was noted that increasing immigration indicated good surface conditions with high-priced labor; but an excessive increase

usually foretold a period of depression. Study of
these data also showed that large steerage bookings
for other countries accompanied by reduced in-
coming steerage passengers, indicated a period of
business depression.

With restrictions of immigration, the demand
for labor is no longer reflected in the figures.
Labor-saving devices are more than making up
for the hundreds of thousands of immigrants we
formerly received each year.

Money is the basis of all trade and is therefore probably the most sensitive of all barometers.
Money is the representative in value of all things
traded in, and the scarcity of it seriously hampers
the manufacturer and the merchant. Low money
rates usually indicate poor present conditions tending toward improved business; while high rates
usually signify very prosperous present conditions,
but often foretell a coming panic. Two sources of
loan statistics are readily available. One is the
" loan and discount " item reported each week by
the leading member banks of the Federal Reserve
System, a good index of the increase or decrease in
the total borrowings of the whole country. The
second is the report of " bills discounted " by the
twelve Federal Reserve banks. When a local
bank is unable to supply its customers with loans,
it may rediscount certain of the notes it holds with
its Federal Reserve bank. In a general way, the
item, " bills discounted," indicates the extent to
which the member banks have had to call upon the
reserve banks for assistance.

In judging the banking situation, we must take into account the *supply* of money, or credit, which the banks have, as well as the *demand* for it. The rental price of money, " interest rates," like the rent of anything else, is governed by the law of supply and demand. The supply of money is best shown by the ratio of the banks' reserves to their liabilities.

Since the inauguration of the Federal Reserve System, bank reserves are held chiefly by the Federal Reserve banks. If it were not for the effect of gold imports, perhaps it would be necessary to watch only the supply of money, or reserves, in the banks. Heavy imports of gold, however, may temporarily inflate reserves without offering a safe basis for credit extension. Any increase in what is called the " reserve ratio," therefore, is always carefully analyzed by the student of fundamentals.

Figures on *Foreign Trade* are also of great value. The foreign trade of the country bears the same relation to the nation as a whole, as the income and expense of an individual bear to the financial condition of the said individual. A man who for any length of time spends more money than he receives is sure to have trouble eventually, and it is the same with a nation. Moreover, as the financial prosperity of the individual is almost in direct proportion to his net income, so the prosperity of a nation very largely depends upon the volume of its foreign trade.

Monthly *Gold Movements* are also important

for study in analyzing money rates, since the amount the banks can loan depends largely upon their gold reserves.

The subject of *Commodity Prices* is very important. The amount of money required to carry on a definite volume of business becomes very much greater as prices increase. For this reason, bankers very carefully watch commodity prices, knowing that high money rates invariably follow a marked increase in commodity prices.

The transactions and *Prices of Stocks* on the New York Stock Exchange are also interesting to merchants as well as to investors. The way money is made on the New York Stock Exchange is by *anticipating* price changes. The leading operators have statisticians continually studying fundamental conditions in order to forecast future conditions, and base their purchases and sales on the information obtained. Therefore a slowly sagging market usually means that the ablest speculators expect in the near future a period of depression in general business; and a slowly rising market usually means that improving business conditions may be expected, *unless the decline or rise is artificial and caused by manipulation*. In fact, if it were not for manipulation, merchants could almost rely on the stock market alone as a barometer, and let these large market operators stand the expense of collecting the data necessary for determining fundamental conditions. Unfortunately, however, it is impossible by studying the stock market alone to distinguish between artificial movements and natural movements. Therefore, although bankers and merchants may watch the stock market as *one* of the barometers, they should give to it only a fair and proportional amount of weight.

Of all statistics compiled by the government the most important to the business man are *Crop Reports*. Most of the government figures refer to what has happened in the past, and some of these figures are published a year or more after the events have happened. In the case of the crops, however, the Government actually forecasts. Therefore, all crop statistics are especially valuable to manufacturers and merchants.

The crops are one of the mainstays of America as nearly 25% of our population is directly dependent upon agriculture. Crop conditions formed the basis of James J. Hill's predictions and business ventures. Mr. Hill, by the way, was a great student of fundamental statistics. The principal crops, grain and cotton, have a tremendous influence upon our wealth. Many industries and mercantile firms are absolutely dependent on the crops, and commodity prices are always more or less dependent thereon. The grain reports and cotton reports issued by the government are watched with great interest. Manufacturers and merchants even watch the weather reports throughout the West, the progress of insect ravages and plant diseases, the condition of the crops in the Argentine Republic, Russia, and other countries. Crop failures are usually followed by a year of uncertain conditions.

Railroad Earnings and Carloadings are very instructive and are used by some in preference to many of the above subjects. Most manufactured goods and even supplies in the local retail stores are shipped by railroads. Therefore, a monthly record of freight which the railroads are carrying serves as a barometer of the business of all the farmers, manufacturers, and merchants of the country. Moreover, the steel companies, the car and locomotive builders, the coal industry, and a hundred other industries are directly dependent on the railroads for their prosperity. Therefore, all merchants should watch railroad earnings and car loadings, and reduce or increase their stock of goods in accordance with what these reports show.

Social and Religious Factors: Although this subject comes last on our list, it might be considered, if suitable figures could be found, by far the most valuable and important to our whole business structure. Business depressions are a direct result of extravagance, recklessness, waste, greed, and irreligion, which develop during the so-called boom times. During periods of depression, we repent of our wasteful methods, we seek to perform true service in order to get the proper remuneration, and again place reliance on the true values in life.

The political factor should perhaps also be included under this heading. Certainly, there is a relation which holds between politics and the business conditions. A study of fundamentals shows that the trend of political factors is more an effect of the other business fundamentals than a cause.

Under this head should also be tabulated statistics on general confidence, such as new securities issued, new incorporations, etc. When confidence is created and we are working toward better business these figures show startling increases. During periods of decline and depression the reverse is true. Such figures are but a meagre measure of this most fundamental group of indicators.

It is an unanswerable argument that the statistics of new members of the nation's leading churches show great gains when the country is in a depression, and declines when the country, in the midst of a boom period, is throwing away money and burning the candle at both ends.

To conclude, each of these twelve subjects is intimately bound up with what are known as " swings," during which all prices change between " high " and " low " in accordance with the Law of Equal Reaction. All financial and commercial trade during the past two hundred years has been divided into distinct movements. Each movement consists of four periods: a period of over-expansion, a period of decline, a period of depression, and a period of improvement. Each period is accompanied by distinct changes in the prices of stocks, labor, and commodities. By comparison with similar periods in previous movements, it is possible with a degree of certainty to determine at about what period in one of these " swings " we happen to be. If the pendulum swings beyond the

perpendicular, we are sure that it must swing back
of the center as far as it swung forward, *because
action and reaction are always equal.*

No country, however, can be prosperous unless
it is progressive. No nation can stand still; it
must go either forward or backward. The normal
demands of our country for new construction must
show an increase each year to have conditions
remain even constant. There must be a distinct increase in order to keep the vast number of our new
citizens busy. Therefore, in comparing the present
with the past, a similar figure does not necessarily
mean the same conditions, but in many instances
may mean an actual falling off. This is very important and must be remembered when estimating an
area to use for comparative purposes in connection
with the Babsonchart which will be described
later.*

* Some firms when interpreting figures on each of the various subjects for
surface conditions, prefer to determine each month what the proper average
figure should be for each of these subjects and note the relation between the
actual figures for surface conditions and these average figures. The average
figure on any one subject is obtained by plotting the yearly figures on that
subject for a period of ten or twenty years and by drawing on that plot a
line showing the average trend for the entire period. Firms using this
system obtain the average figure for any future time, assuming that the general direction of this average line will continue the same. Moreover, in the
case of some subjects, it is often clearer to plot the *relation of present figures
to a ten-year average* rather than the actual figures. This is especially true
with plotting commodity prices and other figures which show only a slight
variation with seasonal changes. The writer, however, believes in this
latter method only as a check upon, and not as a substitute for, the Babsonchart.

CHAPTER II

FOR the investor the amount of money which can be made by the study of fundamental statistics is limited only by the original capital, the number of years the study is continued, and the varying proportions of one's funds invested according to the plan outlined later. Comparative statistics treat of comparative conditions and are used for selecting securities and commodities which are thoroughly safe and which have the greatest prospect of increase in market value under fixed market conditions. Fundamental statistics treat of underlying conditions and are employed for determining these general market conditions and whether or not it is wise to purchase, or to sell, or to do neither.

Major Stock Swing

Many brokers urge customers to attempt to take advantage of minor movements of the stock market; recommending "short selling" for declines and the purchase of securities on margin for advances. Such advice is to be expected from a broker; but with short selling or margin purchases, there are other elements of risk. The investor taking such risks becomes a gambler. Margin trading involves great risks and tends to involve the operator in fatal and excessive complications.

One point, however, which this book would emphasize is: *A capital of a few thousand dollars can be multiplied to a capital of several hundred thousand dollars in twenty to thirty years with but little risk and without selling short or purchasing on margin.* The only requisite is a constant study of comparative and fundamental statistics and sufficient self-control to act only in accordance with what these statistics clearly indicate, refusing to listen to either the optimism or the pessimism supplied by the daily papers and by the many individuals who are always giving free advice.

The above principles apply to bonds as truly as to stocks, and should be studied by the investors who purchase only bonds, as well as those who purchase stocks. Although bonds do not fluctuate as widely as stocks and for this reason do not present as great an opportunity for profit, yet their *minimum* interest yield is absolutely fixed, which is not true of even the most conservative stocks. Bonds are especially recommended to persons dependent upon the income derived from their investments. Furthermore the writer is inclined to advise that all persons should always have a portion of their principal on deposit in a bank, or in high-grade bonds, short-term notes, or commercial paper.

Not only do students of fundamental statistics make large fortunes for themselves and their followers, but such students are the very best patriots which a country can produce. The true patriot is he who studies fundamental statistics and acts in accordance with what they teach, liquidating during a period of reckless prosperity and purchasing very heavily during days of panic and great depression. The real traitor today is he who urges on or follows the crowd during a period of over-expansion, and then locks up his money and refuses to extend aid during the dark days when banks are failing, railroads are becoming bankrupt and the wheels of industry are stopped. Therefore, with every additional person who unites in this work, the next period of over-expansion will be so much less riotous and the next panic so much less severe. There must be a reaction for everything we do, say or think. If it is not a harmful reaction, it is a beneficial one.

Investors must recognize that securities are subject to the same laws of supply and demand as other commodities and are priced at just what people are willing to pay for them. It seems clear, then, as fundamental business conditions change causing a change in the feeling of people and their willingness and ability to buy, that there will be a resulting change in the price of securities. Put in another way we may say that security prices are inclined to vary along with fundamental conditions. Of course, we are considering only trends in this case and not the day-to-day fluctuations which may be attributed to factors impossible to judge.

Changes in fundamental conditions, therefore, are of vital concern to the investor who wishes

to secure the greatest efficiency from his funds.*
These changes are of three different types.

First, there are changes in those factors which
vary with the area movements or periods of prosperity followed by periods of readjustment.
Such full periods have extended in the past over
from less than three to more than eight years.

Second, there is the long-time trend in interest
rates and commodity prices, reflecting war periods
in which undue inflation has taken place.

Third, there is the longer trend movement of the
growth of the country, shown by the X-Y Line.

The successful investor recognizes these changes
in fundamental conditions and builds his plan of
investing around them in such a way that he is safe
no matter what happens. Babson's Reports Incorporated has developed such a plan which is
called the *Continuous Working Plan For Your
Money.*

Part I of this plan recognizes the fundamental
changes which occur during different phases of the
business area movements. It consists of buying
and selling a broad list of stocks in accordance with
the Babsonchart of business conditions and related
stock fluctuations, that is, buying in periods of
depression and selling in times of prosperity and
then holding funds in liquid form until the next
period of depression.

Part II of the plan is to invest in bonds for safety
of principal with regular and assured income.

Part III recognizes the gradual growth of the

* For a complete discussion of the investment of funds see "Investment
Fundamentals" by Roger W. Babson, published by Harper & Bros.

United States by providing for the purchase of stocks in fundamentally sound, growing companies, to hold indefinitely. Intermediate price movements are a secondary consideration and reliance is placed on growth of the company over a long period.

The Babsonchart opposite page 72 shows the relationship which exists between stock price movements and fundamental business conditions. A heavy stock market decline usually precedes a recession in business, and an upward tendency in stock prices precedes a revival of business activity. It is only as one understands the underlying fundamental conditions that one is able to know when to buy and sell according to the Babsonchart plan or Part I of the *"Continuous Working Plan For Your Money."*

Major Bond Swing

On the next page is a copy of the Major Bond Swing, which shows the tendency of interest rates to decline following a catastrophe such as a great war when interest rates have been forced very high and credit greatly inflated. Following a complete liquidation of war time inflation the cycle is continued by a period when the tendency is for interest rates to rise. The years from 1920 to 1928 represented a period of generally advancing bond prices due to easy money rates. Following this came a decline beginning with 1928 and finally a crash in the bond market as England went off the gold standard in the latter part of 1931. Sub-

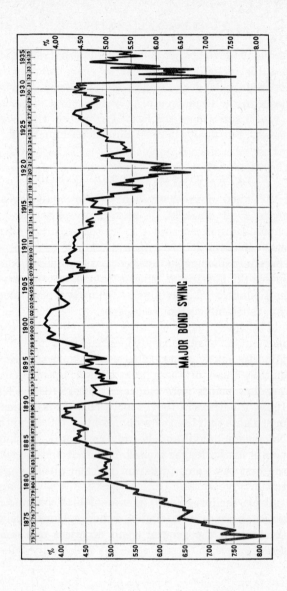

MAJOR BOND SWING

sequent developments in the domestic situation resulted in still lower levels in 1932, followed by revival. The long-swing trend to lower interest rates is the fundamental influence on bond prices. Other causes may temporarily interfere with bond trends, but finally interest rates determine them.

Long Swing of Commodity Prices

A chart of the long swing of commodity prices from 1782 to 1934 is shown on page 36. It should be noticed that during the major upward and downward movement preceding and immediately following our major wars, commodity prices do not run a smooth course. Irregularity and substantial reactions are constantly developing, reflecting current conditions.

The movements of three to seven years supplement a longer phase which covers a period of fifty to sixty years. Since the American Revolution three of these phases have materialized. The low points were reached in 1783, 1848, 1898, 1933; the peaks in 1809, 1865, 1920. It is interesting to note that the years immediately following the Napoleonic, Civil and World Wars mark the high points in the longer phases, and that the lows, in the first two cases, were not reached until twenty to thirty years later.

From the foregoing it is evident that commodity prices have characteristic trends. However, in thinking of the general trend of prices one must remember that all prices do not necessarily follow

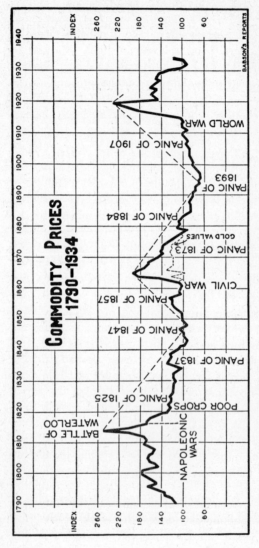

Commodity Prices 1790–1934

INDEX

1790 · 1800 · 1810 · 1820 · 1830 · 1840 · 1850 · 1860 · 1870 · 1880 · 1890 · 1900 · 1910 · 1920 · 1930 · 1940

NAPOLEONIC WARS
BATTLE OF WATERLOO
POOR CROPS
PANIC OF 1825
PANIC OF 1837
PANIC OF 1847
PANIC OF 1857
CIVIL WAR
PANIC OF 1873
GOLD VALUES
PANIC OF 1884
PANIC OF 1893
PANIC OF 1907
WORLD WAR

INDEX 260 220 180 140 100 60

BABSON'S REPORTS

As no continuous index of prices is available for this entire period, we have employed Jevon's index of English commodity prices from 1790 thru 1800, Hansen's index from 1801 to 1825, Juergen's index from 1825 to 1860, Mitchell's index from 1860 to 1880, U. S. Bureau of Labor index from 1880 to 1923 and Fisher's index from 1923 to date. These various indices follow the same trend so closely that they are easily spliced and adjusted to each other. All of the indices used to obtain the composite commodity index have been adjusted to the same base (1913 = 100).

the general trend.   Each commodity has its own
particular trend.

Fundamental Statistics for Merchants and Manufacturers

A knowledge of fundamental statistics is as important to merchants and manufacturers as to investors.   Capital invested in commodities should
not depend upon chance for its development.   To
the merchant or anyone else interested wholly or in
part in the price movement of crops, manufactures,
raw material or merchandise, general figures on
underlying conditions, controlling demand and
supply, are essential.

To know when and in what quantities to buy
commodities as well as when to sell in order to take
advantage of these swings of the market, the
merchant must know what the present conditions
are and which way the pendulum is swinging.
To know how soon to curtail credits extended to
customers, and acquire the cash needed to save
his own credit, when loans cannot easily be renewed, he must watch the Babsonchart which
measures the changes in fundamental conditions.
Keeping his eyes only on the details of his own
business will not enable him to avoid "hard times."
By broadening his study he is able greatly to
increase his profits, as well as to eliminate many of
the losses.

Largely because of the change in the long-time
trend of commodity prices the work of the purchasing agent has been placed on a more profes-

sional plane in the last few years. Evidence of this appears in the special courses for business training which are offered by various colleges and universities. A knowledge of fundamental business conditions as affecting commodity prices is stressed in these courses.

Keen competition in all lines of business has made it necessary to put high grade buyers at the helm, for income statements quickly reflect inefficiency in the purchasing department. The modern purchasing agent must combine a thorough grounding in economic principles with as broad a market experience as possible if he would succeed. He must use all possible aids, both in the form of the internal statistics of his own business and in the external statistics of general business.

The accurate control of inventory, keeping in mind the peculiar price movement of individual commodities, is a very complicated problem. It involves the interest on capital invested in commodities, the valuable storage space required, the possible loss through decline in market value, and in some cases the risk of loss through deterioration. Too many men endeavor to succeed by seeking profits for their companies entirely by driving hard bargains with those from whom they purchase. There is danger in forgetting the real needs of the business and the price movements of the commodities one buys, with disastrous results both for oneself and the company. The wise and successful man operates his purchasing department on a strictly scientific basis, budgeting his inventories in conformity with the carefully determined needs of the business and the movements of commodity prices.

The study of a number of important factors like those described in subsequent chapters of this book results in the discovery of certain clearly defined industrial movements in the past and shows their bearing today in commerce and industry, as well as on the monetary and stock market outlook.

An examination of the Babsonchart at page 72, which shows the physical volume of business and the price index of raw materials, reveals the intimate relationship which exists between them. In periods of prosperity prices tend to rise or to steady perceptibly, while in periods of re-adjustment prices fall. Mathematical proof of this relationship has been established by Dr. Frederick C. Mills of Columbia University.* He made a detailed study of price movements of group indices, and of individual commodities and found that there was a very definite cycle movement in all of these. These cycle movements correspond closely to the area movements of the Babsonchart. Furthermore the general trend of prices in Dr. Mills' study shows the same general increase as that shown in the long-swing of commodity prices covering the same period, that of 1892–1920.

The tabulation of the index figures for the Babson Industrial Commodity Index given on page 41, shows not only the minor fluctuations in prices of this group since 1906, but clearly

* See "The Behavior of Prices" by Frederick C. Mills, published by National Bureau of Economics Research, Inc.

indicates the major movement upward culminating in 1920 and the beginning of a major movement downward at that date.

To estimate the current trends of prices one must work with four distinct movements. These are (a) short-term movements caused by particular conditions affecting supply and demand factors, (b) seasonal movements, especially prominent in agricultural commodities, (c) the fluctuations corresponding with the expansion and deflation of business and (d) the long-time trend.

While the dealer in commodities will be primarily interested in price fluctuations corresponding with general business movements, he must recognize the bigger price waves of about fifty years' duration, the peaks of which have been coincident with great wars. This price movement is even more important when the outlook over a period of years is for lower prices. A heavy inventory may be carried through a temporary, short downward movement, when the long-time trend is upward. But very careful control of inventory must be had when the reverse is true, if serious loss is to be avoided.

The normal human tendency is to center interest in the very short movements in prices. Like the stock market the real profits in the commodity market are in buying and selling right according to fundamental business fluctuations.

In addition to the value of fundamental statistics for determining the trend of demand, supply and prices, they are of even more value for determining

BABSON INDUSTRIAL COMMODITY INDEX*

1908–12 Ave. = 100 (Revised)

	1907	1908	1909	1910	1911	1912	1913	1914	1915	1916	1917	1918	1919	1920	1921
Jan.	115.1	98.5	97.9	104.5	97.0	96.0	117.2	109.3	96.6	135.8	201.2	217.6	229.7	297.8	245.3
Feb.	115.4	96.9	97.9	105.2	97.1	98.3	116.7	109.9	96.8	142.1	207.3	220.2	224.7	313.7	203.4
Mar.	116.0	95.8	96.5	105.8	96.9	99.4	115.5	111.3	97.8	151.4	211.7	226.4	219.9	332.0	191.2
Apr.	115.6	94.4	96.1	106.8	96.2	101.6	114.7	107.9	98.5	157.8	215.4	236.0	218.6	334.8	180.8
May	115.7	93.6	97.6	105.4	96.0	103.9	113.8	104.0	100.4	157.0	223.6	239.9	222.5	337.4	172.5
Jun.	115.8	92.9	99.0	103.3	96.3	104.8	111.8	103.2	104.6	156.0	230.9	242.4	232.9	337.0	163.6
Jul.	115.4	92.9	98.5	102.4	96.3	106.9	111.1	103.3	104.2	153.2	234.5	245.1	239.1	336.3	156.7
Aug.	113.2	94.1	100.2	100.4	96.1	108.2	113.7	105.0	107.0	143.6	232.8	247.2	247.5	326.8	153.9
Sept.	110.3	94.6	101.4	100.9	95.7	110.5	113.8	100.3	111.3	143.9	223.3	248.1	248.6	314.8	154.7
Oct.	108.0	94.8	103.4	100.3	95.4	113.0	112.3	95.8	114.0	148.4	210.3	245.6	252.2	302.7	167.5
Nov.	106.1	96.1	105.5	100.6	95.0	114.2	112.0	95.1	121.1	171.4	211.4	242.9	260.0	277.0	177.6
Dec.	102.4	97.3	104.5	97.7	94.7	115.5	110.2	95.9	129.4	189.8	214.5	237.9	280.5	257.5	178.9

	1922	1923	1924	1925	1926	1927	1928	1929	1930	1931	1932	1933	1934	1935	1936
Jan.	185.4	195.9	186.2	178.9	185.2	176.4	163.3	169.3	154.9	129.2	107.4	97.7	136.5	132.7	135.7
Feb.	182.3	210.2	193.9	190.2	185.7	173.7	163.4	167.5	151.7	128.5	106.1	94.1	137.3	131.6	135.5
Mar.	182.4	215.4	195.6	189.7	182.1	163.0	163.2	167.7	149.7	122.2	104.6	95.0	137.2	130.3	136.0
Apr.	178.8	213.2	192.8	183.5	180.7	157.2	163.2	164.8	150.1	119.3	104.0	95.9	137.6	130.9	136.4
May	188.6	204.2	188.0	183.3	181.7	156.8	164.6	164.1	146.0	115.6	103.1	101.8	137.6	132.0	137.0
Jun.	189.9	198.1	178.8	183.3	183.2	158.7	164.6	163.7	144.8	110.5	100.8	109.4	136.2	133.0	137.1
Jul.	188.1	194.0	175.1	187.0	182.4	158.4	165.2	163.3	143.4	111.2	100.8	121.1	135.8	133.3	138.4
Aug.	185.6	191.5	173.2	187.5	183.8	161.6	167.0	163.6	141.3	111.5	103.6	128.6	134.8	132.4	138.2
Sept.	185.9	187.5	171.8	187.9	184.2	165.3	167.5	163.6	140.6	112.7	107.1	133.7	133.8	131.9	139.2
Oct.	189.0	187.4	169.5	188.0	184.2	165.1	167.8	161.6	138.2	112.7	107.1	133.6	133.0	131.0	140.6
Nov.	190.0	182.2	172.1	189.7	179.7	164.0	167.0	159.8	134.0	111.1	105.4	136.2	132.5	135.2	143.8
Dec.	192.4	180.4	176.2	187.7	178.8	163.9	169.5	157.4	132.8	109.7	101.4	136.0	132.1	136.1	146.0

*This index includes four grades of hides and leathers, print cloth and cotton yarn, newsprint, boxboard and pulp (mech. and chem.), petroleum (10 fields), wool and worsted yarns, rubber and lumber, iron and steel, bituminous coal, non-ferrous metals (copper, lead, spelter, tin), and building materials (cement, lime, bricks, glass). Each group has a weight of 10% of the total in making up the index.

the amount of credit which manufacturers and merchants should at any time extend to customers.

Most successful manufacturers and merchants have found that the system of "fixed" credit limits for customers is absolutely wrong in principle; unjust to customers; unfair to the sales force and a source of danger to the firm. Instead, a system of "flexible" credit limits should be used by which credits are increased and decreased, in accordance with the relative position and size of the latest area of the Babsonchart of business conditions explained in the following chapter. This system invariably results in greatly increased sales and yet insures that a firm shall be in a strong financial position at a time of panic or business crisis. These various practical applications of fundamental statistics cannot, however, be explained in detail in this volume.*

Bankers and Fundamental Statistics

When we realize that during the years 1930–32 there were 5,099 bank suspensions and that during the years 1921–1933 there were 16,006 bank suspensions, which equalled 53.2% of the total number of banks in existence in 1920, we can get some idea of the reason why bankers also need to study fundamental statistics.

In the first place the banker must understand the phase of the major swing through which he is passing. He must know, as must the merchant

* For a complete discussion of the practical applications of fundamental statistics, see "Business Fundamentals" by Roger W. Babson, published by B. C. Forbes Publishing Co., New York, and "Investment Fundamentals" by Roger W. Babson, published by Harper & Bros., New York.

or manufacturer, how fundamental statistics are affecting his customers' business and especially how those statistics are affecting the price of the commodity—money — in which he deals.

The period between 1892–1920 constituted the latter portion of a major swing in interest rates and commodity prices. During this period there was an increase in the dollar value of practically all goods and an upward trend in interest rates. In 1920 a different phase of the major swing began and some practices that were profitable during the former period ceased to be effective.

In addition to the suspensions mentioned above, following 1920 many banks suffered severe losses on loans made on expanded inventories manufactured and purchased at peak prices just before the re-adjustment took place. They in fact, without desiring it, suddenly became merchants who had to liquidate goods they had taken for their loans. The result of these huge losses was that bankers began to feel more keenly the necessity of studying fundamental conditions in order to avoid further losses. Many of the larger insti-tutions have gone to great expense and employed their own statisticians and economists to study these conditions. In addition they secure the point of view of independent economic and sta-tistical services which are able to give a more detached and unbiased point of view.

Again to provide adequate protection to their customers and to themselves, bankers must know the relation of credits to the business cycle. The position to be taken at any time depends upon the outlook as shown by fundamental statistics.

Conservative banks build up reserves and curtail credits during periods of over-expansion, when the public is willing to loan to anybody and to buy anything and then draw on those reserves and expand their credits during periods of depression when the public refuses to loan even to solvent borrowers or to purchase even the highest-grade securities. Moreover, for performing these two functions such banks receive a twofold reward, namely; the market rate of interest on the loans and securities held, and also every few years a large profit on the sale of securities. Moreover, banks which do not fulfill these two functions not only fail to serve fully their true purpose in the community, but also make very much smaller profits and assume very much greater risks.

That many banks heretofore have not efficiently performed these functions is shown in the failure figures above mentioned. While inability to obtain the necessary statistics for correctly judging the trend of conditions may have been excusable in earlier years, now that such statistics may be obtained at small expense from a central agency,* this cause for failure is overcome.

An Understanding of the Law of Equal and Opposite Reaction is of great Value in the Study of Credits.

* In order that firms may keep accurately informed as to present and future conditions my statisticians accumulate and analyze the necessary facts and figures used in determining the same. These figures, which are of great value in connection with the purchase of merchandise, the discounting of commercial paper and the investment of money, we can supply to our subscribers.

R. W. B.

CHAPTER III

A LL that has been said up to the present regarding Fundamental Statistics has been to show their great value to bankers, merchants and investors. It is now time to show how the subjects heretofore mentioned are studied, and what justification we have for using the laws upon which this work is based.

All readers at once associate the name of Sir Isaac Newton with an apple falling from a tree. This is because Sir Isaac was the first who asked why apples fall down instead of up, which question led to his discovery of the law of gravitation. It is evident from a study of Newton's life, however, that he may have considered his greatest work, not the discovery of the law of gravitation, but rather his research into the Law of Action and Reaction.* Newton felt that his studies of the law of gravitation were practically complete, and nothing new would be discovered from further investigation thereof. He was sure, however, that he had only made a meagre investigation of the Law of Action and Reaction, and that research into that law would be rewarded by new and wonderful discoveries. Briefly, the Law of Action and Reaction is, *"To every action there is always opposed an equal reaction."*†

* For brevity this law is often referred to as the Law of Equal Reaction.
† See page 15 of Newton's Mathematical Principles of Natural Philosophy — Mott's Second Edition.

This is one of the most fundamental laws of the universe, underlying as it does all the sciences, from astronomy to chemistry. At the present time, it is usually taught to young people in connection with the study of physics under a chapter relating to mechanics.

There is one simple illustration of this law, however, as applied to mechanics, to which I wish to refer: namely, the spring. Every one who has used a spring gun, knows that in loading the gun he himself has pushed back the spring, yet he is likely to think that the gun has more energy than he has. This idea, however, is a fallacy. It is impossible for a person to store in any spring more energy than he has in his body. The spring has simply the energy that one expends in pressing it down; while in shooting the bullet, the spring simply expends the energy which was put into it.

If there is one thing which science teaches, it is that this Law of Action and Reaction cannot be eliminated. We may dread it and attempt to ignore it, but it is always in operation in thousands of diversified ways. Whether making a balloon ascension or raising our feet in walking, we are working in accordance with the Law of Action and Reaction.

The study of hygiene is comparatively in the same stage in which that of mechanics was a couple of centuries ago. As a matter of history, it has been only in recent years that fundamental laws have been scientifically applied to the study of the human body. Instead of grasping the fact that the same laws apply to men as to commodities, physicians used to doctor with different methods and various drugs, hoping to hit something, by hook or by crook, that would perform a cure. Recently, however, there has been a great change, and they have learned that men are simply machines, and that to do good work they themselves must be good mechanics. This means that instead of bleeding a patient and filling him up with drugs, as they did years ago, physicians now look upon their patients as machines and realize that the machine needs to be kept clean, well oiled and supplied with fresh power. The great heart specialists are now simply utilizing Newton's Law of Action and Reaction as applicable to the pump, while other specialists are realizing that other organs of the body are nothing but individual sewerage systems, power plants, and various other mechanical contrivances.

Moreover, physicians recognize Newton's Law of Action and Reaction in its relation to sleep, breathing, eating, exercise, etc. For instance, every man has a certain normal line of sleep; that is, he requires a certain amount of sleep, which varies with different individuals at different ages, but which for a given individual at a given age, is a constant factor. Furthermore, for all a man varies from this normal line of required sleep in one direction he must compensate by varying a corresponding amount the other side of the line. This can be illustrated by considering the X-Y Line of our regular Babsonchart* as representing the normal

* See chart inserted opposite page 72.

amount of work which a given man can average, the outline of the shaded areas representing the amount of work that he actually does. Whenever the man performs an abnormal amount of labor, causing him to lose sleep, a black area is formed above the X-Y Line. It then becomes necessary for him to rest a corresponding amount, and this causes the red area to go below the X-Y Line. When any man attempts to ignore the Law of Action and Reaction and remain above his normal X-Y Line too long, he suddenly becomes ill, and is forced to go to bed and make up his required amount of rest. This Law of Action and Reaction applies in the same way to man's breathing, food and exercise. Our bodies are like the spring rifle; we get out of them only what we put into them.

Not only are certain physicians making great progress today through the use of Newton's Law of Action and Reaction, but psychologists as well are employing it in their experiments. It is a fact well known to students of Newton's investigations that the great scientist found this law to apply not only to mechanical and astronomical phenomena, but also believed it to apply to affairs more remotely removed from such sciences. McLaurin, in his famous treatise, entitled *Sir Isaac Newton's Philosophical Discoveries,** discussing Newton's ideas concerning even spiritual manifestations, and referring to the Deity, says:

"The establishing of the equality of action and reaction, even in those powers which seem to sur-

* Page 388, edition of 1748.

pass mechanism, and to be more immediately derived from Him, seems to be an indication that
those powers, while they derive their efficacy from
Him, are, however, in a certain degree circumscribed
and regulated in their operations by mechanical
principles."*

A student of this treatise will see that Newton
believed that the voluntary actions of men *en masse*
are subject to the Law of Action and Reaction.   We
look upon a mob as the last thing which would
work in accordance with scientific law, but psychologists tell us that the mob is one of the best
illustrations of Newton's Law of Action and Reaction. In our study of history we look upon the
French Revolution as something abnormal, but it
could have been foretold by applying this law.
Moreover, if some way could be found to multiply

* Notwithstanding the developments of the Action and Reaction Theory
in the mechanical, chemical and economic worlds, however wonderful
and revolutionary they at times appear, nothing interests the writer so
much as the study of its application to the teachings of Jesus. For centuries, people have mechanically read over the philosophy of Jesus, that
" whatsoever a man soweth, that shall he also reap," without recognizing
the scientific basis existing for these words as applied to spiritual matters.
We have read about " overcoming evil with good," and have considered
the Golden Rule as a splendid altruistic motto for life, but the scientific
aspect of these precepts has never properly been emphasized. When,
however, it is generally realized that the purpose of life is to acquire true
happiness, and that religion is simply a force to aid us in such acquisition,
the relation of the Law of Action and Reaction to these teachings will
be recognized. Then scientists will be employed in religious work, as they
long have been in connection with material studies, and as they are now
becoming interested in biology and the study of the human body.
    The fundamental teachings of the church relating to conduct have been
respected, but have not been considered practical in their application
to everyday life. Consequently, the precepts of the Hebrews and the
Sermon on the Mount, as well as the words of other great religious leaders,
have not been taken seriously as scientific teaching. A study of Newton's
Law of Action and Reaction, however, in connection with the fundamentals of religion, shows that a scientific basis exists for faith, obedience,
sacrifice, and everything else which the great prophets have emphasized
as essential. This is referred to in Emerson's essay on " Compensation "
as follows:
    " Always pay; for, first or last, you must pay your entire debt. Per-
sons and events may stand for a time between you and justice, but it is
only a postponement. You must pay at last your own debt. Benefit

the intensity of the strained conditions existing prior to this revolution by the length of time that these conditions existed, it could doubtless be shown that the product thus obtained is approximately equal to the intensity of the French Revolution multiplied by its duration. Owing to the same law, the Napoleonic Wars were a natural reaction from the Revolution. Similarly, every intelligent police captain, engaged in handling acute situations, such as existed in London during the Suffragette activities, realizes the application of the Law of Action and Reaction to his work. By considering the number of persons engaged in a certain uprising and the intensity of that uprising, he is able to figure very closely when the next uprising will occur.

One of the most spectacular examples of this law is shown by the history of Japan. Many persons wonder how the Japanese nation has been able to

is the end of nature. But for every benefit which you receive, a tax is levied. He is great who confers the most benefits. But the benefit we receive must be rendered again, line for line, deed for deed, cent for cent, to somebody.

" The physiologist has observed that no creatures are favorites, but a certain compensation balances every gift and every defect. A surplusage given to one part is paid out of a reduction from another part of the same creature. If the head and neck are enlarged, the trunk and extremities are cut short. Every excess causes a defect; and every defect an excess.

" This Law of Compensation will not be balked of its end in the smallest iota. It is in vain to build or plot or combine against it. Things refuse to be mismanaged long. If the government is cruel, the governor's life is not safe. If you tax too high, the revenue will yield nothing. If you make the criminal code sanguinary, juries will not convict.

" The law of nature is: Do the thing, and you shall have the power: but they who do not the thing have not the power. Everywhere and always this law is sublime. The absolute balance of Give and Take, the doctrine that everything has its price; and if that price is not paid, not that thing but something else is obtained, and that it is impossible to get anything without its price — this doctrine is not less sublime in the columns of a ledger than in the budgets of states, in the laws of light and darkness, in all the *action and reaction of nature.*"

Some day there surely will be a great religious revival which will far exceed, both in intensity and permanency, anything which has ever been witnessed before. Moreover, this will be due to a general recognition of expand so spectacularly during the years since Commodore Perry opened its ports to world commerce. The Japanese are held up as world wonders for the tremendous progress which they have made in less than two generations. The explanation, however, is very simple when the Law of Action and Reaction is considered. For centuries that nation had been bottled up and had been gradually accumulating energy. Suddenly, the doors of opportunity were thrown open and the same result occurred psychologically as occurs mechanically when a charge of dynamite explodes. Furthermore, a mathematical equality exists between the product obtained by the multiplication of the number of years that Japan was bottled up and the intensity of that period, and the amount of its recent advancement multiplied by its duration. The book entitled, "The Great Illusion," by Norman Angell, illustrates on every page the effect of Newton's Law of

the fact that the fundamental teachings of Jesus are based on purely scientific grounds, especially upon Newton's Law of Action and Reaction, and that the Golden Rule is simply a statement of this law in general terms applicable to the man in the street.

All that we take away from others must, in some way, at some time, be given back. All that we do for others will, in some way, at some time, come back to us. We all have our normal X-Y Lines, and all that we raise ourselves through covetousness above this X-Y Line must be made up below it. Life is the same as the boy's spring gun; we can get out of it only what we put into it, although we can increase our capacity just as the boy could remodel and increase the capacity of his gun. We can *raise the slope* of our X-Y Line of happiness, but to attempt to go above this line artificially is of no avail, as it must be made up by an equal reaction at some later date.

Moreover, it is interesting to think what it means to keep on our X-Y Line. Scientifically, this simply means dealing justly, and doing unto others as we would that they should do unto us. For a long time artists have personified Justice as a woman holding a pair of scales, without realizing the scientific fact that the primary Law of Action and Reaction underlies both moral justice and the mechanical scales. When we deal justly we keep on our line of growth, but whenever we deal unjustly we get off this line, and some day we must compensate therefor. *Whatever we do that raises the X-Y Line of civilization is good, and reacts upon us as good; but whatever we do that lowers the X-Y Line is evil and such performances react upon us as evil.*

Action and Reaction upon nations and communities, which effect is vividly demonstrated in the great European War.

In this connection the following quotation of Prof. Wilhelm Ostwald* will be of interest:

" No large enterprise of a technical or industrial nature is undertaken nowadays without a very comprehensive knowledge of what its future is to be. We are not afraid to invest millions of dollars in a work which at the moment, when the expenditure is determined upon, has no other existence than a prophecy in the form of calculations and drawings made by engineers. But we know for a certainty that when the directions in the calculations and blueprints are carried out, a structure will arise possessing all the foretold properties, whether it be a bridge, a steamship, or an electrical plant.

" While in the technical pursuits prophecies of this sort have been developed to an extraordinary degree of accuracy, it is somewhat more difficult to gain foreknowledge and power of prophecy in the economic world. That is why the few who possess this quality to a greater extent than others, those who are able to foresee the future with greater certainty than others, easily achieve economic superiority. They conduct their transactions in accordance with their prophetic capacity, and so are able to pocket greater gains than their competitors. This ability to see into the future depends upon knowledge of the natural laws involved.

" Just as mathematics long ago succeeded in separating even the most complicated movements into their simple periodic component parts, so the statesman must learn to decompose the totality of human movements into the simple wave elements produced by self-regulation in the various fields of human activity. In this way politics can be transformed from a mere knack, as it has been regarded since olden times, into a science like technology with the power of sure and far-reaching prophecy."

That the law of equal reaction applies to economic or business conditions is indicated along two main lines, physical and psychical. This is because the conditions which prevail in the business world

* Professor Ostwald's work in the field of chemistry has given him an international reputation. He formerly held the chair of chemistry at Leipzig University.

have as their effective causes both physical and psychical factors. For example, rainfall is an important physical factor that affects business trends. This result is reached through the effect of rainfall on the crops which are always an influential factor in determining conditions. The records of the weather bureau show that dry and wet years do not alternate indiscriminately, but rather follow a clearly defined wave movement. This is to say that we have a series of years of sub-normal precipitation followed by a series of super-normal precipitation. An attempt has been made to show that sun spots were the cause of these variations in rainfall and that these followed an oscillatory motion, rising, increasing in size and activity, then gradually dying down. Whether or not sun spots can be used to forecast periods of sub-normal and super-normal rainfall, the fact is that weather bureau statistics show the existence of such periods. This means that whatever effect crop conditions have on economic movements is exerted in accordance with the law of equal reaction.

But more important than the influence of rainfall are the psychical factors. Prosperity has a well-understood and clearly definable effect on men's minds. So also has a period of depression or adversity. Business conditions depend chiefly on what men do. What men do depends on what they believe and think; I mean that men act according to their real beliefs and valuations — not necessarily according to what they *say* they believe and think.

This becomes clear if we follow through the usual sequence of business events. Let us assume that we are in a period of depression. Mills are idle or running half-time, there is little demand for goods, and prices are low. Problems of unemployment are worrying our legislators. There is little or no profit in doing business and therefore little business done. Much capital lies idle, and money rates are low. The fact that a considerable number of people are out of employment and others have had their wages cut, reduces the buying power of the people as a whole. But this reduction of consumption is not caused by reduced buying power alone. The psychical effect of " hard times " is to induce economy. People have had their wages reduced, have been out of work themselves or seen others out of work. They become fearful of the future and are impressed with the advisability of saving something for a rainy day. Furthermore it is easier to save if everybody else is doing it. In a period of expansion, free expenditure is popular. We have to spend more to " keep up with the Joneses," but in hard times the " Joneses," like ourselves, have had their pay reduced. So we can reduce our expenditure without having their ostentation flaunted before our eyes. Economy, being a necessity, is made a virtue, and we are not ashamed to practise it.

This wave of economy and resulting saving is not confined to the rank and file. The capitalist class is hit by the reduction of dividends and the lowering of the rate of interest. Hardest hit of all are the business enterprisers — those who organize and direct industry, who take the responsibility of ownership and contract to pay fixed interest to capital and fixed wages to labor. They rely on the difference between the expenses of production and the price of the finished product for their share in distribution. When prices first commence to fall, this class acts as a buffer and stands considerable loss before reducing wages and closing plants.

Economies which result in a lowered demand for all goods, affect with special force the demand for luxuries. Hence those business enterprises that cater to the demand for luxuries suffer most. Failures are numerous; those firms that are high-cost producers, whether because of poor natural conditions, over-capitalization, or inefficient management, are forced into bankruptcy. In fact, the only firms that survive such a period of readjustment are the efficient low-cost producers of the wares that people want and will pay for. Their business is in sound condition, their credits not over-extended, their natural advantages at least reasonably good, their capitalization low and management efficient. In short, the whole commercial fabric is on a sound and practical basis.

The cutting off and giving up of luxuries has two important effects. By throwing out of employment persons engaged in the production of luxuries, it forces them to seek employment in the production of more necessary commodities, thus helping to lower the price of the latter to the consumer. The

effect of the increase in savings which results from
the popularization of economy is always a large
increase in bank deposits, especially in the savings
banks. Thus funds and credit accumulate and are
available for use when the tide turns.

The other psychological effect of hard times is
the increase in temperance and industry. Both of
these are due in part to the economy referred to
above. People realize the necessity of clinging to
a job. When there are many candidates for few
positions, those who have positions know that
should they fail to give satisfaction it would be an
easy matter to replace them. This is equally true
of the business enterpriser. He is dependent for
his business upon the patronage of his customers.
Competition is keen and buying is slack. His
success in business is measured by his ability to
please his customers. This all leads to a powerful
realization on the part of all classes that the only
road to success is the road of service. It is clearly
seen at such times that wealth is the natural reaction from service. Thus temperance, industry,
regulated plain living, and a willingness to serve go
to characterize to a large degree all classes of the
population. It is just this psychical condition
which lays the strongest foundation for a period
of prosperity. Such conditions cannot fail to forecast improvement.

Ordinarily some specific event serves as the immediate stimulus to the inevitable upswing. That
event may be a war, the opening of new lands,
bumper crops or an abnormal increase in the cir-

culating medium.   The accumulation of savings is
certain, sooner or later, to burn holes in the pockets
of the savers.   That is human nature.   In any
case, the primary element in the stimulating factor
is the new demand for goods.   This new demand
raises the price of those goods upon which the demand falls; and since expenses of production do
not rise at first or in equal degree, a considerable
" spread " is thereby created between the price of
the finished product and the expenses of production.   This means profit for the business enterprisers in the lines affected.   The wheels, therefore,
begin to hum, more help is taken on, the mills work
full time and the demand for necessary raw material rises.

If the new demand be sufficiently powerful so
that it cannot be satisfied by the operation of the
existing plants, other enterprisers with adaptable
facilities are induced to enter the field.   This means
a call for more material, for labor, and as additions
and new constructions are planned, a demand for
building material, plants and machinery.   As when
a stone is thrown into the water, the ripples spread
out in wider and wider circles, so the new demand
for goods soon spreads out through the various
relations of interdependence until it has affected
the whole economic fabric.

With the general advance in the cost of living,
wage-earners are led to demand that the price of
their services be increased to correspond with the
rising scale of commodity prices.   Demands for
increased wages are generally granted because the

price of goods is such that employers would rather pay a high rate than lose business by a strike.

Just as a period of depression carries its antidote in the sound psychological conditions which are created by depression, so a period of over-expansion produces within itself a poison which destroys the prosperity. Excessive prosperity makes men extravagant and careless. Rising prices show large profits on the books of the business enterprisers. Burning with a desire to make still more profits, they extend their plants and embark eagerly upon new business ventures. Increased income leads to an increase in personal expenditure. The employee who has steady work and who has seen his wages advance is filled with optimism, buys an automobile, builds a shack in the woods or at a popular beach. Similarly, his employer buys a couple of high-priced motor cars and sends his family to Palm Beach for the winter.

A large market develops for luxuries of all kinds. Business enterprisers push on into this field also and the demand for new equipment still increases. As the natural reaction of adversity is economy, thrift, industry and temperance, so the reaction of prosperity is to make men extravagant, wasteful, self-indulgent and careless. High prices are relied upon to make good the loss by waste and inefficient management. There is little effort to please the customers when the books are already filled with orders for the year ahead. Labor, while insisting on an increase of remuneration, grows increasingly careless as regards the quality of ser-

vice given in exchange.   Every man knows that if
he is rebuked or his work criticised, he can easily
find employment elsewhere.

A decrease in productivity is the inevitable result.
The willingness to serve is then forgotten and in
its place comes the notion that the high road to
wealth and prosperity is the path of speculation.
The air is full of stories of brokers' clerks and
messenger boys who secured bargains in stocks or
land and in consequence are now buying motor
cars and country estates.   Industry, perseverance
and honest labor are at a discount and each one
hopes to make his fortune by a lucky strike.   There
is no idea that can possess the human mind that
has a more destructive effect on those qualities
that are necessary for efficient production.

With increased production and rising cost of
raw materials and labor, the " spread " between the
price received for the finished product and the
expense of production is gradually reduced.   It
ultimately becomes manifest that there has been
a disproportionate investment in fixed capital in
certain lines of industry.   The great expansion in
industry which characterizes a period of so-called
prosperity always produces a strain on financial resources.   It takes more money to finance a business
enterprise on a high scale of prices.   The amount
that banks will loan on stocks and bonds is based on
their market values, this amount rising and falling
as the market value increases or diminishes.   Similarly, also, the amount that can be borrowed on
real estate and equipment depends upon the esti-

mated value of the security. The value of stocks
depends not upon their earnings, but upon their
expected earnings. It is also possible to borrow
more on the plant that is making large profits and
expects to continue to do so, than upon one that is
earning but little. Thus all along the line credits
open and expand in proportion to expected earnings.
When the rising costs of production result in reducing profits in the lines in which they first advanced,
the high-cost producers in these lines find themselves in a weak position. The demand for funds
makes the interest rate high toward the close of
a period of over-expansion and this high cost of
funds is a further check on the progress of industry.
Creditors at this point begin to take alarm. Stocks
are widely distributed on narrow margins, and conditions are ripe for a decline.

When the decline comes, the contraction of
values necessitates a contraction of the credit
which had been built up on the basis of the former
inflation. Loans are called, and securities must
be sold to meet them. Money rates rise and a
panic ensues, accompanied by the failure of an
increasing number of business enterprises. Commodity prices fall. Just as when prices are advancing everyone is anxious to buy in anticipation of
further advance, so when prices begin to fall everyone is anxious to sell in anticipation of further
decline. Thus demand collapses as the selling
pressure increases. Since retailers will not order,
wholesalers cannot, and manufacturers find themselves forced to curtail production. The keynote

of this period is disappointment. Business enterprisers are disappointed at the failure of the expected profits. Investors are disappointed at the
failures of those enterprises in which their money
was invested. Wage earners are disappointed,
first because their increased wages will not buy
as much as they had expected; later, because the
high wages and easy positions fail to be maintained.

When expansion is checked and the volume of
business falls off, the demand for funds is also reduced. The interest rate falls because there is little
profit in employing funds and we are entering upon
another period of reaction. The duration of this
reaction is dependent upon the time necessary to
liquidate the unhealthful condition which the profits
and period of over-expansion have created. If the
reaction is very intense this may be accomplished
in a comparatively short time; if less intense the
time will be longer. Not until the unsound business conditions and the disastrous psychological
effects of too much prosperity have been liquidated
and corrected can the foundations be laid for another boom.

There have always been periods of depression,
periods of over-expansion, and intermediate periods,
as everyone already knows.* There is absolutely
no dispute regarding this first point. As to the
duration of these periods there is a distinct difference of opinion. It is the general impression that
the great major trends are of about twenty years'

---

* See Monetary Commission volume on " Crises," by Prof. O. M. W.
Sprague of Harvard, a foremost authority on " Applied Economics."

duration, and the minor movements average
41 months' duration, with possibly still other
swings of about ten years' duration. Probably
the most interesting of the older works on this was
by Samuel Benner, who, from 1875 to 1884, formu-
lated a most elaborate system of charts and who,
without doubt, clearly foretold the panics of 1884
and 1893, and the prosperous years intervening.
Many other men have devised other charts and
theories, some based on supposed economics and
others based on superstition, but all have been
found to fail, and have been forgotten.*

Upon careful examination all these charts and
theories are found to have two great defects; and
it is chiefly because the Area Theory herein discussed eliminates these two defects that the theory
and the Babsonchart described in the following
pages deserve attention.

Reaction Equals Action

The first defect in the old theory of Benner and
other writers consisted in the fact that they based
their calculations simply on either *time* or *intensity*,
instead of on their product. There is no law in
physics or nature that any action or any reaction
must come with any definite *regularity*. There is,
however, as before indicated, a law under which
mechanics, medicine, and other sciences move,
namely that " action and reaction are equal."
This is absolutely true; but when the student at-

* Recent scientific contributions to the literature on these movements
have been made by Mitchell, Copeland, Moore, Jones and others.

tempts to go one step farther, he generally fails.
For instance, we may say that a certain reaction
amounts to one hundred foot-pounds, but whether
the body weighs one hundred pounds and is moved
one foot or weighs only one pound and is moved
one hundred feet, we have no way of knowing until
we learn one factor.

In other words, to say that a period of over-
expansion or period of depression will last any given
time, irrespective of the business activity of the
country during such time, is contrary to all basic
law. Yet upon such reasoning most of our predecessors have worked, while the others believed that
a change in conditions comes when figures for pig-
iron, bank clearings or commodity prices reach a
certain point. They entirely ignore the *product* of
time and intensity. Only by multiplying one by
the other can the true reaction be ascertained.
Time, then, may be compared to space, and intensity may be compared to weight, and their
product to space multiplied by weight, or to " foot-
pounds."

For this reason, when studying a Babsonchart
like that at p. 73, which is based on a representative and comprehensive number of business indicators, able bankers and merchants today do not only
study height or length, but study *area*. That is,
such men believe that the shaded portions *above*
the average line of growth X-Y, shown in the plot,
should approximately equal in *area* the following
shaded portion *below* said line. Thus, if the country
is enjoying a condition of only medium activity,

prosperous conditions may be expected to extend over a longer time than if tremendous over-expansion exists, and vice versa.*

All Subjects Must Be Considered

The second great error heretofore made by these economists consisted in the fact that each man seemed to focus his attention on only one or two subjects, instead of making a composite interpretation of all. Some would study bank clearings, some foreign trade, others gold movements, production statistics both for agriculture and industry, and so on, believing that, as the figures on their particular pet subject or subjects changed, it was possible to forecast future conditions. Many still believe it is possible to utilize certain subjects in this way, but all such systems are absolutely wrong. No one of these subjects, when studied independently, serves to foretell the great changes in conditions which have occurred since 1860. Some of the subjects seem to work out better than others, but all of them entirely fail to give proper warning in all instances.†

* See " Cours d'Economie Politique," by Vilfredo Pareto, Vol. II.

† For illustration, " gold movements " formerly was used as one of the very best barometers of future conditions. During heavy imports of gold (such as occurred in 1878–1882) the United States enjoyed unparalleled prosperity and after said imports declined and the exports of gold exceeded the imports (as in 1882–1883) followed the panic of 1884. This same rule worked most admirably in forecasting the prosperous times of 1888–1890, the panic of 1893, and the prosperous times of 1898–1902. The rule, however, did *not* work in forecasting the panic of 1903 nor the prosperous years following, and the heaviest imports of gold the United States ever enjoyed preceded the panic of 1907. Of course the reason for these huge imports in 1906–1907 is now well understood; but any one, who in 1906 simply studied the bare figures, without knowing that such importations were artificial, would have been justified in expecting that 1907 and 1908 would be years of great prosperity. On the other hand, such an error would not have been possible if a study had simultaneously been made of the other leading subjects.

However, a study of all these subjects reveals the fact that there has not been a single case when a change in conditions has not been fully and plainly foretold by a *majority* of these subjects.

Four general rules can be worked out for each subject — one rule for each of the four periods of over-expansion, decline, depression and improvement, respectively. These rules are given in detail for each of the subjects treated in Chapters IV, V and VI. The basis of these rules is that very high figures, such as appear during a period of over-expansion, foretell a panic or period of decline. Very low figures, such as appear during a depression, foretell a period of improvement.

General Considerations

From the foregoing it is evident that it is better to reduce all figures to a single summary plot, in order to ascertain the *"area"* above or below the normal Line X-Y, although the separate charts on the different subjects may be again referred to as a check and interpreted in accordance with the laws just outlined. If both the Babsonchart and the individual interpretations foretell the same change, this change may surely be expected to come to pass; while if both do not foretell the same change, one may assume that *at this moment* conditions are uncertain, although a little later this uncertainty may not exist.

This practically completes the diagnosis, although as a further study, it is interesting to refer back to

previous history and ascertain what changes, after
such conditions as exist today, have followed in the
past. This is accomplished by referring back to
points in the various past business trends when (1)
the same area above or below the normal line
existed as exists today; and (2) when a majority
of the individual subjects foretold the same conditions which they foretell today.

In connection with this study there is a certain
sequence of events which is a distinct aid to bankers,
merchants and investors. This sequence is similar
to the various stages of disease with which physicians are so familiar. Sometimes one stage of the
disease " runs " longer than usual; *but the sequence
is usually about the same*. Likewise, it is not always possible to judge correctly the exact duration
of each period of increase or decline in prices; but
by a study of fundamental statistics it is always
possible to ascertain approximately in which of the
following periods we are.

The prices of stocks usually continue to rise
after the prices of bonds begin to fall. Industry, as
a whole, generally follows several months behind
stock prices. The prices of commodities generally
stop rising at about the time business reaches its
height. Interest rates are likely to continue to rise
until the prices of land values have declined
sharply. This latter event usually completes the
decline in prices that precedes and accompanies a
panic. Conditions in other countries and crop
conditions in this country also have much to do
with the date and extent of these periods.

In short, this study of fundamental statistics consists simply in ascertaining present conditions and interpreting them with the view of forecasting future conditions. It is like the work of a physician when he examines a man for life insurance. The physician first ascertains the man's present conditions and his mode of life. Applying his knowledge based on previous history of what usually follows such conditions, he makes a forecast of the man's probable length of life. That action and reaction are equal and that history usually repeats itself is the foundation of both the science of medicine and the great business of life insurance.

These fundamental principles apply equally in the field of economics and hence the merchant and the investor should give the subject of fundamental statistics his most careful attention and consideration. Those who study the figures on these fundamental subjects each week obtain a barometer figure for present conditions. The Babsonchart is really a graphic picture of such statistics which are gathered from many authoritative sources, tabulated and kept up-to-date.

In the first portion of this book is described the meaning of fundamental statistics and their use. In this chapter is outlined the theory underlying the work and the reason why such statistics may be depended upon. Now a few words must be given to explaining the mechanical work of compiling and reducing these figures to one single "Business Index" such as is the basis of the Babsonchart.

Construction of Babsonchart

In the Babsoncharts for the United States and for Canada* the need of direct and definite results leads to seeking a systematic, comprehensive and reliable practice, so that an accurate basis of comparison with the period selected as the base may be established at the outset. The course usually followed by the leading bankers, merchants and investors when studying fundamental statistics is to collect data covering a long period of years, and relating to such subjects as those listed later which for the U. S. Babsonchart are grouped under seven main headings: Manufactures, Mining, Agricultural Marketings, Building and Construction, Electric Power, Railway Freight, Foreign Trade.

As our knowledge of the Law of Action and Reaction increases and as more statistical data become available we are continually revising our studies to secure the best possible measure of business conditions. The revised Babsonchart of the physical quantity, or volume, of United States business is described below. In this new volume study the difficulty of deflating subjects reported in terms of dollars has been practically eliminated. Data were selected for the series to be combined in this chart, which would include, — (1) monthly figures of quantity; (2) cover all the principal fields of

*See Chapter VIII for a complete description of the Babsonchart of Canada which gives a monthly index of the variation of the physical volume of business activity from 1915 to date.

business activity; and (3) include a large part of the total activity in each field.

The Subjects.—The Babsonchart is based on 54 different subjects tabulated on insert page 69. They are carefully weighted, and carried back over more than a quarter century. In addition to its use as a measure of general business activity it can be broken down into its component curves or to represent the groups of Production of Basic Materials, Agricultural Marketings, Manufacturing, Distribution, etc. The Babsonchart represents the physical volume of business as measured by quantitative subjects. However, in the case of one subject, New Building, statistics have not been collected in terms of physical volume for more than a few years back. Hence it was necessary to compute volume figures from the value figures by allowing for changes in building costs. These changes have been obtained by the use of the Babson Index of Building Construction Costs, computed from our price indices of the materials going into residential and other types of construction. The variation in labor costs was obtained from our weighted index of building wage scales, which not only allowed for the proportion for each type of labor contributing to ordinary building construction, but was also weighted in proportion to the contribution to the total building in the United States of the seventeen principal cities of the country from which the wage rates were obtained.

Weighting.—The United States Census figures for 1923 thru 1927 are the primary bases of the weight-

ings indicated in the table at page 69. Both the
value of products and the number of people engaged in each line were considered, the final weighting chosen being based solely on the value added
to the products in the particular phase of business
activity being discussed. Reweighting can therefore be made, if necessary, at each census of manufactures.

Improvements and Revisions.—Considerable difficulty was experienced in carrying some of the series
back to 1904. We are indebted to a number of important companies, both railroad and industrial, for
supplying for certain years unpublished data pertaining to their business. Several departments of
the United States Government also have supplied
us with special studies. As to future changes, at
the close of any business depression completing an
area movement, there can be substituted any new
and better series that have become available
for the measurement of any particular phase of
business activity. Thus we can take advantage
of new statistical data to increase the accuracy
of measurements of each different phase covered
by the study.

To accomplish our purpose the following requirements for the Babsonchart were set up:

1. It must include as many major phases of busi-
    ness activity and industrial divisions as can
    be adequately and reliably represented by the
    series available.

2. It must be adjusted for seasonal variation so

that any month may be compared directly with any other month.

3. It must give each series its proper importance in the index. This importance must be determined on the basis of the "value added" by the industry represented by the series.*

4. It must adjust for the shifting relative importance of constituent items and of the major groups during the period covered by the chart, and it must provide adequately for incorporating such changes in the future.

5. It must show the actual index of activity—not merely the deviations from some unrevealed "normal," so that the long-time trend of activity can be seen and comparisons made between different periods, or between the growth of general business activity and one's own business.

6. It must adequately meet the many problems of logic and statistical technique which arise in its calculation.

The work on the Babsonchart proceeded so as to meet all of the above requirements in the most satisfactory manner with known materials and statistical methods.

Adjustment for Irregular Months.—In those cases where industries did not work 365 days a year and where we could ascertain with a fair degree of accuracy the holidays observed, adjustments were made for the working day irregularities by com-

* This is, in most cases, substantially the value of products less the cost of materials, supplies, fuel and power.

piling the series on the basis of average daily output.

Seasonal Adjustment.—The original monthly series were individually adjusted for seasonal variation by seasonal indexes determined on a seven-year moving basis. Ratios were computed of each month to the twelve months' average in which it "centers." Arranging these ratios according to months, the arithmetic mean of the "middle" three ratios for the respective months in each seven-year period was used as the seasonal index for that month in the middle year of the period.

Formula Used.—The formula used in the calculation of this index is the aggregative number "53" in Professor Irving Fisher's book, "The Making of Index Numbers," shifted to a physical volume index. In its form to give price it is $\dfrac{\Sigma P_1 Q_0}{\Sigma P_0 Q_0}$; to give volume it is $\dfrac{\Sigma Q_1 P_0}{\Sigma Q_0 P_0}$; where $Q_1 =$ current quantity; $P_0 =$ base value added; (average during the years 1923–27); $Q_0 =$ base quantity similarly derived; and Σ indicates the summation of the corresponding products of all series that are being combined.

The base period chosen for the revised Babson-chart is the five-year post-war period 1923–27. It was the best five-year post-war period for which census data were available at the time that this study was made, and represents a fair average of conditions. No pre-war base for a study of the physical volume of business was to be considered for we have put behind us forever the former levels of business activity.

The X-Y Line.—The X-Y Line is determined by the Method of Averages calculated for different cycles;—D, E, F, G, and H estimated. These center points are connected by a suitable trend line. It represents the net growth of United States business, showing a rather steep ascent during the early World War period. Economists and statisticians always disagree as to the proper location of such a line, and we are not presenting this study as a final conclusion. The net growth of business is something to which every business man should give careful attention. Up to the beginning of the war in Europe, the long-time growth of American business continued at a fairly steady pace. From 1914 to the time the United States entered the war, there was an entirely new situation—a tremendous demand for American goods without corresponding foreign competition. Prices rose to high levels, stimulating the greatest development in that length of time that American producing facilities have ever known. After the United States entered the war the advantage was reduced. Production, already high, was expanded at a less rapid pace. The X-Y Line herewith presented is in keeping with these facts.

Some statisticians prefer to eliminate the " net growth " or secular trend from each of the individual subjects before they combine them into a single index figure. This is done by various mathematical processes. Of course, when the growth element is eliminated, it then is possible to use a horizontal base line instead of a sloping X-Y Line when comparing the index figures. To the casual observer it appears that the statisticians who use this method avoid the difficulties of locating an " X-Y " Line. This is not the case; they have to calculate how much of the increase in the business records they believe represents normal growth before they can subtract that amount from the original statistics.

We have felt that it is very much better not to attempt to subtract the growth factor from the figures, but to represent it on the chart by the X-Y Line. There are several important advantages: (1) It permits every one to see what allowance is being made for normal growth. This in itself is valuable information. (2) It makes it possible for one to compare the figures of his own business with the Babsonchart without first correcting them to eliminate the growth factor. (3) In times of sudden change, such as occurred during the war, mathematical methods of subtracting growth from the original data all fail.

The ratio scales used for the chart give a true representation of proportional movements in all curves. Equal vertical distances between any points represent equal percentage changes.

Use of the Babsonchart. A copy of the Babsonchart is shown opposite page 72. The line marking the irregular contour of the black and red areas is formed by the Business Index calculated for each month as described above. Thus is traced out the month-by-month changes of business conditions.

The X-Y Line not only serves to define the areas of over-expansion and depression in general business, but it also furnishes the standard toward which every business man should work. It represents the approximate rate at which business can be carried on indefinitely without the necessity of periodic readjustment and wasteful depression. It shows the net gain made by the nation as a result of the right use of land, labor, and capital in all forms. By "right" use of these factors is meant that use which brings about efficient production of wealth, together with a consumption of this wealth which is productive, not wasteful.

The dotted black line shows the movement of the Babson index of wholesale industrial commodity prices using for a base period the average price level of the years 1908 through 1912 equal to 100. Of course this shows but a small portion of the major commodity price swing which culminated in 1920. It does show that the minor movements have a definite relation to the Babsonchart areas. Furthermore it brings out the necessity in any careful study of an individual business of considering the changes in physical volume of production as well as in dollar sales.

Different industries are related differently to the area movement of the Babsonchart and for many of the more important we are able to furnish indices showing this relationship. With the knowledge of the present position of business in relation to the X-Y Line and also of the relationship of his particular industry to the Babsonchart a business man has the essential factors required for an estimate of the trend of his sales.

The vertical red lines on the Babsonchart represent the monthly high and low of the average price of 50 stocks (40 until 1928) and the solid black line, the average yield of 60 bonds. Although during these years the stocks have usually discounted the black area, yet this cannot be depended upon. Previous to 1903 there also were instances when the black area rose and fell first.   Therefore, the only safe method is to study both of these together, giving the most weight to the Babsonchart.

Although the main use of the barometer figures is to plot the " area " mentioned earlier in this chapter, the figures themselves are also useful. If, during a period of depression, the final business index for a long period shows a continuous but slow increase, the country is usually facing improved conditions, however poor business may appear to the average merchant.   On the other hand, during a period of over-expansion, if the business index continues to increase abnormally, there is likely to be a change for the worse at any time.

The fundamental principle to be remembered, however, concerning the Area Theory is as follows: If the line, X-Y, truly represents the normal development of the nation's business, and if the black areas truly represent the actual course, then the sums of the areas above and below the line X-Y must, over sufficiently long periods of time, be equal.

Current Interpretations

But in addition to collecting data to deduce barometer figures therefrom, some merchants and bankers have the monthly figures on each of the more important subjects interpreted each month for what they signify.

Such interpretations are made in accordance with the rules given in Chapters IV, V and VI, and show how many subjects signify a " Continued Improvement," how many signify " No Improvement " and how many signify " No Change." Figures on the majority of the necessary subjects can be obtained not oftener than monthly, and therefore final totals need be studied in detail but once each month. If there has been a normal growth or change,— sometimes a favorable showing requires an increase or sometimes a decrease,— the figures on a given subject are considered as signifying satisfactory conditions; but if a growth or a change is not normal, the figures are considered as showing unsatisfactory conditions. In other words, satisfactory conditions require a *normal* change and figures of much less than normal or much more than normal are considered unsatisfactory.

The whole industrial organization of the country is governed by the law that reaction equals action. In a rapidly growing country like America, the figures to be normal *must increase in proportion to the increase in population, intelligence, industry and righteousness.* Great and sudden increases or decreases are distinctly abnormal and are always

significant of a coming change: a change for the
better in time of depression, when present conditions are very unsatisfactory; or a change for the
worse during a period of over-expansion when
present conditions are apparently very satisfactory.
When a man or a nation is in a *normal* condition,
there may be nothing to be anxious about; but
when a man or a nation *overworks* or "lives too
high," or in any way becomes strained or careless,
trouble is sure to follow.

This same principle is illustrated by interest
rates.* For instance, when interest rates gradually
increase and surplus reserves gradually decrease
after a period of depression, the combination is
significant of improved present conditions; when
commercial paper is discounted at very low rates,
it is certain that the country is not prosperous,
that many factories are idle and many men out of
work. As the mills resume operation and as business becomes more active, money rates increase
and surplus reserves decrease. Then, as money
rates increase too much, and the surplus reserves
decrease to very low figures, the change is significant of unsatisfactory future conditions. In other
words, when money rates are *below* normal it shows
business is *dull*, but may be better; and when
money rates are *above* normal, it shows that business is good, but will soon be worse.

Of course if these data were obtained by each investor, merchant or banking house independently,
it would require a force of clerks to collect, analyze

* See the very valuable book on this subject by Professor Irving Fisher
of Yale University: The Rate of Interest; The Macmillan Co.

and sort the mass of figures; but as the data may now be obtained from a central agency, all of the drudgery is eliminated. The investor or merchant may simply note the barometer figures as they are made up each week, thus keeping in constant touch with conditions; and by reference to the monthly figures once a month, these conditions may then be interpreted in accordance with the rules mentioned. Moreover, the average banker, merchant or investor is satisfied to depend upon the Babsonchart Business Index and reports furnished by this central agency, simply making a personal detailed examination at desired intervals.

However, no matter what the time and money expended in studying fundamental conditions, the investigator always finds the subject absorbingly interesting, the more so because such studies indicate what may be expected of the future.

If, during a period of depression, uncertainty and discouragement, the Babsonchart and individual charts show distinctly that the country is about to enter a period of over-expansion, investors buy stocks, merchants buy goods, and bankers extend loans. The result is that, when good business returns, such investors and merchants find that they have purchased very much below the prevailing prices and obtain many times the profit that they otherwise would.

On the other hand, during a period of great expansion and extravagance, when everybody is buying goods or securities and there is a general increase of indebtedness, if the Babsonchart and

the other charts foretell a change for the worse,
investors sell their securities for cash, merchants
reduce their merchandise and outstanding credits,
and bankers reduce loans or place a large part of
them " on call." These statistics, therefore, both
serve as an insurance against loss and also enable
men to be prepared to take advantage of the very
low prices which are sure to prevail during the
formation of an area of depression below the line
of normal growth.

POTENTIAL PROFITS IN STOCKS

To those unfamiliar with the long swings of the
stock market, it may seem impossible to increase
one's principal from $6,000 to over $600,000, more
than 100 times its original value, during an investment lifetime. Statistics show, however, that such
profits have been possible. As fundamental statistics become more complete and more soundly
interpreted, investors can approach nearer and
nearer to the profits outlined herein. The following tabulation traces the long swings of the stock
market averages.

That there might be no possibility of bias in
the selection of stocks, we have confined ourselves
to the Dow-Jones market averages of 30 industrials*
and of 20 rails from 1896 to date. We have been
obliged to carry back these averages ourselves
to 1893, but have held, in so far as possible, the
same stocks that Dow-Jones used.

We have not taken the lowest point for purchase, nor have we taken the highest point for

* 20industrials prior to October, 1928, and 12 industrials prior to
August, 1914.

sale, for in the exercise of ordinary judgment it is impossible to pick the absolute lows and highs. Instead we have assumed purchase at the average price of the rail group and of the industrial group for the low month of the stock market movement, and have sold at the corresponding average prices of the high month of each swing.

We have bought the same number of shares of each stock in the average except where there was a balance of capital remaining which would enable us to purchase one additional share each of all the rails, or of all the industrials which make up the average.

In 1893 the purchase of 4 shares each of the rails and 5 shares each of the industrials required, with commissions, a total of $6,046. Dividends and rights while the stocks were held, and interest at savings bank rates on these dividends to April, 1899, totaled $2,065. Upon selling in April, 1899, the same stocks (less commissions and taxes) brought $11,294, giving a total principal at that date of $13,359. Placing this sum on deposit for a year, the current savings bank interest brought $506, giving a total principal of $13,865 for investment at the next low month of the market, in June, 1900.

The table continues the transactions, carrying the original $6,000 to over $600,000.

We emphasize that the following table represents the goal or objective of the long-pull plan. As statistics become more complete and analysis more accurate, potential profits will be more fully realized.

POTENTIAL PROFITS

1893	July	Original principal invested @ 49.09 for rails, @34.22 for industrials .	$6,046
		Dividends, and interest @ 4%	
1899	April	Stocks bought 7/'93, sold @ 85.80 for rails, @ 74.94 for industrials	13,359
		Investment to date (including balance on interest) . . .	
		Interest 1 year @ 3¾% on investment to date	
1900	June	Available for stock purchase @ 76.49 for rails, @ 56.53 for industrials	13,865
		Dividends, and interest @ 3½%	
1901	June	Stocks bought 6/'00, sold @ 116.02 for rails, @ 77.17 for industrials	20,618
		Investment to date (including balance on interest) . .	
		Interest, 2 years @ 3½% on investment to date	
1903	Nov.	Available for stock purchase @ 91.95 for rails, @ 43.81 for industrials	22,101
		Dividends, and interest @ 3½%	
1906	Jan.	Stocks bought 11/'03, sold @ 135.36 for rails, @ 98.72 for industrials	39,033
		Investment to date (including balance on interest) . .	
		Interest, 1½ years @ 3½% on investment to date	
1907	Nov.	Available for stock purchase @ 84.27 for rails, @ 55.74 for industrials	41,094
		Dividends, and interest @ 3½%	
1909	Aug.	Stocks bought 11/'07, sold @ 131.59 for rails, @ 97.78 for industrials	71,689
		Investment to date (including balance on interest) . .	
		Interest, 2 years @ 4% on investment to date	
1911	Sept.	Available for stock purchase @ 111.96 for rails, @ 76.61 for industrials	77,598
		Dividends, and interest @ 4%	

1912	Oct.	Stocks bought 9/'11, sold @ 121.96 for rails, @ 92.24 for industrials	91,990
		Investment to date (including balance on interest)	
		Interest, 2 years @ 4% on investment to date	
1914	Dec.	Available for stock purchase @ 89.85 for rails, @ 54.97 for industrials	99,573
		Dividends, and interest at 4%	
1915	Dec.	Stocks bought 12/'14, sold @ 106.47 for rails, @ 97.00 for industrials	144,253
		Investment to date (including balance on interest)	
		Interest, 2 years @ 4% on investment to date	
1917	Dec.	Available for stock purchase @ 75.31 for rails, @ 70.17 for industrials	156,144
		Dividends, and interest @ 4½%	
1919	July	Stocks bought 12/'17, sold @ 88.26 for rails, @ 109.70 for industrials	233,528
		Investment to date (including balance on interest)	
		Interest, 1½ years 4¼% on investment to date	
1921	June	Available for stock purchase @ 68.95 for rails, @ 69.21 for industrials	248,734
		Dividends, and interest at 4½%	
1923	Mar.	Stocks bought 6/'21, sold @ 88.89 for rails, @ 103.87 for industrials	377,918
		Investment to date (including balance on interest)	
		Interest, ½ year @ 4½% on investment to date	
1923	Oct.	Available for stock purchase @ 79.23 for rails, @ 88.11 for industrials	386,421
		Dividends, and interest @ 4½%	
1925	Oct.	Stocks bought 10/'23, quoted @ 103.23 for rails, @ 150.65 for industrials	654,240
		Investment at that date	
1929		Note—At the high point of the market in 1929 when Babson's famous warning was issued, these holdings were worth over	**$1,000,000**

POTENTIAL PROFITS IN COMMODITIES

A knowledge of fundamental statistics is as important to merchants and manufacturers as to bankers and investors. This does not refer to the short-swing trader dabbling in the commodity exchanges or to the company engrossed with inventory speculation. Rather it means that the long swings of commodity prices offer almost as great possibilities of gain or loss as the stock market.

Capital invested in commodities should not depend upon chance for its development. To the business man interested wholly or in part in the price movement of crops, manufactures, raw material or merchandise, figures on underlying conditions, controlling demand and supply are essential.

The tabulation below should be examined carefully. The commodities used in this problem include: Iron, wheat, corn, cotton, sugar, wool, coffee, rubber, pork, copper. Remember that such figures measure not only potential profits, but inversely the potential losses thru ignoring fundamental conditions and price movements. Not only to business men but to investors, commodity price trends are extremely important.

In the figures below we did not include storage charges, insurance and other costs; on the other hand we did not take actual highs and lows but only the average of prices for the whole year. The results represent a capital growth thru commodities of 400% in a brief business career.

POTENTIAL PROFITS IN COMMODITIES

Original Purchase, 1914	$16,535
First Sale, 1920	35,873
Second Purchase, 1921 (1.8 x orig.) . . .	35,873
Second Sale, 1925	50,857
Third Purchase, 1932 (5.16 x orig.) . . .	50,857
Present Value	83,056

CHAPTER IV

WEALTH, NEW BUILDING, CHECK TRANSACTIONS, FAILURES AND LABOR CONDITIONS

WHEN interpreting subjects from the Graphic Outlook based upon our statistical tables and charts treated in this and the two following chapters, one must remember that it is first necessary to decide in which of the four periods the country is: whether in a period of depression, a period of improvement, a period of over-expansion, or a period of decline. This is due to the fact that the same change in the figures of a given subject usually signifies different results under different periods; for example, during a period of depression an *increase* in Bank Clearings is a favorable sign, but during a period of over-expansion a great increase is a dangerous sign. This problem, however, is readily solved by reference to the Babsonchart.

After deciding in what period we are, each set of subjects must be interpreted in accordance with certain rules. Usually with each given subject a *decrease* signifies one thing, an *increase* signifies another, while *no change* signifies a third. Therefore, the figures on each subject should be examined *independently* to ascertain whether the figures show a decrease, an increase, or no change. The new figure, whatever it is, will then be interpreted according as it shows " more satisfactory conditions," " less satisfactory conditions," or " uncertainty." After reaching this conclusion, relative to what the figures on the subject under consideration signify, a note should be made of the result.

Each subject can be treated in this manner and a conclusion reached. All of these conclusions may then be summarized and count taken of how many subjects signify an improvement, how many signify a decline and how many signify something else. All of these are then averaged, though a greater " weight " may be given to one subject than to another; and a conclusion reached as to the duration of the present period and the nature of the next change.

In short, the study of Fundamental Statistics consists simply of (1) obtaining the latest figures on each subject, noting their trend; (2) comparing both the figures and the trend with normal figures and normal trends for said subject; and (3) deducing one final conclusion as to whether the figures and their general trend are becoming more or less normal, considering the areas of the Babsonchart and the Law of Equal Reaction.

In this study, although theoretically the proper method is to consider each subject independently, yet the only safe method is to consider what they, *as a whole*, indicate. This can best be seen by a study of the Babsonchart. Therefore, although the directions given in these three chapters are very valuable for use as a check upon what the Babsonchart indicates, yet no independent subject should be allowed to overshadow what the Babsonchart indicates, viz.: the Babsonchart always shows at a glance in what minor period we are and what period may next be expected; and gives an approximate idea of how long it will probably be before this next period of depression or over-expansion will be upon us.

Therefore, in all cases, the " area consumed," as shown by the Babsonchart, must also be carefully considered.

Let us now turn directly to a study of such subjects as relate especially to mercantile conditions.

WEALTH, BUILDING AND REAL ESTATE OPERATIONS

"Wealth," according to the late Theodore E. Burton, "comprises all things which are alike useful, limited in supply, and transferable. All wealth is produced from or created by land, labor or capital. Land includes every form of nature in earth, seas or air, together with the natural forces which may be set at work. It is the source of our so-called 'raw materials.' Labor includes physical strength and exertion, and the mental qualities which furnish them with method and ingenuity.

" Capital, technically defined, is wealth withheld from immediate consumption for the purpose of producing wealth in the future. It includes food, clothing and fuel for support of those engaged in production of wealth, necessary seed for planting, raw materials for the finished products of manufactures or, if we look at the subject from the standpoint of the employer or capitalist, money for wages and the purchase of supplies. These may be included in the term ' circulating capital.' There is also fixed capital, which includes tools, machines, factories, buildings occupied or used by those engaged in productive employment, improvements upon land, likewise ships and railways with all their equipment. Nations are rich or poor not in proportion to the amount of land or natural resources which they have, but in accordance as they have an abundance or lack of capital."

The above describes what is technically known as " wealth." A concrete example of what constitutes wealth may be found in the following tables. The figures are made up by the Bureau of the Census, Washington, and as reported for the census years, are carefully compiled records of actual values as appraised under the general terms, real and personal property. The 1932 estimate of U. S. wealth is not yet available in itemized form. However, the National Industrial Conference Board, using the census estimate as a basis, has computed the national wealth in 1929 as $362 billion, and in 1932 as $247 billion. This sharp drop was due primarily to the fall in prices rather than any proportionate change in the volume of physical assets.

ESTIMATED WEALTH OF THE UNITED STATES

(000 omitted)

	1904	1912	1922
Real property taxed....	$55,510,228	$96,923,406	$155,908,625
Real property exempt..	6,831,245	12,313,520	20,505,819
Live stock............	4,073,792	6,238,389	5,807,104
Farm implements and machinery..........	844,990	1,368,225	2,604,638
Gold and silver coin and bullion.............	1,998,603	2,616,643	4,278,155

	1904	1912	1922
Manufacturing machinery, tools, etc........	$3,297,754	$6,091,451	$15,783,260
Railroads and their equipments.........	11,244,752	16,148,533	19,950,800
Motor vehicles........	....	....	4,567,407
a. Street railways, etc. (itemized)			
Street railways........	2,219,966	4,596,563	4,877,636
Telegraph systems.....	227,400	223,253	203,896
Telephone systems.....	585,840	1,081,433	1,745,774
Pullman and private cars...............	123,000	123,363	545,415
Pipe lines.............	....	....	500,000
Shipping and canals....	846,490	1,491,117	2,951,484
Irrigation and canals ..	....	360,865	....
Privately owned water works...............	275,000	290,000	360,885
Privately owned electric light and power stations...............	562,851	2,098,613	4,229,357
Total.............	4,840,547	10,265,207	15,414,447
b. All other property (itemized)			
Agricultural products ..	1,899,380	5,240,020	5,465,796
Manufacturing products	7,409,292	14,693,862	28,422,848
Imported merchandise..	495,544	826,632	1,548,666
Mining products.......	408,067	815,552	730,296
Clothing and personal ornaments..........	2,500,000	4,295,009⎫	39,816,001
Furniture, carriages, etc.	5,750,000	8,463,216⎭	
Total............	18,462,282	34,334,291	75,983,607
Grand total	**107,104,212**	**187,300,000**	**320,803,862**

Though the census figures are the only statistics which give the actual value of property in the country, since a complete statement is made only once in ten years, the needs of fundamental statistics lead to the adoption of certain other reports which may be expected to serve as barometers of the conditions termed wealth by our first proposition.

Building statistics, including road and municipal construction, give us the most interesting figures on this subject. Because a new house costs

$10,000, all land on the same street improves and the valuation of the whole city is some thousands of dollars greater at the next census. A factory erected on the same street might reduce the real estate value as residence property, but might so benefit the city as a whole as to greatly increase its entire wealth.

The difficulty of obtaining accurate reports of building has been an obstacle heretofore in the way of systematic study of the subject. The laws of cities and states are so different, that the returns from building permits alone are not always reliable as a basis. But from the field of the contractor another set of figures is to be had. The best of these have been developed by the F. W. Dodge Corp., of New York. The business of such firms is to make a thorough canvass of the principal fields of construction activity in order to furnish accurate information of business openings for contractors and supply firms of all kinds. Reports gathered by this very thorough system have been published from time to time for many years; but have only recently been segregated and tabulated. These reports cover the new work, both in private and municipal building and railroad construction. The values given are conservative and the result of careful inquiry by trained observers.

Fire losses, as reported monthly, include all fires, and show the total destruction of timber, rolling stock of railroads, wharfage and shipping, as well as buildings of all kinds. As in the case of construction or building statistics, the amounts given in these fire loss tables cannot be compared directly with the census figures on wealth. Sometimes the insurance loss is given, sometimes the assessed valuation, sometimes an estimate, as in buildings and contents under appraisal. The direct loss by forest fires is hard to determine exactly, while the indirect losses, so well known to the students of forestry, cannot be calculated for use at frequent intervals. The monthly record which is obtainable, however, is a valuable indicator of conditions likely to contribute to the improvement or decline of business and should, for that reason, be watched. Conditions of poverty following fires, or general improvement as a result of new construction, are both necessary and valuable barometers of business and show where to increase or decrease investment in land, labor and capital.

Another factor of importance, and bearing a relation to the second group of subjects we are considering, is the real estate business. To understand rightly the financial condition of this country, we should know the history of real estate booms and watch for increased rents either of land or buildings. During the hard times of 1907–8 and 1930–33, many of the leading manufacturers reduced their rents fifty per cent, some more and some less. By such means, they hoped to keep their employees on hand for renewed production. Such action was an attempt to meet the wage-earner half way. Some chains of stores went into bankruptcy, as a result of long high rent leases, or to cancel such leases. Raises are usually

seen in times of improvement and especially
towards the culmination of a period of expansion
when rising wage-scales attract the attention of
the house owner who raises his rents, and reaps
his harvest, at the same time when commodity
prices and security markets are rising. A study
of the statistics will show that real estate values
are very good business barometers. New land
developed, irrigation systems introduced, and a
variety of similar factors may seem to be the
causes of booms here and there; but none of these
enterprises can be carried on without the active
investment of capital under sound fundamental
conditions.

So, for the purposes of fundamental statistics,
beside the official figures on wealth, there should be
included these three subjects: (1) new building,
(2) fire losses and (3) real estate values. These
subjects give us a gauge of conditions more frequently than once in ten years.

As the business man is much more interested in
the relation of wealth to prosperity than in any
definitions, it is interesting to note history and
ascertain how the wealth of the country has affected
conditions in the past. Let us, for example, study
the relation of " Miles of New Railroad " to general
conditions, using these construction figures as
illustrative of " New Building."* The first great
crisis which this country experienced was in 1837;
it was preceded by six years of great activity. The

* This is done because it has been impossible to obtain good records
strictly for " New Building " previous to 1902.

railroad mileage of the country had grown from 23 miles in 1830 to 1500 miles in 1837. Simultaneously with this growth in railroad mileage, new towns had been founded, new factories had been opened, desert lands had become taxable, farm property and the wealth of the country had rapidly increased. If the reader will turn to the records of this time, he will find that there was a greater increase of wealth between 1832 and 1837 than during any previous ten years of our history. A great number and variety of new enterprises were started, the bank deposits were large and there was great interest in trading, shipping, manufacturing and real estate. In fact, this great increase in real estate speculation resulted in a similar increase in the assessed valuation of both city and country property.

The second great crisis came in 1857, and was likewise preceded by a period of great increase in new construction. Immediately following the panic in 1837 there was a period of great depression and, although conditions improved in 1844 and 1845, there was no great advance until the discovery of gold in 1849. By 1852, California was actually sending millions of dollars worth of gold to New York. Shipping received a tremendous impetus both on account of the trade with California and on account of the Crimean War in 1854 and 1855. There was also a great increase in railroad mileage, which advanced from only 5600 miles in 1847 to 24,500 miles in 1857. In other words, in 1830 there were but 23 miles of railroad and in 1837, the year of the panic, this had been increased to 1500 miles. During the ten years between 1837 and 1847, only about 4000 miles of new track were constructed, yet in the ten years from 1847 to 1857 about 20,000 miles were constructed. When studying such figures it appears very easy to have prophesied a panic for 1857. With the building of these 20,000 miles, thousands of new towns were settled, millions of acres of hitherto untaxed land became taxable as farm land, and a vast number of manufacturing and other enterprises were started. The result was another great increase in wealth equalled only by the increase which preceded the panic of 1837. As a still further result, came the panic of 1857, causing bankruptcies, suicides, and widespread destitution.

The third great crisis came in 1873. Like its predecessors, it had many causes among which, beyond a doubt, was the great increase in new building construction and new miles of railroad. The Civil War had been accompanied by great destruction of property and a consequent reduction in wealth. This was due partly to deterioration of values and the depreciation of the currency; but largely to the fact that the attention of the people had been turned away from productive industry. Ploughshares had been turned into swords with the accompanying decrease in production. When the Civil War was over, both the South and the North again gave their attention to agriculture, manufacturing and commerce, with the result of an unprecedented rebound. During the early sixties, taxable property decreased; during the early seventies it rapidly increased.

If later panics (that is, the panics of 1884, 1893, 1903, 1907, 1921 and 1930) are studied, the same law will be found to hold true. Furthermore, by inverse reasoning from these same figures it will be found that years of over-expansion may likewise be anticipated.

Another set of building statistics have recently become available through the efforts of F. W. Dodge Corporation. These are figures of contracts awarded for each of the eleven main classes of building, as follows: Business buildings; Educational; Hospitals and Institutions; Industrial; Military and Naval; Public buildings; Public Works and Utilities; Religious and Memorial; Residential; Social and Recreational; Miscellaneous. By studying these figures it is possible to judge what class of building is running above or below normal.

BANK CLEARINGS AND CHECK TRANSACTIONS

Bank clearings are divided into two main classes:

(a) Total Bank Clearings and Check Transactions of the United States.

(b) Bank Clearings and Check Transactions of the United States excluding New York City.

In every large city, and many small ones having more than two banks, there is an institution known as a " clearing house." Each day at some given hour, the representatives of all the banks in the city or town meet at one of the banks to exchange checks drawn on one another and such a bank thus serves as a temporary " clearing house." To illustrate: If customers of the Gloucester National Bank deposit during the day $20,000 in checks drawn on the Gloucester Safe Deposit and Trust Company and customers of the Trust Company deposit checks to the amount of $15,000 drawn on the Gloucester National Bank, instead of the Gloucester National sending a messenger to collect the $20,000 from the Trust Company and the Trust Company sending a messenger to collect the $15,000 from the Gloucester National, representatives of both banks meet and exchange checks and the Trust Company gives the Gloucester National a check for $5,000 to balance the account. This process of settlement is not of great importance in a city having only two or three banks, but the average importance increases rapidly as the number of banks increases. In large cities such as New York, Chicago, Philadelphia and Boston, the " clearing house " occupies a separate building and has regularly salaried employees.*

Up to August 15, 1916, the clearing houses above mentioned conducted the entire clearing business of the country. On that date, however, the Federal reserve banks assumed the functions of clearing houses and extended the existing clearing facilities to many outlying districts, which up to that time had not been served by the clearing houses. Under the new plan each of the twelve Federal reserve

* For further particulars as to the details of clearings and the business of clearing houses refer to Jas. G. Cannon's most complete book on the subject, entitled " Clearing Houses," and also to " The Principles of Money and Banking " by Conant. For a very simple and condensed statement, refer to pages 80–86, inclusive, of " Money and Investments " by Montgomery Rollins. The changes in the clearing system brought about by the Federal Reserve law should also be considered.

banks handles checks for all the banks in their respective districts which agree to remit to them at par. This includes checks on all national banks throughout the country, and checks on a large number of state banks and trust companies. Eventually the Federal reserve banks expect to be able to collect checks on practically all the commercial banks throughout the country. Therefore, by taking the reports of the Federal reserve banks, together with those of the clearing house associations, we have a much more comprehensive record of bank clearings than formerly. Of course some allowance must be made for this change when comparing current figures for bank clearings with those previous to August, 1916.

As to-day, practically all payments are made by check and all business is carried on through the banks, the volume of money handled by the banks by check increases or decreases in constant ratio with the general volume of business of the country, *provided that the prices of the commodities and securities traded in remain constant*. Therefore, as the banks pass their business through the clearing houses, a report on bank clearings is a very good barometer of present business conditions.

Some people make the mistake of assuming that by studying clearing house statistics solely one can easily *forecast* business conditions. A study of these statistics *is an aid* in forecasting conditions, both along lines above mentioned and in connection with Prof. Irving Fisher's " Equation of Exchange "*; but taken by themselves they are of

* See Professor Fisher's book " The Purchasing Power of Money."

little value.   On the other hand, some critics do not
care " to know about present conditions, but desire only to forecast future conditions." This
point of view is also illogical, as a knowledge of
present conditions is a necessary step toward forecasting future conditions.

Were it not for the systematic reports received on
bank clearings, our knowledge of business would be
less complete.   By a study of these clearings, as
they are reported each week, one is in immediate
touch with existing conditions throughout the
country and is also able to study the "velocity
of circulation," which, as it increases, is a form of
credit inflation.   In making use of these statistics
two methods are used:

1. The bank clearings are plotted for each week
for a number of past years with a horizontal scale
for weeks and a vertical scale of billions.   With
one-half inch to a week this makes a plot about
thirty inches long.   It is customary to have each
year under the preceding year, a thing easily done,
as each plot is of the same length, although the
angle of fluctuations is not constant.   This gives
comparative plots for several complete years,
directly under which appears a plot for the present
year up to the receipt of the last report on bank
clearings.   This not only gives the merchant a
bird's-eye view of the situation for the present
year, but also an idea of what may be expected at
different periods during the year.   During some
periods of the year, poor figures on bank clearings
are not, in reality, as unsatisfactory as if they had

occurred at other seasons. The principal use of this plot, however, is to study the fluctuations of the last portion of the plotted line for the current year. In other words, the business man notes whether the variations of the last few months plotted for the current year is upward or downward, and also how said variations compare with similar months of previous years, or in other words, with *normal* figures. If the plots for these previous years can be combined into one plot for an assumed normal year for purposes of comparison, the work is greatly simplified. This may seem to be a simple method of procedure, but when fully comprehended and carefully studied, it will be found to furnish not only a bird's-eye view of present conditions, but, in conjunction with a study of other subjects, the best possible idea of whether general business is becoming better, worse, or simply holding its own.

2. The other plan is more mathematical and more readily operated. Instead of plotting the figures for a series of years, merchants simply tabulate the totals as shown in columns 3 and 4 of insert at end of Chapter VII.

Column 3 is for the bank clearings of the *entire* United States, and column 4 is for the United States *with the exception of New York City.* (*In practice, these figures are subdivided into months and only the past eight or ten years are studied.*) As a second step, the merchant notes from the monthly tables the actual figures received for the current year to date and estimates the probable clearings for the remainder of the year. This may be illustrated somewhat as follows: The merchant notes what proportion the clearings for January, February and March have heretofore borne to the clearings of the entire year. (A novice might think it was simply necessary to multiply the clearings of three months by four in order to have an estimate for the entire year, but such a method is not correct, since it does not provide for the seasonal changes before alluded to.) By making a study of the relation that these three months bear to the entire year for several years back, it is possible to make a very good estimate for the entire current year even if only three months are reported. Having made this estimate, one compares it with the total figures for previous years and forms an opinion as to the probable business conditions for the current year. If the study is dropped at this point, these figures would be of no value, but the merchant revises this estimate each month, as new figures are received, and also notices whether the revised figures are increasing or decreasing. In other words, by this second method, the one universally recommended, the merchant studies the statistics to note whether each succeeding estimate is an increase or a decrease over the previous estimate. If the new estimate is an increase, this shows that business conditions are improving as marked by an upward line on the plot. If the new estimate is a decrease, it shows that business is decreasing, as marked by a downward line on the plot. If the new estimate is practically the same as the last one, this indicates that there may be no change either for the better or for the worse, as marked by a horizontal line on the plot.

The remaining point to be considered on the subject of bank clearings is the reason for separating the subject into the two main classes as per the preceding tables. The reason for this subdivision is as follows: The clearings of New York alone are nearly one-half of those of the entire country. If these clearings were simply a result of commercial business transactions, that is, the transactions of merchants, manufacturers and business men, there would be no reason why the New York clearings should not always be included with the clearings of other cities. The facts of the case, however, show that an exceedingly large percentage of New York clearings is affected by the transactions of bankers or is intimately related to the stock exchange transactions. This may be clearly shown by plotting two lines, one for the transactions of the New York Stock Exchange and the other for the bank clearings of New York. These lines, although very " zig-zag," are almost parallel to each other, and when one rises the other follows, and vice versa. For this reason, during dull times on the stock exchange, bank clearings of the United States *including New York* may show a decrease, even though general business throughout the country is increasing, while during a very active period on the New York Stock Exchange, the bank clearings of the entire United States *including New York*, may show an increase, even though general business throughout the country is decreasing.

For this reason, in order to judge correctly the

general business of merchants and manufacturers throughout the country, it is best to consider the bank clearings of the United States *excluding New York City*. If the figures for the United States *with the exception of New York City* have been properly studied and a conclusion drawn, it is also well then to note the figures for the entire country, including New York City. If the figures for New York City confirm the conclusion arrived at when not including New York City, then the result may be considered absolutely correct. The most successful merchants *tabulate, each month, the sum of the figures for New York and those excluding New York, after first multiplying the latter by 4 or 5, as suggested by Prof. Irving Fisher of Yale University.*

Note 1. There are two exceptions which may be taken to using bank clearings as an index. One is the fact that, as banks consolidate, the ratio is improperly changed. This is not true of check transactions. The other is that bank clearings are increased by the increased cost of commodities and securities, as well as by the increased volume of trade.

The other objection, that an increase in clearings does not necessarily mean an increase in the *volume* of business, is a valid criticism. It is, therefore, well always to note the change in the Commodity Price Index, which index shows how much allowance should be made when studying bank clearings.

Moreover, as a check on one's conclusion, it is well to note the railroad tonnage and car loadings figures, as the latter are wholly dependent upon the *volume* of business, and are independent of rates or prices.

Note 2.   It is pointed out also that clearings reported by one city may be reported also by another city.   For example, the business of a branch house may be reported in the clearings of the city in which it is located and again as part of the business cleared by the main office in the home city.   Just what the percentage of duplication is, it is impossible to determine, but it is probably small compared with the total clearings of the country.

From data compiled by the Federal Reserve authorities, it is possible to get a record of total check transactions which is even more comprehensive than bank clearings.

BUSINESS FAILURES

Every great crisis has been made known to the public by one or more large failures, sometimes accompanied by the exposure of dishonest methods, sometimes by political or national calamity; more often by the failure of some bank or number of banks in endeavoring to finance industries or new corporate undertakings.   So failures,— that is large, single failures,— stand as signals of sharp crises, and the beginning of depression.   They may be followed by other large failures and many small ones, so quickly that the total both in the number of failures and in liabilities for the panic year is swelled, as in 1893, far above the limits of other years just preceding and following it; or the failure record may move slowly and may require more than a year for any great change. Failure statistics, therefore, are of use principally in determining the probable length of a period of depression as shown by the following figures. Note that after a crisis in no case has over-expansion returned until failure statistics have again become normal.

FAILURE STATISTICS FOR THE UNITED STATES

Table I

Compiled from R. G. Dun & Co. figures.

Year	Number Failures	Liabilities	Average Liabilities	Liabilities per firm in business	Per cent failing
1857	4,932	$291,800,000	$59,200	No report	
1858	4,225	95,700,000	22,600	before 1866	
1859	3,913	64,400,000	16,500		
1860	3,676	79,807,000	21,700		
1861	6,993	207,210,000	29,600		
1862	1,652	23,049,000	14,000		
1863	495	7,900,000	16,000		
1864	520	8,579,000	16,500		
1865	530	17,625,000	33,300		
1866	1,505	53,783,000	35,700	$336.	.94
1867	2,780	96,666,000	34,800	462.	1.33
1868	2,608	63,694,000	24,400	230.00	.94
1869	2,799	75,054,000	26,800	212.00	.79
1870	3,546	88,242,000	24,900	207.	.83
1871	2,915	85,252,000	29,200	178.00	.61
1872	4,069	121,056,000	29,800	229.	.77
1873	5,183	228,500,000	44,100	410.	.93
1874	5,830	155,239,000	26,600	258.	.97
1875	7,740	201,060,333	25,960	339.78	1.21
1876	9,092	191,117,786	21,020	305.15	1.33
1877	8,872	190,669,936	21,491	302.60	1.36
1878	10,478	234,383,132	22,369	259.49	1.55
1881	5,582	81,155,932	14,530	108.65	.71
1882	6,738	101,547,564	15,070	129.94	.83
1883	9,184	172,874,172	18,823	210.23	1.06
1884	10,968	226,343,427	20,632	261.94	1.21
1885	10,637	124,220,321	11,678	137.28	1.16
1886	9,834	114,644,119	11,651	124.60	1.01

Year	Number Failures	Liabilities	Average Liabilities	Liabilities per firm in business	Per cent failing
1893	15,242	$346,779,889	$22,751	$290.65	1.28
1894	13,885	172,992,856	12,458	155.25	1.25
1895	13,197	173,196,060	13,124	145.06	1.09
1896	15,088	226,096,834	14,992	190.57	1.31
1900	10,774	138,495,673	12,854	119.63	.92
1901	11,002	113,092,376	10,279	94.63	.90
1902	11,615	117,476,769	10,114	94.85	.93
1903	12,069	155,444,185	12,879	122.33	.94
1904	12,199	144,202,311	11,820	111.33	.92
1905	11,520	102,676,172	8,193	78.75	.85
1906	10,682	119,201,515	11,159	86.52	.77
1907	11,725	197,385,225	16,834	139.75	.82
1908	15,690	222,315,684	14,169	153.58	1.08
1909	12,924	154,603,465	11,964	104.01	.80
1910	12,652	201,757,097	15,947	133.16	.80
1911	13,441	191,061,665	14,215	125.28	.81
1912	15,452	203,117,391	13,145	129.85	.98
1913	16,037	272,672,288	17,003	168.68	.99
1914	18,280	357,908,859	19,579	216.19	1.10
1915	22,156	302,286,148	13,644	180.49	1.32
1916	16,993	196,212,256	11,547	114.90	.99
1917	13,855	182,441,371	13,168	105.26	.80
1918	9,982	163,019,979	16,331	95.44	.58
1919	6,451	113,291,237	17,561	66.21	.38
1920	8,881	295,121,805	33,231	151.20	.49
1921	19,652	627,401,883	31,926	325.53	1.02
1922	23,676	623,896,251	26,351	314.61	1.19
1923	18,718	539,400,000	28,817	270.24	.94
1924	20,615	543,200,000	26,350	265.32	1.01
1925	21,214	443,744,000	20,918	210.18	1.05
1926	21,773	409,232,000	18,795	189.59	1.01
1927	23,146	520,104,000	22,448	239.00	1.07
1928	23,842	489,559,624	20,533	221.76	1.08
1929	22,909	483,250,196	21,094	219.38	1.04
1930	26,355	668,283,842	25,357	306.82	1.21
1931	28,285	736,309,102	26,032	346.45	1.33
1932	31,822	928,312,517	29,172	447.04	1.53
1933	20,307	502,830,584	24,761	247.96	1.00
1934	11,724	230,198,000	19,635		1.00
1935	11,510	183,013,000	15,900		1.00
1936	9,145	147,426,000	16,121		1.00

For example, note in the above table the year
1857, both in number and liabilities. Note that
the crisis is indicated in the amount of liabilities,

for while in 1858 the number of failures is still large, there is a reduction of liabilities amounting to more than 67 per cent. The next three years show depression by a relatively large number of failures; but they are of lessening average amount of liabilities. That statistics of failures may indicate not only the length but the general character of a depression is proved particularly well from the course they take from the crisis year of 1873 to the height of the depression in 1878, and for a shorter period from 1893 to the culminating year of 1896. From the preceding table it is also evident that, while the average of liabilities per failure is less, the *number* of failures is often larger toward the end of a depression than during the crisis year.

From this table also we have another view of the usefulness of failure statistics during those years in which the percentage of failures to the total number of firms in business is available.

Thus we find that up to 1878 the possibility of loss, that is the ratios of " liabilities " to the " number of firms actually in business," was large or increasing from year to year, as was also the case from 1893 to 1896; while, on the other hand, the effects of the crisis of 1903 gave place very quickly to prosperous conditions, surpassing any known in thirty years previous. Furthermore, from the " per cent of failures " to the firms in business we find, that such figures as 11,002 for the failures, in 1901 and 10,478 for 1878 mark two degrees of depression more widely different than they would seem at first glance, and that the high number of

11,725 of 1907, or even 15,690 in 1908, indicate conditions much less severe than does the 7,740 of 1875. The 1931–32 figures confirm the severe depression in every respect. Note the sharp contrast of the 1934 and 1935 recovery period!

But as the study of the past, however interesting as pure history, is here to be regarded only as a means of understanding the significance of current changes, the points above mentioned are of value only in connection with the present day figures.

Statistics of the year are available in different forms. Divided into months, as is the customary way for merchants to compile them, there is meaning to be found in the year's record on lines similar to those used in the annual tables. The following table for liabilities, expressed in millions, serves as illustrations: The " number " omitted from these tables will be found on the Statistical Supplement* from 1914 on as will also the percent of failures to firms in business. For an additional table, the "percent to the firms in business" is recommended.

FAILURE LIABILITIES, IN MILLIONS
Table II

Month	1906	1907	1908	1909	1910	1911	1912
Jan.	$11.952	$13.628	$27.099	$14.008	$32.015	$24.090	$19.770
Feb.	10.859	10.283	27.064	16.734	27.435	17.086	21.477
Mar.	10.949	8.163	21.542	13.718	13.628	18.474	21.763
Apr.	8.059	11.082	20.316	16.825	17.752	16.924	16.874
May	12.992	9.965	13.643	14.383	9.590	13.469	15.277
June	7.850	16.445	14.708	12.607	11.817	13.652	12.847
July	6.919	12.334	14.222	9.527	13.790	12.150	16.098
Aug.	8.821	15.197	23.782	9.620	12.442	11.116	16.153
Sept.	6.255	18.935	17.298	8.446	15.933	11.900	13.280
Oct.	10.553	27.414	15.898	12.529	18.977	19.270	15.762
Nov.	11.980	17.637	12.599	9.812	11.324	15.266	15.646
Dec.	12.006	36.296	14.139	14.625	17.039	17.659	18.164

* The above figures are by Dun Co.

Month	1913	1914	1915	1916	1917	1918	1919
Jan.	$22.972	$39.374	$49.641	$25.863	$18.283	$19.279	$10.736
Feb.	28.141	22.354	32.405	18.744	16.618	12.829	11.489
Mar.	25.718	21.493	23.658	16.885	17.406	17.672	13.595
Apr.	18.445	20.549	43.518	18.383	12.587	14.271	11.450
May	16.863	23.447	21.053	19.466	11.772	13.135	11.957
June	20.767	57.881	18.313	11.929	18.055	10.607	9.483
July	20.325	20.377	18.935	11.647	17.240	9.789	5.507
Aug.	20.848	43.468	17.734	20.129	18.085	7.985	5.932
Sept.	22.662	23.018	16.208	11.569	11.903	17.407	8.791
Oct.	20.245	29.702	25.522	10.775	12.812	13.980	6.872
Nov.	24.199	25.489	15.694	14.105	13.635	13.815	9.177
Dec.	31.480	30.899	19.605	16.745	14.044	12.249	8.300

Month	1920	1921	1922	1923	1924	1925	1926
Jan.	$7.240	$52.137	$73.796	$49.210	$51.273	$54.354	$43.651
Feb.	9.763	60.853	72.608	40.628	35.942	40.123	34.176
Mar.	12.699	67.409	71.608	48.393	97.651	34.005	30.623
Apr.	13.224	38.568	73.059	51.492	48.904	37.189	38.487
May	10.826	57.066	44.403	41.022	36.591	37.027	33.543
June	32.991	34.639	38.242	28.678	34.099	36.701	29.408
July	21.906	42.774	40.010	35.721	36.813	34.505	29.680
Aug.	28.377	42.904	40.230	34.335	55.154	37.159	28.130
Sept.	29.554	37.021	36.908	28.699	34.296	30.687	29.990
Oct.	38.915	53.059	34.647	79.302	36.099	29.544	33.231
Nov.	30.758	53.470	40.265	50.292	31.124	35.922	32.694
Dec.	58.872	87.502	58.069	51.615	45.279	36.528	45.620

Month	1927	1928	1929	1930	1931	1932	1933
Jan.	$51.290	$47.634	$53.877	$61.185	$94.610	$96.860	$79.101
Feb.	46.941	45.070	34.035	51.326	59.610	84.900	65.576
Mar.	59.891	54.814	36.355	56.846	60.387	93.760	48.500
Apr.	53.156	37.985	35.269	49.059	50.868	101.069	51.098
May	37.785	36.116	41.215	55.541	53.371	83.764	47.972
June	34.465	29.827	31.374	63.130	51.656	76.931	35.345
July	43.150	29.586	32.425	39.826	60.998	87.190	27.481
Aug.	39.196	58.202	33.746	49.180	53.025	77.031	42.776
Sept.	32.786	33.956	34.124	46.947	47.256	56.128	21.847
Oct.	36.236	34.990	31.313	56.296	70.660	52.870	30.582
Nov.	36.146	40.601	52.045	55.260	60.660	53.621	25.353
Dec.	51.062	40.744	67.465	83.683	73.213	64.189	27.200

Month	1934	1935	1936
Jan.	$32.905	$14.603	$18.104
Feb.	19.445	15.217	14.089
Mar.	27.228	15.361	16.271
Apr.	25.787	16.529	14.157
May	22.561	14.339	15.375
June	[23.868	12.918	9.177
July	19.326	16.523	9.903
Aug.	18.460	13.266	8.271
Sept.	16.440	17.002	9.819
Oct.	19.968	17.185	8.441
Nov.	18.350	14.384	11.531
Dec.	19.911	15.686	12.288

This table gives examples of what may serve as types of years. Thus, 1903 had what was called "the rich man's panic," beginning with the stock market in the summer of that year and continuing into the next as shown very clearly by the table. The presence of business trouble is first indicated in July of 1903, when the amount of liabilities is very much increased; and this increase and this ratio remain practically unbroken for ten months. Normal years, also, such as 1905 and 1906, show heaviest liabilities between October and March, any increase between these points coming just before or just after the fiscal year.

While Table II is not in itself sufficient, the points just raised show the practical value of such figures. Even without knowing anything of the exact causes, a man with these figures at his hand could not have failed to think a little when, in the report for June, 1907, liabilities ran over 100% higher than in 1906 and nearly as much higher than 1905. As the new figures were received each month, and liabilities for the month of September reached an aggregate of nearly $19,000,000 compared with $8,039,947 for the same number of failures in September, 1905, the change in ratio told something as to the approach of bad times. The statistics for 1929 did not foreshadow the calamity ahead; but the decreases in the winter of 1932–33 indicated revival.

The following table, compiled by Bradstreet's, gives an analysis of failures from the depression year of 1907 to the depression year of 1931.

For example, a large percentage of failures is
due to lack of capital, and if figures show that
this cause is increasing year by year, it means

PERCENTAGE OF FAILURES AND LIABILITIES CLASSIFIED
AS TO CAUSE — UNITED STATES (PER CENT)

	Number				Liabilities			
Failures due to	1907	1906	1905	1904	1907	1906	1905	1904
Incompetence......	22.6	22.3	24.4	23.1	8.9	15.5	21.6	14.1
Inexperience......	4.9	4.9	4.8	5.1	3.2	2.2	2.1	3.2
Lack of capital....	37.1	35.9	33.4	32.2	18.4	30.9	33.0	31.8
Unwise credits.....	2.3	2.6	3.5	3.4	3.1	2.1	4.2	4.8
Failures of others ..	1.4	2.0	2.2	2.5	3.3	8.8	4.5	8.2
Extravagance......	.9	1.0	1.1	.8	.5	.9	1.2	.7
Neglect...........	2.5	2.2	2.9	3.1	.5	1.5	1.1	1.6
Competition.......	1.2	1.0	1.5	1.3	.4	.4	.9	1.0
Specific conditions..	16.3	17.3	16.3	19.1	51.7	17.9	15.5	22.7
Speculation.......	.7	.8	.7	.8	4.9	3.6	7.7	5.3
Fraud............	10.1	10.0	9.2	8.6	5.1	16.2	8.2	6.4

	Number				Liabilities			
Failures due to	1911	1910	1909	1908	1911	1910	1909	1908
Incompetence......	27.0	26.6	24.2	21.6	23.5	21.3	20.9	16.0
Inexperience.......	4.1	4.4	4.9	4.0	2.2	1.9	2.6	1.8
Lack of capital....	31.4	33.9	34.5	34.2	28.3	27.9	28.6	27.2
Unwise credits.....	2.0	1.7	1.9	2.0	2.2	1.9	3.2	3.7
Failures of others ..	1.3	1.0	1.2	1.8	4.2	3.1	5.9	5.0
Extravagance......	.9	.7	.9	1.0	1.2	.5	2.3	.9
Neglect...........	2.2	2.5	3.0	2.2	1.3	.9	2.1	.8
Competition.......	2.9	2.6	2.5	1.8	4.8	1.9	1.4	1.7
Specific conditions..	16.9	14.4	15.3	18.9	20.7	21.1	20.2	31.3
Speculation.......	.7	1.0	.8	1.0	2.7	7.4	4.4	4.7
Fraud............	10.6	11.2	10.8	11.5	8.9	12.1	8.4	6.9

	Number				Liabilities			
Failures due to	1915	1914	1913	1912	1915	1914	1913	1912
Incompetence......	29.9	28.0	28.6	30.2	17.3	13.4	18.4	26.8
Inexperience.......	5.4	5.6	5.1	4.6	2.4	1.9	2.0	3.0
Lack of capital....	27.5	29.4	29.2	29.7	28.4	31.6	24.9	33.5
Unwise credits.....	2.4	2.5	2.6	2.0	3.9	3.2	16.0	2.6
Failures of others ..	1.0	1.8	1.9	1.3	9.2	16.7	11.4	4.9
Extravagance......	.6	.9	.8	.7	.6	.6	.6	.9
Neglect...........	1.9	2.2	2.0	2.0	1.0	1.0	.7	1.0
Competition.......	5.7	3.0	2.3	1.9	3.3	1.2	.9	1.3
Specific conditions..	18.9	16.4	15.3	16.5	24.7	19.8	14.0	13.8
Speculation.......	.4	.7	1.1	.8	2.2	3.5	2.7	3.4
Fraud............	6.3	9.5	11.1	10.3	7.0	7.1	8.4	8.8

	Number				Liabilities			
Failures due to	1916	1917	1918	1919	1916	1917	1918	1919
Incompetence......	33.2	35.5	36.5	38.2	21.8	25.3	26.9	22.6
Inexperience.......	6.0	6.8	6.7	5.6	4.4	5.2	4.7	4.8
Lack of capital....	30.3	31.9	33.2	30.3	31.9	32.7	30.8	25.5
Unwise credits.....	1.9	1.9	1.3	1.3	2.6	1.8	1.8	3.9
Failures of others ..	.9	1.0	.9	1.7	4.6	5.9	3.3	3.3
Extravagance......	.6	.6	.6	1.1	.6	.6	.6	1.2
Neglect...........	2.4	2.2	1.5	1.7	1.0	.8	.9	.8
Competition.......	4.2	2.1	1.2	1.1	2.5	2.1	.8	.8
Specific conditions..	13.4	.9	11.9	11.3	19.3	14.2	19.8	20.5
Speculation.......	.4	.4	.4	.7	3.9	1.5	1.2	2.3
Fraud......	6.7	5.7	5.8	7.0	7.4	9.9	9.2	14.3

Failures due to	Number				Liabilities			
	1920	1921	1922	1923	1920	1921	1922	1923
Incompetence.....	32.5	32.0	34.2	33.7	13.3	22.2	21.6	20.0
Inexperience.......	6.6	5.7	4.7	4.7	3.3	2.9	1.9	2.7
Lack of capital....	32.3	29.3	30.8	34.2	26.6	21.9	24.4	31.8
Unwise credits.....	1.6	1.1	1.3	1.2	3.7	3.9	1.5	3.6
Failures of others..	1.2	1.1	1.2	1.5	.8	1.8	2.5	4.6
Extravagance......	1.2	.4	.7	1.3	.3	.3	.6	1.5
Neglect...........	1.3	1.3	1.1	1.2	.5	.4	1.0	.5
Competition.......	1.3	.9	1.1	1.4	.3	.3	1.2	.7
Specific conditions..	14.4	23.2	20.9	16.3	45.5	42.1	37.0	26.6
Speculation........	.6	.3	.3	.3	1.9	1.1	1.8	2.1
Fraud.............	7.0	4.7	3.7	4.2	3.8	3.1	6.5	5.9

Failures due to	Number				Liabilities			
	1924	1925	1926	1927	1924	1925	1926	1927
Incompetence.....	34.4	36.9	33.9	34.5	30.0	27.7	18.9	20.4
Inexperience.......	4.7	4.0	5.1	5.2	1.5	1.8	3.4	5.2
Lack of capital....	33.3	33.0	32.7	34.9	25.5	28.8	29.7	32.9
Unwise credits.....	1.1	1.3	1.7	1.4	3.1	3.0	2.6	4.4
Failures of others..	1.5	1.3	1.2	1.3	3.3	4.9	2.7	4.0
Extravagance......	1.6	1.9	1.3	.5	.7	1.1	.7	.4
Neglect...........	1.3	1.3	1.5	1.1	.4	.6	1.1	.4
Competition.......	1.9	2.0	2.6	2.4	2.2	.9	1.4	1.6
Specific conditions..	15.9	14.8	15.8	14.8	26.7	26.1	32.9	25.9
Speculation........	.5	.2	.4	.3	1.5	.9	1.5	1.1
Fraud.............	3.8	3.3	3.8	3.6	5.1	4.2	5.1	3.7

Failures due to	Number				Liabilities			
	1928	1929	1930	1931	1928	1929	1930	1931
Incompetence.....	31.4	31.4	26.3	21.7	18.9	18.1	12.8	13.8
Inexperience.......	4.8	4.9	5.3	4.8	2.3	2.2	2.2	5.1
Lack of capital....	35.8	37.2	31.6	31.5	34.4	33.1	14.9	15.0
Unwise credits.....	1.3	2.1	3.5	1.7	2.3	7.5	2.2	.9
Failures of others..	1.3	1.5	3.4	2.3	3.7	7.8	6.7	9.4
Extravagance......	.4	.5	.7	.4	.3	.4	.2	.6
Neglect...........	.8	.9	.9	.5	.4	.4	.2	.2
Competition.......	3.6	3.9	3.5	2.3	2.4	2.2	2.1	.5
Specific conditions..	17.7	15.6	22.4	33.9	31.4	25.1	55.2	52.9
Speculation........	.2	.3	1.2	.1	.6	1.2	1.8	.8
Fraud.............	2.7	1.7	1.2	.8	3.3	2.0	1.7	.9

In severe depressions, many failures are attributable to the depression itself. Note large figures for "specific conditions."

clearly that the beginnings of new enterprises must be increasingly well supported, as it grows more difficult to add to inadequate capital when money rates are high or when competition makes it imperative to expand. The U. S. Department of Commerce has issued bulletins analyzing the causes of failures in various trades. Those studies are more thorough and highly recommended.

As Bradstreet's table excludes all losses except those strictly commercial (that is, it includes only those failures involving loss to creditors of individual firms or corporations engaged in legitimate mercantile occupations), they cannot be compared, figure for figure, with the tables from other sources; but believing that the figures due to failure in insurance, real estate, brokerage, etc., do have a distinct effect upon general business conditions, the analysis of these also should be a part of a study of the whole subject.

Another law recognized by merchants and already suggested in this discussion, is that small firms do not feel the effect of a panic or depression until some time after the effect is felt by the larger firms. For this and other reasons, the study of this subject is especially valuable as a guide and protection to small merchants and storekeepers.

In conclusion I will repeat that figures on business failures are of greatest value to all in determining what the length of the present " period " will be, and how soon one's own business and that of others, in which he has greater or less investments of capital, may be expected to show a change. When the flood begins to subside from its high water mark, a study of the rate at which it is subsiding, and a knowledge of the condition of each tributary stream assists very much in estimating the time when seed may be planted in the rich bottom land, now under water, or *inversely* as the case may be. We need not carry this figure of speech further in order to show that it contains the idea upon which merchants rate the study of *Business Failures* as of fundamental importance to their progress.   For such study is but a part of a system by which they may know exactly the conditions upon which the next move should be based, and upon the result of which depends the subsequent course of the business life of each individual.

LABOR CONDITIONS

The general subject of labor conditions is of importance in diagnosing present business conditions and in forecasting changes which may be expected. But labor interests involve so many factors and include so wide a field of investigation that, with the statistics heretofore available, it has been very difficult to compile figures that were sufficiently complete to tabulate for comparative purposes.

During the past few years important statistical contributions have been made by the United States Bureau of Labor Statistics, New York State Industrial Commission, Wisconsin Industrial Commission, Massachusetts Bureau of Statistics and certain others.   Annual statistics of union wage scales in certain trades are also available.

While these records are by no means complete, they show what can and eventually will be done to secure accurate information on labor conditions. The difficulty with all these records today, however, is that they extend back over only a short period of years.   They are valuable for determining the present trend, but great care must be taken in drawing conclusions as to their indications of the future.   The record of immigrants arriving and departing is practically the only available subject which has reflected the labor situation during earlier years.

The data furnished by the Department of Labor are very important inasmuch as they cover such a wide geographical distribution and unlike the Massachusetts data include a diversified list of industries. This work was started by the United States Bureau of Labor Statistics in July, 1915, and for recent years, monthly data are available.

The index includes in its distribution approximately six hundred to eight hundred thousand wage earners and includes the automobile, iron, steel industries, textiles, boot and shoe, tire, chemical, clothing and in all about fifty industries. The data show the number on the payroll as well as the total amount of the payroll, in a manner similar to the index numbers on employment conditions used on our Statistical Tables and Charts. Taken in conjunction with the New York figures, it is now possible to get a survey of employment covering almost a million and a half men.

Further impetus to the gathering of labor statistics by the Federal Government was given thru the appointment of Miss Frances Perkins as Secretary of Labor in the Roosevelt administration in March, 1933. As Industrial Commissioner in the New York State Department of Labor, Secretary Perkins established an enviable record and was particularly interested in gathering and compiling data affecting employment, wages, hours of labor, payrolls, strike, and other vital statistics concerning the human element in industry. Under her direction, the State of New York took the lead in making available a vast array of data and presented it in a timely and valuable way so that the figures have been of specific use to business men.

President Roosevelt so valued her services while he was Governor of New York that he broke a precedent and made her the first woman cabinet officer. As soon as she took office as Secretary of Labor, she began to expand the work of her department and it is already showing results in the form of increased and more detailed data on various aspects of labor statistics.

About 1914 we began publishing the reports on current strikes which appear in the Strike Chart shown on the insert.

When this record was started it was considered not quite good form to publish reports of strikes. It was felt that a man's strikes were his own property and many employers resented newspaper publicity on strikes as completely as a man would resent publicity about his domestic troubles.

These, when tabulated over a term of years, give a report that possesses high value. By charting these strikes, it is possible to show the trend of strike activity from year to year; to show the pre-war normal level of strikes; to compare the present with that level, and to show at any time exactly where we are in this matter of labor disturbances.

The personal element, human temperament and so on, enter into strikes to such an extent that we have wide variations from any standard. Still, taking a ten-year survey, it is possible to draw many valuable conclusions from the strike reports.

The attitude of labor all over the United States changes radically as we go from expansion to depression, or vice versa. When jobs are many and men are scarce, labor assumes a more or less arrogant air. By "more or less," we mean that the greater the urgency of the labor market, the more powerful labor becomes. During the phenomenal period of the World War this fact was illustrated to the extreme. Never before in the history of the United States has labor had such an advantage in the market as it had during those years. Four million men were withdrawn from the productive forces of the country and put into our army and navy. Other millions were engaged in supplying these forces with sustenance and war material. The balance were left with the ordinary production work of the country on their hands. Furthermore, immigration was suspended and the ever-fresh supply of cheap labor was thus cut off.

In consequence the workers had the advantage all on their side. They were for the most part loyal and intent on serving their country. But the urgency created by mounting living costs, coupled with the power that conditions gave them, resulted in a nation-wide move on the part of labor to better its conditions.

The outstanding symptom of this development is the frequency of strikes. All through the war and during the period of post-war expansion the strike curve was far out of normal. Labor used its economic power and employers were generally unable successfully to cope with this power. The majority of the strikes were successful.

It should be noticed that any marked change in the number of strikes accompanies a corresponding change in the business situation. So long as the reported strikes remain above the normal, we know that the advantage in the industrial struggle lies with the employees. When these conditions reverse, the change will show itself in the reports on strikes and wage changes. If we had no other data on business conditions it would still be possible to make a fairly good picture of fundamental business from the strike statistics.

As a barometer of labor conditions, immigration and emigration figures previous to the war were extremely good. In peace times the steamship lines maintained a balance in the supply of labor between the United States and Europe. Labor, like water, seeks its own level, when both living expenses and wages are considered. Of course, if it cost five times as much to live in New York as in Italy, the Italian laborer would not come to this country for simply five times the wages that he received at home, provided the demand for labor was the same in each country. Therefore, living expenses, as well as wages, must be considered. On the other hand, if the Italian could obtain wages in New York equal to ten times what he received in Italy, he would board a steamer for the

United States, even with the expenses in New York five times as great as at home. Such high wages the Italian could always obtain in America in times of over-expansion, and especially in times just preceding the culmination of a period of over-expansion.

The important part which immigration played as a barometer of labor conditions thruout the United States ended with the enactment by Congress of the immigration restriction law in 1924. This eventually served to reduce the flow of immigration into the United States to a mere trickle.

There is also another reason why these various figures are of interest; namely: because the number of aliens entering or leaving the country was not only a barometer of business conditions, but it was also influential in the trend of such conditions. When a foreigner entered this country, he usually brought a little money, for he knew that he would need a place in which to sleep while here and must have some food and clothes. On the other hand, when leaving the country he took from circulation a certain amount of money which was almost invariably many times what he brought into the country. In addition, he directly reduced the income of some landlord and the business of some small grocer and dealer in second-hand clothing.

CHAPTER V

BANKING, FEDERAL RESERVE SYSTEM,
FOREIGN TRADE, FOREIGN EXCHANGE, GOLD
AND COMMODITY PRICES

MONEY IN CIRCULATION

THIS subject may, at first thought, seem uninteresting and of little concern to the merchant or manufacturer; yet, as a matter of fact, the " Amount of Money in Circulation " is of vital interest not only to the merchant and manufacturer, but also to the humblest store-keeper and day laborer.

The trade of the corner grocery store is regulated by the amount of money in circulation in the neighborhood; and the amount of money in circulation in the neighborhood is dependent upon the amount circulating in the entire country. As the local banks in every small town have deposits in some large city such as New York, Chicago or St. Louis, money cannot be abundant in one city and scarce in another, except for a very short time. The banks of the various cities are so related through the Federal Reserve System, that money — like water — immediately seeks its own level. As a result, all parts of the country must prosper or suffer in accordance with the amount of money in circulation. The storekeeper must, therefore, study figures of the entire country, and not simply the conditions in his own town or in his own neighborhood.

The amount of money in circulation is, in fact, of equal importance to the large merchants and to the manufacturers. The small retailer who buys only what goods he can sell immediately, ceases purchasing as soon as his business diminishes. This immediately affects the business of the manufacturer, who in turn ceases to purchase from the large producers. Since the small manufacturer buys new material only as needed for actual manufacture, he ceases to purchase in direct proportion as he reduces his help. The great merchants and manufacturers do not feel the effect, possibly until later; but when the blow does come, they feel it to a greater extent than the small dealer. It may be plainly seen, therefore, that the amount of money in circulation directly affects every one, whether laborer, clerk, small storekeeper, merchant, large manufacturer or the railroad company which transports for all.

The Terms Defined.

In the discussion of this subject, two different " amounts " are referred to, viz.:

1. The *gross amount* of money per capita, whether hoarded or in use.

2. The *net amount* of working money in circulation.

These two amounts may be defined as follows:

" The *gross* amount of money per capita " includes all money in the United States whether it is in the bank or buried in the ground, at work or idle. All money in the safe deposit boxes and in the

pockets of individuals is counted in this item.
This amount of money in circulation formerly
stood at about $35* per capita, based on the esti-
mated population of the United States. The gross
amount of money per capita simply represents the
total of the gold and silver coins and bills and bank
notes in existence, wherever located in the United
States. It has been estimated that in order to keep
this figure in the vicinity of $34 or $35 per capita,
it is necessary to create or import about $50,000,000
net in coin and bills each year.

The " net amount of working money " means the
amount in actual use in making payments from
day to day plus the sum of checks drawn against
bank deposits. When a farmer deposits in his
bank, money received from the sale of cotton in
Liverpool, he increases the gross amount of money
in circulation but not the net unless the bank loans
the money out to someone else. When he checks
this out to an American firm in payment for fertilizer he increases the net amount of active money
but not the gross. Should he draw this money out
and hoard it he does not affect the gross amount of
money in the country but may indirectly affect the
net by curtailing the loaning power of the bank.

But " the net amount of working money in circulation " is affected in another way, namely: by
the amount of money that each man is carrying in

* Rose after the World War (November, 1920) to $59.77. Beginning
July 1, 1922, the form of circulation statement was revised so as to exclude
all forms of money held by the Federal Reserve banks and Federal Reserve
agents. This change results in showing a per capita circulation at the
peak in November, 1920, of $52.36. On May 1, 1923, the circulation was
$42.04, whereas under the method heretofore used it would have been
$52.61.

his pocket. If a man carries eleven dollars in his pocket instead of one dollar, he seldom realizes that the act is affecting the financial condition of the country; but if 15,000,000 working men in the United States should do this same thing, it would make a difference of $150,000,000 in the net amount of working money in circulation, or more than $500,000,000 in the banking resources of the United States. Thus the net amount of working money in circulation represents the amount which is actually in the banks or actually at work in commerce and industry; it does not include idle money stowed away in pocketbooks or safe deposit boxes.

Experience has shown that the " *net* amount of working money in circulation " cannot be forecast by figures, but is dependent rather upon sentiment. In other words, instead of being dependent upon the financial condition, it is dependent rather upon the sentiment of the people. This net amount in circulation may remain practically constant for years until some large failure, scandal or rumor of war comes, when the people lose confidence and money stops circulating. In such cases, everybody holds all he has in his possession and free circulation is stopped or retarded. Thus the *net amount* of working money is often independent of the *gross amount* of money in circulation. Should a rumor be published in the morning papers that some great financial institution is in a critical condition, the *net* amount of money in circulation would immediately be affected to a greater extent than would be possible through years of legislation; but the *gross* amount of money would remain constant. Furthermore, such rumors, failures or scandals are the best warnings of impending contraction of the net amount of money in circulation. The study of statistics in such instances is of little value. In other words, as soon as such a thing happens, the merchant may be reasonably certain that his trade will be diminished, and the effect of his curtailment will be felt by the manufacturers, the middlemen and the railroads.

On the other hand, the merchant should be equally on the watch for the time when confidence will be restored and when the people will decide to part with the money they have been hoarding. As it is human nature to hoard money in case of trouble, it is also human nature to forget this trouble quickly. Moreover, people seem unable to withhold money from circulation beyond a certain length of time; they become uneasy under the loss of interest, and it finally occurs to them that their money is in more danger in their houses than when deposited in a bank. Thus periods of financial stringency, which were caused by the temporary withdrawal of money from circulation, were invariably followed by a great increase in the net amount of working money. *Nevertheless, the business of the merchant does not increase directly in proportion to the increase of the net amount of working money.* While business falls off as soon as the *working* money decreases, the reverse is not true.

When mills are closed and people are out of employment, they acquire frugal habits, and after the mills again start, they do not at once begin to spend; but they deposit their savings in a bank. The fact remains, nevertheless, that after these periods of fright, money becomes very plentiful with the banks and interest rates becoming correspondingly low, with a slow but gradual increase in business. As the efficiency of money depends upon its rapidity of circulation, a contraction in the net amount of working money always causes a decrease in general business which requires some time to return to a normal state.

In the case of the "*gross* amount of money per capita," entirely different laws prevail. To quote from the late Theodore E. Burton's admirable book entitled "Crises and Depressions":—"Paradoxical as it may seem, the starting point for crises and depressions may be found in abundance rather than in scarcity, whether in money or in capital." Here he refers to the "*total gross amount of money per capita*" or the figures which are studied under fundamental statistics. The best statistics available may be obtained from tables prepared each month by the U. S. Government. In general, these figures usually show a continued increase up to a certain point, at which time a panic or a depression comes over the country. *This is due to the fact that panics and depressions are so often caused by over-prosperity. Therefore, this gross amount of money per capita is a good barometer of prosperity.* If the gross amount of money in circulation, as reported by the government, shows a steady increase per capita for several years and the country is prosperous — mills running overtime, labor in great demand, and everybody happy and contented — then the merchant and manufacturer should be on the watch for a turn in the tide. In other words, too large an amount of money per capita is sure to be followed by a period of disaster.

REPORTS OF THE COMPTROLLER OF THE CURRENCY

Each national bank is required to make three reports a year to the Comptroller of the Currency. The reports are verified under oath by the president and cashier and are attested by at least three directors of each bank. They give in detail the resources and liabilities of all national banks at a date specified by the Comptroller, and always previous to the date of the call. Each report must be mailed to the Comptroller within five days after the request is made for it. Such reports are the basis of a most useful examination of the banking situation, as they include not only figures from all national banks but also annual supplementary figures relative to other banks.

These figures should be studied both independently and in their relation to one another. In other words, the " ratios " should be studied and compared. This is one of the principal features of these reports as used in connection with the study of " Fundamental Statistics." They will be found more fully explained under the headings of "Loans," " Reserves," etc.

LOANS OF THE BANKS

In analyzing reports of the Comptroller of the Currency, four distinct lines of investigation are followed, namely:

(a) The ratio of bank " Loans " to bank " Resources."

(b) The ratio of bank " Loans and Investments " to bank " Resources."

(c) The ratio of " Reserves " of the banks to the " Deposits."

(d) The ratio of the " Reserves " of the banks to the " Resources."

These four distinct subjects should be studied independently before making any deduction or forecasting business conditions. It is also instructive to study the relation of loans to deposits. Then (a) should be compared with (b), and (c) with (d). In order to save time and space, the first two are here treated together, and the second two are treated together under another heading.

Bank Loans: Bank loans include notes, discounts, overdrafts, and all other forms of so-called liquid assets. Banks when first organized were expected to serve two purposes: they were to receive money on deposit and they were to loan it to depositors, with the understanding that all deposits could be withdrawn and all loans called for payment at any time. The most ideal conditions are to be found where banks still keep most closely to the standard above laid down. All of the assets of a bank other than cash on hand, etc., should consist of loans that can be liquidated within six months. Therefore the term " Loans and Discounts " would include all notes, etc., which are either payable on demand or are payable within six months or a year at the utmost.

Investments: In reality, a bank is loaning money to a corporation whether it purchases its fifty-year debenture bonds or its six-months' notes. In either case the security is the same and the interest may be the same. For an investor, the fifty-year bonds if properly secured, are often a more practical purchase than the notes; but for a bank the same statement cannot be made. Strict adherence to the original principle of banking often demands that a bank shall refuse to purchase the bonds of a corporation of which it may willingly accept the notes.

Notes when purchased by banks may be listed under the head of " Loans and Discounts," but bonds so purchased must be listed under the head of " Investments." The national law forbids the purchase by national banks of real estate, except as a building site, but purchase of real estate mortgages has been encouraged recently by medium of the Home Owners' Loan Corp. and various new banking and recovery legislation. Logically there seems to be no reason why a national bank should be allowed to buy fifty-year bonds and forbidden to purchase improved real estate, but the fact that the prohibition is made shows that the spirit of the law is against all forms of permanent investments. Therefore, by such reasoning, all stocks, bonds and notes, which do not mature for six months or more, come technically under the head of " Investments." As there is no law which states exactly the difference between " Loans " and " Investments," banks differ regarding the definition, many banks placing under the head of loans, even such short term notes as do not mature for two or three years.

Resources: The " Resources " of a bank are the same as the resources of any individual or nation. They include the notes, discounts, loans, stocks, bonds, real estate and other property which the bank holds. When a bank makes an appraisal of its total assets, figured on a conservative basis, the resulting figure represents the " Resources." The greater the proportion of " Loans " to " Resources," the less normal are banking conditions.

We think that the above definitions in themselves are sufficient to convince the reader of the truth of the following statement:

(1) *The banking situation of the country becomes more critical as the proportion of loans to resources increases, and improves as the proportion of loans to resources decreases.*

If all national banks confined themselves to loans and discounts, and made no permanent investments, excepting to the extent of their capital, it would be a very easy matter to judge the conditions in accordance with the above rule. As, however, practically all banks place a large amount of funds in more permanent investments, that item must be independently analyzed and the above rule must be supplemented by the following:

(2) *With a given ratio of loans to resources, conditions become more critical as the proportion of investments to resources increases, and conditions improve as the proportion of investments to resources decreases.*

In other words, provided a constant relation exists between the funds loaned and the total resources, the general banking situation is strengthened whenever a bank disposes of long term bonds and reinvests the money in high grade commercial paper; conversely the general banking situation is weakened whenever a bank purchases long term bonds with money received from deposits or from the payment of high grade commercial paper. Therefore, anyone studying these conditions should note two things:

(1) Whether the proportion of " Loans " to " Resources " is increasing, decreasing, or remaining fixed.

(2) Whether the proportion of " Investments " to " Resources " is increasing, decreasing, or remaining fixed.

Although the most careful students consider these terms separately, we think it is generally safe to combine the two ideas in the one general rule, as follows:

As the ratio of "Loans and Investments" to "Aggregate Resources" increases, the banking situation becomes more critical; and as the ratio of the two combined items to "Aggregate Resources" decreases, the banking situation improves.

The accompanying table shows the record of the national, state and private banks and trust com-

panies of the United States which have reported to
the Comptroller since 1865. A study of these
figures, with the other subjects, would have made
it possible to forecast nearly every period of depression and every period of over-expansion which this
country has experienced since the Civil War.
These figures cannot be expected to foretell the exact time when crises or panics will occur, owing to
sudden catastrophes, but they forecast the large
swings. They clearly show when conditions are becoming abnormal and expansion is going too far.
These figures date back only to the Civil War, as
the system of national banks was not established
until 1863. Consequently, this is the only period
which gives satisfactory data to form a basis for any
theory regarding the relation of banking conditions
to general business, and conversely, the effect of
business conditions upon banking conditions. The
latter clause is added because, although strained
banking conditions cause a recession in general
business, it has always been found true that great
activity in business has caused strained banking
conditions.

Therefore, when business has been very active
and the country very prosperous, bankers may
surely anticipate strained and critical banking conditions. Conversely when strained banking conditions have existed for a certain period, business men
may be sure of a reaction. The figures show that
after a period during which there was a more or less
noticeably rapid increase in the ratio of " Loans and
Investments " to " Resources," there followed in-

variably a period of depression until the ratio was
reduced to a normal point.   From 1887 to 1897 the
" Loans and Discounts " increased only 43% and
the " Investments " 73% against an increase in
aggregate resources of 50%.   This was a normal
and healthy increase and all observers were sure
that the country was preparing for a period of
marked expansion, but between 1897 and 1907 the
" Loans and Discounts " increased 155% and the
" Investments " 153% against the increase in " Resources " of 151%.   It was due to these figures that
the bankers and investors who carefully study all
fundamental statistics were sure that the country
was entering a period of decline. Such figures
showed a period of depression to be absolutely necessary in order to give the banks an opportunity
to recuperate and again enjoy healthy and normal
conditions.   These figures are still more dangerous
when it is considered that during the period between 1887 and 1897 the aggregate " Resources "
showed an increase of 50%, even though the market
value of securities was not increasing.

During the ten years between 1897 and 1907, the
increase in aggregate " Resources " was largely due
to the inflated prices and the growing market value
of securities held, and possibly not much to larger
numbers of investments. These changes have
been irregular rather than constant and have
caused varying conditions of strength and weakness
in the banking situation; the growth of loans and
investments was much more rapid than the Babsonchart Index of the Physical Volume of Business.

The above figures would appear somewhat different if figures of all private banking houses, such as J.P. Morgan & Co., Kuhn, Loeb & Co., and others were included, but nevertheless they are sufficient.

Referring to earlier years, we see that in 1873 the ratio of " Loans " to " Resources " first exceeded 50% and in fact reached a ratio of 52.71%. Consequently, a panic occurred in that year. The ratio of " Loans " to " Resources " continued to increase to 54.13% and 54.55% in 1874 and 1875 respectively, and the prolonged depression was probably due to this continued increase. Moreover, this item remained practically unchanged until 1876 when the liquidation was completed. " Loans and Discounts," which in 1873 were $1,439,900,000, after reaching $1,748,100,000 in 1875, were reduced in 1879 to $1,507,400,000. This condition of the banks enabled them to loan money at low rates of interest and again accommodate legitimate enterprises. Consequently, business increased marvelously from 1879 to 1883.

During this period, however, loans had again rapidly advanced,— as is shown by the table,— and remained practically fixed between 1883 and 1885. During this period, that is in 1884, a sharp panic occurred which might readily have been anticipated. Although distress was felt in every part of the United States, it lasted only a short time in comparison with that of 1873. The banks were able to reduce their ratio of " Loans and Investments " to " Resources " so quickly that the ratio which stood at 77.96% in 1884 was reduced to

72.83% in 1885. Consequently, business became again more active, mills resumed operation and railroad earnings began to increase.

In 1886, the new period of over-expansion, with advancing prices, was in full swing. This movement continued without any marked change until the early nineties when " Loans " reached a very high proportion, 60.57%. Large crops in this country, with small crops abroad, helped to postpone trouble for a time, but a depression came in 1893 when the ratio of " Loans " to " Resources " was even higher than in 1890, namely 60.74%. All business men and investors who were then studying these figures were absolutely sure that a panic would ensue.

Another disturbance came in 1903 which, although short, was certainly severe. Railroad earnings decreased, mills shut down, many men were thrown out of employment and money rates were very high. Again the western farmer came to the rescue of the country, and owing to bountiful crops and other reasons, mills again started and business improved. This continued until 1907. During these years, however, there was no real improvement in the banking situation except for a short time. In 1904, money was very cheap, but only temporarily. Banking conditions became worse and worse so that students of the situation were sure that the improvement from 1904 to 1906 would be followed by a depression in 1907 when the banks might again have an opportunity to recuperate. This recuperation was completed in

1908, and very soon banking conditions were again normal. In 1920, 1925, 1928 and 1929 the inflation of debt and bank credit went from bad to worse.

The great value of these data to the investor is self-evident. When the ratio of " Loans and Investments " to " Resources " is abnormally high, the country is abounding in a false prosperity and securities are selling at high prices, the wise investor sells his securities and places his money on deposit in strong banks. On the other hand, when the ratio of " Loans and Investments " to " Resources "* is low, and when, although business is dull and mills are not running, his general knowledge of the situation shows that fundamental conditions are sound, the investor will withdraw his money from the banks, purchase high grade stocks and bonds and hold them until business again becomes active.

While in the previous table we have given aggregate figures for all banks, in order to show general banking conditions, such figures are also of service relative to the condition of two or more banks. A depositor should select a bank whose ratio of " Loans " to " Resources " is comparatively small and should especially avoid banks with large " Investment " accounts,— so large as to show a policy not in agreement with sound management.

A very small figure for " Loans " is not a good sign, neither is a very large figure. The former

---

* Some prefer to substitute " Deposits " in place of " Resources," and in that way check their conclusions, as the " Loans " should not much exceed the " Deposits."

signifies stagnation, the latter over-extension. It is important that the figure be normal, and that it bear a proper relation to the figure for "Deposits," — thus giving a sound, safe amount for "Reserve." See also the discussion of the Federal Reserve law, page 153.

SURPLUS RESERVES OF THE BANKS

The figure for "Surplus Reserve" often indicates:

(a) The Price of Money.
(b) The Supply of Money.

The price is determined by the relation of the supply and the demand; that is, when more persons wish to borrow than to loan, interest rates advance; and when a larger number wish to loan than to borrow, the supply is greater than the demand and interest rates decline. For this reason, money rates are usually high during the periods of business activity and low during periods of depression. The *price* of money, however, is not as important a factor as the *supply*. In other words, provided the merchant can obtain the money when needed and in sufficient quantities, an abnormal interest rate is less harmful in its effects than the inability to get money at all.

A variation in the rates for borrowed money has a more direct effect upon the market for stocks and bonds than upon the market for merchandise. When the speculator can borrow money at three or four percent to purchase securities paying five or six percent, the temptation is to borrow and make the purchases, thus increasing the demand and consequently the market price for the securities. Under such circumstances, there is a profit on the " interest account," even though there is no increase in the value of the investments. On the other hand, this increased incentive to purchase does not exist when money commands six or seven percent and securities are selling on a four or five percent basis, for then the " interest account " shows a loss. Those who have securities upon which they are borrowing money are tempted to sell them in order to stop the loss in interest. Consequently, the supply of securities exceeds the demand and the price declines.

As previously stated, this question of " interest rates " is entirely secondary to the question of " supply." It is not interest rates that cause the merchant to fail or the speculator to sacrifice his stocks, but rather his inability to renew his loans on any terms whatever. Many great periods of declining prices have been solely due to this cause, namely, a lack of supply of money, and the speculator is not the only one to feel the effect of such times. The weekly statement of reporting member banks, used in connection with the Federal Reserve bank statement, Comptroller's Reports and Foreign Money Rates, forms the best barometer of the *supply* of money. Previous to the Federal Reserve system the statement of the New York Clearing House Banks was the best barometer.

As to the current *price* of money, this may be
definitely determined each day by referring to the
money articles on the financial page of most daily
papers. The figures under what is known as " call
rates " or " call money " denote the rates which the
stock exchange houses and bond dealers are required to pay for money on loans which may be
called any day and on which the rates may change
from day to day. Sometimes this figure is more
and sometimes less than the figure for " time rates."
" Time rates " apply to loans maturing at a fixed
date, such as six months or a year. When the
bankers having money to loan think that all rates
are to strengthen in the near future, then the call
rate is less than the time rate, and when the bankers
having money to loan think that all rates are to
decrease in the immediate future, then call rates
are higher than the time rates. Some of the
shrewdest borrowers take time money when the
bankers are encouraging the people to take call
money, and vice versa, on the principle that the
bankers know more about the situation than their
customers. However, this question of money rates
is too complicated to present here in detail, especially since, as has been stated, the price of money
can be easily ascertained at any time by referring
to the daily papers.

The *supply* of money is the most vital question
as, unlike the price, it is not so subject to manipulation. This supply, as above stated, was formerly
best indicated by the weekly New York Bank Statement. This was simply a statement of the New

York banks and did not include statements from any of the other twenty thousand banks in the United States, nor the great banking institutions of foreign countries. We now have what is in the way of becoming a complete weekly bank statement. It now includes the statements of over six hundred of the principal member banks of the Federal Reserve System. From this statement, together with the statement of the twelve Federal Reserve Banks, we can note weekly the amount of available money and follow closely the expansion or contraction of credits, as shown by the relation between reserves and deposits, and between reserves and loans.

So long as the " Surplus Reserve " decreases, a corresponding increase in money rates may be expected; but if the " Surplus Reserve " increases each week, a decrease in money rates may follow. Since the demand for stocks often increases as the interest rate decreases, money and the stock market often strengthen with the publication of what is known as a " good bank statement," namely, a bank statement which shows an increase in the " Reserve Item." On the other hand, as an increase in money rates often forces a sale of stocks, due to the calling of the loans, a " poor bank statement " is often followed by a drop in the market prices. When the New York bank statement is published on Saturday, the change in interest rates cannot come until the following Monday. However the trader realizes this and bases his transactions on it. The first sellers after a poor bank statement

are supposed to obtain the best prices, and the
first buyers after a very good bank statement are
supposed to obtain their securities at the lowest
prices.

AGGREGATE RESOURCES

Before the enactment of the Federal Reserve
Banking Act a large part of the reserves of national
banks was kept either on deposit in Reserve Cities
or in cash. The banks in reserve cities, in turn kept
their reserves partly in cash and partly in demand
deposits in central reserve cities, especially New
York. Hence the ratio between cash in the banks
and " Deposits " and between cash and " Resources " was of great importance for judging the
banking situation.

The surplus cash always tended to gravitate to
New York where it was employed partly in commercial loans. But chiefly these funds were loaned
on stock exchange collateral for financing stock
speculation. Any financial disturbance or any
great general demand for money which causes the
withdrawal of funds by the depositing banks in
other sections, had a cumulative effect on the cash
held by the New York banks. Hence the ratio between cash and resources and between cash and
deposits of the New York banks in years past had
always been an especially good indicator.

Under the Federal Reserve System, however, the
banks which are members of the system now have
to carry all of their legal reserves with the Federal
Reserve Bank in their respective districts. To

some extent country banks still deposit funds in New York, but as such deposits cannot be counted as legal reserves, they are not nearly as large as formerly.   The Federal Reserve Banks have the authority to transfer funds among themselves in case of distress in any particular locality.

Having already explained the relation that " Loans and Investments " bear to the money situation, let us study the effect that " Reserves " have on the money situation.   Of course, it is usually true that the greater the amount of " Loans and Investments," the smaller the amount of " Reserves " and vice versa.   For this reason the following rule is already self-evident.

The banking situation grows more critical as the ratio of reserves to deposits decreases, and the situation improves as the ratio of reserves to deposits increases.

National banks are now compelled by law to maintain a reserve on deposit with the Federal Reserve Banks equal to from 7% to 13% of their demand deposits (according to the city in which the bank is located) and 3% of their short time deposits running over 30 days and any amount over this required reserve is called a "Surplus Reserve."   As this surplus reserve declines, money rates increase, merchants and manufacturers are limited in borrowing, and speculators are compelled to dispose of stocks and bonds in order to pay their loans.   On the contrary, as the surplus reserve increases the banks become sounder and are ready to loan money to investors, manufacturers, and merchants at lower rates of interest.   This subject is explained more in detail a few pages hence.

Periods of depression and over-expansion in the past often could have been anticipated by a study of the ratio of " Cash " to " Deposits," since under the old National banking act reserves were held wholly in cash by the New York banks, while country banks carried 40% of their reserves in cash. Whenever a great decline in the ratio of cash to deposits or aggregate resources occurred there always followed a period of contraction of credits; and conversely as this ratio increased lower interest rates have always followed. The following table shows the ratio of cash to the deposits of the National, State, Savings and other banks and trust companies from 1865 through 1933. After 1916 the ratio is no longer indicative, owing to the change above described; especially is this so after 1933.

Year	No. of Banks Reporting	Individual Deposits	Total Cash in Banks	Ratio of Cash to Individual Deposits
1865	1,960	$641,000,000	$199,400,000	31.11
1866	2,267	815,800,000	231,900,000	28.30
1867	2,279	876,600,000	205,600,000	23.45
1868	2,293	968,600,000	200,700,000	20.72
1869	2,354	1,032,000,000	162,500,000	15.74
1870	2,457	1,051,300,000	187,700,000	17.85
1871	2,796	1,251,600,000	194,000,000	15.50
1872	3,066	1,353,800,000	177,600,000	13.12
1873	1,968	1,421,200,000	218,200,000	15.35
1874	1,983	1,526,500,000	252,200,000	16.52
1875	3,336	1,787,000,000	238,700,000	13.36
1876	3,448	1,778,600,000	226,400,000	12.73
1877	3,384	1,813,600,000	230,500,000	12.71
1878	3,229	1,717,400,000	214,600,000	12.50
1879	3,335	1,694,200,000	216,300,000	12.77
1880	3,355	1,951,600,000	285,500,000	14.63
1881	3,427	2,296,800,000	295,000,000	12.84

Year	No. of Banks Reporting	Individual Deposits	Total Cash in Banks	Ratio of Cash to Individual Deposits
1882	3,572	$2,460,100,000	$287,100,000	11.65
1883	3,835	2,568,400,000	321,000,000	12.50
1884	4,111	2,566,400,000	321,200,000	12.51
1885	4,350	2,734,300,000	414,300,000	15.15
1886	4,378	2,812,000,000	375,500,000	13.00
1887	6,179	3,308,200,000	432,800,000	13.09
1888	6,647	3,422,700,000	446,100,000	13.03
1889	7,203	3,778,100,000	499,100,000	13.21
1890	7,999	4,062,500,000	478,300,000	11.77
1891	8,641	4,796,800,000	479,100,000	11.41
1892	9,338	4,664,900,000	568,400,000	12.58
1893	9,492	4,627,300,000	515,900,000	11.15
1894	9,509	4,651,200,000	688,900,000	14.81
1895	9,818	4,921,300,000	631,100,000	12.82
1896	9,469	4,945,100,000	531,800,000	10.84
1897	9,457	5,094,700,000	628,200,000	12.33
1898	9,485	5,688,200,000	687,800,000	12.09
1899	9,732	6,768,700,000	723,300,000	10.69
1900	10,382	7,238,900,000	749,900,000	10.36
1901	11,406	8,460,600,000	807,500,000	9.54
1902	12,424	9,104,700,000	848,100,000	9.31
1903	13,684	9,553,600,000	757,200,000	8.97
1904	14,850	10,000,500,000	990,600,000	9.90
1905	16,410	11,350,700,000	994,100,000	8.76
1906	17,905	12,215,800,000	1,016,400,000	8.32
1907	19,746	13,099,600,000	1,113,700,000	8.51
1908	21,246	12,784,511,169	1,368,300,000	10.70
1909	22,491	14,035,500,000	1,452,000,000	10.34
1910	23,095	15,283,400,000	1,423,800,000	9.32
1911	24,392	15,906,300,000	1,554,200,000	9.77
1912	25,195	17,024,067,607	1,572,953,479	9.24
1913	25,993	17,501,006,000	1,560,709,447	8.92
1914	26,765	18,557,978,467	1,639,219,163	8.83
1915	27,062	19,195,151,304	1,457,702,138	7.59
1916	27,513	22,844,801,601	1,486,118,322	6.51
1917	27,923	26,058,000,000	1,502,502,000	5.77
1918	28,880	27,716,000,000	896,571,000	3.23
1919	29,123	32,629,000,000	997,353,000	3.06
1920	30,139	37,268,000,000	1,076,378,000	2.89
1921	30,812	34,791,000,000	946,567,000	2.72
1922	30,389	37,144,000,000	829,892,000	2.23
1923	30,178	39,984,000,000	797,101,000	1.99
1924	29,348	42,924,000,000	911,500,000	2.12
1925	28,841	46,715,000,000	951,286,000	2.04

Figures as of June report or thereabouts.

Year	No. of Banks Reporting	Individual Deposits Demand and Time	Total Cash in Banks	Ratio Cash to Deposits
1926	28,146	$48,827,000,000	$996,520,000	2.04
1927	27,061	51,062,000,000	1,007,896,000	1.97
1928	26,213	53,245,000,000	887,845,000	1.67
1929	25,330	53,158,000,000	819,928,000	1.54
1930	24,079	53,564,000,000	865,970,000	1.62
1931	22,071	50,485,000,000	884,327,000	1.75
1932	19,163	41,180,000,000	791,627,000	1.92
1933	14,624	36,676,000,000	672,556,000	1.83
1934	15,835	41,870,000,000		
1935	15,994	45,766,000,000		
1936	15,752	51,335,000,000		

The present banking law has changed the reserve requirements and the method of handling these reserves so as to deprive these subjects of some of the importance they formerly possessed. Under the present system the member banks are required to keep reserves as follows, plus the temporary increase of 50% in those figures, according to recent ruling to paralyze accumulated excess reserves.

1. " Country " banks — not less than 7% of the aggregate amount of its net demand deposits and 3% of its time deposits.

2. If in a reserve city, a net balance not less than 10% of its net demand deposits and 3% of its time deposits.

3. If in a central reserve city, a net balance equal to not less than 13% of net demand deposits and 3% of time deposits.

It is provided in every case that the amount of required reserve shall be kept as a balance to the credit of the member bank in the Federal Reserve Bank of its district.

Beside this reserve kept in the Federal Reserve Bank, it is obvious that any bank must keep a fund of cash on hand as " till-money " to meet the daily demands of its business. Experience has shown that about 3% or 4% of the deposits is ordinarily a safe amount in good times for the country as a whole, while large city banks need only about 2%. With the growth of the " checking habit" the amount of till-money required is steadily declining. Some of the importance formerly possessed by the relation between cash and deposits, and cash and resources of the national banks now attaches to these items in the combined statement of the twelve Federal Reserve Banks.

DEPOSITS OF THE BANKS

The rule governing the ratio of " Reserves " to " Deposits " holds good, except when deposits are increasing too rapidly, owing to increased prices of securities, real estate and commodities. Besides studying the ratio which we have described, the deposits should be watched independently for changes, as deposits should not increase too rapidly. The weekly statement of the New York banks will serve this purpose. A very simple illustration shows how a report of large deposits, without any intentional misstatement of facts, may hide potential weakness.

A few years ago a miser died in a certain town, which may be called Graniteville. The executor of his estate found $5,000 in gold stored away in the house, and deposited it with the Graniteville Trust Company, thereby increasing the deposits of that company by $5,000. Shortly after, John Smith borrowed of the trust company $4,500 of the amount deposited in order to buy stone with which to build a block of buildings. The local granite company, having outside income sufficient to pay its operating expenses, deposited the entire $4,500 received from Smith with the Graniteville Trust Company; so the deposits of the trust company became $9,500 greater. Soon after, Mr. Jones came into the bank and borrowed $4,200 with which to buy stone to build a block in another part of the town, and upon receipt by the granite company of Jones' $4,200 the granite company made another deposit with the trust company, increasing the deposits to $13,700.

The following day a Mr. Brown, by means of a loan from the trust company, bought stone, and the granite company further increased its deposits to $17,500. This same method of procedure was continued until the $5,000 in gold which was originally deposited resulted in increasing the deposits of the trust company by $50,000 and the loans by $45,000. Moreover, this $5,000 enabled the granite company to suppose it had $45,000 in cash on deposit in the trust company, and provided for the building of several stone blocks in the city. In other words, the deposit of this $5,000 in gold resulted in creating an apparent wealth in Graniteville of about $100,-000. This story shows not only the risks of great increases in " deposits," but also the importance of

gold importations in times of stringency, owing to
the advantage of having on hand as much currency
as possible.

When the miser's estate was settled, this $5,000
was turned over to his only daughter, who had the
same hoarding disposition as her father. She immediately withdrew in gold the $5,000 from the
Graniteville Trust Company and placed the same
in a safe deposit box with the following result. The
Graniteville Trust Company, in order to show its
proper " Reserve," was obliged to demand payment
of all the loans made to Smith, Jones, Brown, and
the other men. In order to pay these loans, all of
these men were obliged to sell the buildings which
they had erected and, in order to protect the price
of granite, the granite company was obliged to purchase these buildings, which necessitated the withdrawal of their deposits from the trust company.
Thus the withdrawal of this $5,000 in gold resulted
in a $50,000 decrease in the deposits of the trust
company, caused the $45,000 of cash assets of the
granite company to vanish, and caused half a
dozen or more citizens to lose their property, and
possibly enter bankruptcy.

The principle should be clearly kept in mind
when studying the " Deposit " item of the bank
statement. Large " Deposits " are not necessarily
a healthy sign. Neither very large nor very small
" Deposits " are normal. The best bank statement
is the one where the figures for " Deposits " are
normal and bear a proper relation to " Loans,"
thus showing a proper " Surplus Reserve."

MEMBER BANK STATEMENTS

Since the inauguration of the Federal Reserve System the plan of bank statements has been very much improved. The following is a table of the items upon which a representative number of certain member banks report each week. The specific amounts shown are purely illustrative. Although only member banks in 101 leading cities report for this statement, they are the larger banks and represent approximately 75% of the total reserve of the Federal Reserve members.

Loans on Securities.	$3,304,000,000
All other Loans and Discounts.	5,039,000,000
Total Loans and Discounts.	8,343,000,000
U.S. Securities owned (Inc. U.S. guaranteed)	10,083,000,000
Other Securities owned.	3,369,000,000
Total Loans, Discounts and Investments	21,795,000,000
Reserve with Federal Reserve Banks.	4,416,000,000
Cash in Vault.	382,000,000
Balances with Domestic Banks	2,252,000,000
Demand Deposits—adjusted.	14,258,000,000
Time Deposits.	5,047,000,000
Government Deposits.	752,000,000
Inter-bank Deposits	5,784,000,000
Borrowings . . . . .less than	1,000,000

Explaining the items in the order in which they are given:

The loan items are highly important. Loans are divided into two classes, according to the nature of their security. (1) Loans secured by United States government obligations show the amount of government paper including refunding issues of notes and bonds still held by the banks; and loans secured by other stocks and bonds reflect the trend of financing in the security markets. (2) " All Other Loans and Discounts " represent very largely commercial and real estate accommodations.

" United States Securities Owned " represent primarily Liberty Bonds and certificates of indebtedness.

" Other Securities Owned " represent the investments of the banks in other than U. S. Government securities.

" Total Loans, Discounts and Investments " are the total of the four items given above and also include all bills rediscounted with the Federal Reserve Bank and discounted bills.

" Reserve Balances with Federal Reserve Banks: " As explained in the preceding pages, only reserves which are held with the Federal Reserve Banks are counted in the members' legal reserve. This item, together with the " Cash in Vault," represents the liquid resources of the bank. In calculating ratios between reserves and deposits or reserves and loans the reserve item should include cash in vault.

" Demand Deposits " represent deposits subject to check without notice, as contrasted against " Time Deposits " which are not subject to check.* For practical purposes, however, ratios between loans and deposits and reserves and deposits can be calculated without considering "Time Deposits," except to set aside the 3% reserve against them.

* Bankers in California and some other states allow limited checking privileges against savings or time deposits.

" Time Deposits " are more in the nature of deposits of a savings bank, the depositor being required to furnish 30 days' notice before he can withdraw his funds. " Government Deposits " — still another classification — during the war assumed large proportions but have since declined and should fall off gradually as the government's activity in rediscounting operations decreases.

"Borrowings", including funds borrowed from correspondent banks and bills payable and rediscounts with the Federal Reserve Bank, indicate the amount of indebtedness which the member banks have with other banks or the Federal Reserve Bank and show the extent to which they have had to resort to the Federal Reserve Banks for assistance. Recently this item is practically nil.

The item " Loans and Investments " should be compared with the reserves of the member banks. Reserves should be compared with the net demand deposits of the member banks. These ratios have approximately the same meaning as the ratios of loans to cash and cash to deposits under the old banking system.

Total effective deposits is the sum of demand, time, government, and inter-bank deposits, less balances with domestic banks.

* * * *

THE COMPTROLLER'S REPORTS UNDER THE FEDERAL RESERVE SYSTEM

In the items of the Comptroller's Reports, which cover the whole country, certain changes have also occurred which students must take into account when comparing current figures with past figures. Loans have greatly increased. The reduction in reserve requirements theoretically released about $500,000,000 in cash, against which more than $2,000,000,000 in loans could be made which would not have been possible under the old system. The importation of about $1,137,944,000 of gold in 1915 and 1916 was also a strong factor for expansion in loans. Considering the change in the law and these gold imports, loans of the national banks during the first year and a half under the Federal Reserve System increased nearly $1,000,000,000 and war financing afterwards caused them to increase much further.

" Cash " is much smaller. Whereas under the old system banks were required to hold 6%, 12½% or 25% of their deposits in cash (according to the class of bank), they must, under the new system, hold only 7%, 10%, and 13% respectively, of their demand deposits and 3% of their time deposits in the Federal Reserve Bank, and only such cash as till-money as the daily demands of business compel: about 3% or 4% or less. According to distribution of deposits on October 31, 1914, therefore, the law authorizes an average reduction of about 8% in cash holdings; but since the 1932–33 experience bankers will probably not hold so little cash on hand. However a large reduction in " cash " took place under the new system.

" Investments " were not changed a great deal by the Federal Reserve System. While one of the chief aims of the system is to turn the banks from long term investments, such as bonds, etc. (which constitute " Investments "), to short term business paper, many banks continue to carry a " back log " of good bonds among their holdings. After the Federal Reserve Act went into effect a large amount of bond buying was carried out by all classes of banks, but this was not due (directly, at least,) to the change in system, but rather to the obligation laid upon the banks to help the government finance the war. The longer the war lasted the greater was the amount of government securities that the banks were obliged to carry. This development has continued due to the increase in proportion of saving deposits.

" Aggregate resources " were expanded on account of the increase in the " loans " item. " Surplus " was not directly affected by the new system. The " surplus " of a bank, as in any other business concern, is the " nest egg " which it saves out of its earnings, and the earning capacity of the banks has not been greatly altered. Deposits of course are much larger.

The Glass-Steagall Bank and Currency measures permitting issuance of bank notes against U. S. government bonds, coupled with inflationary possibilities, tends to increase deposits without a corresponding increase in loans.

THE FEDERAL RESERVE BANK SYSTEM

For many years it was evident that the banking system of the United States was inadequate to

meet the great financial needs of the country, not
only due to certain defects but because the former
system lacked certain necessary provisions which
go to make an efficient banking system.   Although
the present law embodies changes which are far
reaching and of great importance, still its frame-
work is for the most part that of the old banking
system, the good features of which have almost
without exception been retained.   Briefly, the new
system has five prime purposes which are named
below, although it also seeks to make many other
important corrections.

(1) The creation of a joint mechanism for the extension
of credit to banks which possess sound assets (especially in
times of emergency) and which desire to liquidate them for
the purpose of meeting legitimate commercial, agricultural,
and industrial demands on the part of their clientele.

(2) The creation of an elastic currency which will contract and expand directly with the demands of business; also
the ultimate retirement of the present bond-secured currency, with suitable provisions for the fulfillment of government obligations to bondholders.

(3) The establishment of a public discount market for
commercial paper and a better market for farm land mortgages which will furnish the merchant, the manufacturer
and the farmer with better facilities with which to care for
their financial needs.

(4) The provision for better extension of American banking
facilities in foreign countries to the end that our trade abroad
may be enlarged and that American business men in foreign
countries may obtain the accommodations they require in
the conduct of their operations.

(5) To establish a more effective supervision of banking
in the United States and to secure the co-operation of the
nation's banking power for the mutual protection and profit
of the banks and the public.

In each of the above aims is embodied the desire
to utilize the credit of the country to its greatest
extent, at the same time providing against dangerous inflation.

The greatest defect in the old system was in the matter of bank reserves. First, because of the lack of centralization of reserves which would combine the power of all the country's banks to withstand the strain of financial crises. Hitherto each bank had been rather a unit in itself. By law it was required to reserve a certain percentage of its deposits, part of which had to be held in its own vaults while the remainder could be deposited with banks of either of the three central reserve cities, New York, Chicago or St. Louis, and also in reserve cities where it drew about 2% interest. This resulted in a large accumulation of funds in these cities, especially in New York where they were loaned to a large extent against stock exchange collateral. In case of sudden financial stringency, the outside banks were unable to call in their reserves because the central reserve city banks themselves could not liquidate their funds.

The Federal Reserve system has attempted to correct this condition by providing a series of twelve great reservoirs, one reservoir for each district, from which the banks of that district can draw in time of need. These reservoirs are called Federal Reserve Banks. In reality each reserve bank is an association in itself, having as members all of the national banks and any other banks which wish to join it. Instead of these member banks depositing a portion of their required reserves in New York, Chicago or St. Louis banks, they are required to carry them with their respective Federal Reserve Bank. Instead of having to depend simply upon their reserve in an emergency, member banks can at once convert their commercial paper by having it rediscounted with the Federal Reserve Bank. The proceeds they may have credited to their accounts, thus creating a balance with the Federal Reserve Bank which counts as reserve, or they may take out Federal Reserve notes to pay out over their counters as cash.

Thus the great advantage to the member banks in " pooling " their reserves with the Federal Reserve Banks is at once evident. All of our worst panics in the past have started in a single section, and, like a great fire, have spread over the country because other depositors, becoming frightened, began to draw their balances from their banks, causing the so-called " runs " and creating a general panic. By extending the proper aid to the banks first affected, the worst features of most of our nation-wide panics could have been quenched with comparatively little difficulty.

To accomplish its next prime object, that of supplying an elastic currency, the new law has provided a currency which can be based partly on commercial paper. This currency is known as *Federal Reserve notes*. These notes are issued only by Federal Reserve Banks to their member banks in return for gold or eligible paper which their member banks deposit with them. Thus when business activity increases, as in the fall of the year, the amount of commercial paper offerings will increase so that collateral for the new currency will automatically become available. Moreover, as business demands decrease, the currency will also decrease; for when the discounted paper which is furnished as collateral falls due, it must be collected. Since a member bank has indorsed the paper, the reserve bank will presumably deliver it to the member bank for collection and the latter will, in so far as possible, deliver national bank notes or Federal Reserve notes. If, however, business demands still continue heavy when the collateral paper falls due, the member bank may substitute other collateral in its place or the Federal Reserve Bank may keep the Federal Reserve notes outstanding through the security of its gold reserve.

These restraints in themselves, however, could never prevent inflation. *The great responsibility for safety lies with the bankers and the officials of the system.* First, all loans will be carefully scrutinized by the individual bankers. If, however, the situation gets beyond their control, the Reserve Bank of the district should take a hand. Rates for rediscount will be raised and commercial paper offered as collateral will be more carefully scrutinized. Finally, if over-expansion continues, the Federal Reserve Board, which will keep a close watch wherever trouble is evident, should reject the Reserve Bank's applications for notes, and insist that a higher rate of discount be charged the member banks of the district affected, and if outside help is needed, it will require higher reserves of members, in accordance with certain provisions of the 1933 Farm Act.

In short, the supervision of the nation's banking by men of ability and experience is the law's greatest provision against abuse. Hence the great importance of keeping it out of politics.

If the reader wishes a still more complete discussion of the law, we would refer him to the book written by Prof. Edwin Walter Kemmerer, entitled "A B C of The Federal Reserve System," the book by Professors Conway and Patterson, entitled "The Operation of the New Bank Act," also "The Federal Reserve Act" by C. W. Barron, "The Federal Reserve System" by Henry Parker Willis, and to the Act itself, which is in very readable form.

IMPORTS OF MERCHANDISE INTO THE UNITED STATES

Connected with fundamental statistics and very closely related to one another are the three following subjects:

Imports of Merchandise into the United States.

Exports of Merchandise from the United States.

Balance of trade between foreign countries and the United States.

Each of the three subjects is absolutely dependent upon the others and, were it not for the separate tables connected with each subject, it would doubtless be simpler to treat all three in one comprehensive section entitled " Imports, Exports, Trade Balances and Volume." Owing, however, to the fact that it is absolutely necessary for the banker or merchant to divide the figures into three separate tables and not allow them to be combined in any way, each is here treated independently.

No detailed definition need be given of the imports of the United States except that the word import refers to the valuation of the raw material, manufactured goods and all other products purchased from abroad and entering any port or crossing any boundary of the United States. It may be mentioned also that although the figures published by the Government are correct for *comparative* purposes, they are, as a matter of fact, low. For this there are two reasons: first, there is a large quantity of goods brought into this country of which no record is ever made; and secondly, the " values " are placed by the importers at the lowest possible figures in order that the charge for duty will be as little as possible.

(Figures in the following table prior to 1867 are for the fiscal year ending June 30. After that year they are for the calendar year.)

TABLE OF UNITED STATES IMPORTS

Year	Imports	Per Capita	Year	Imports	Per Capita
1860	$353,616,119	$11.25	1877	$480,246,300	$10.37
1861	289,310,542	9.02	1878	431,812,483	9.07
1862	189,356,677	5.79	1879	513,602,796	10.52
1863	243,335,815	7.29	1880	696,807,176	13.88
1864	316,447,283	9.30	1881	670,209,448	13.06
1865	238,745,580	6.87	1882	752,843,507	14.36
1866	434,812,066	12.26	1883	687,066,216	12.81
1867	371,476,175	10.23	1884	629,261,860	11.48
1868	368,006,572	9.94	1885	585,868,673	10.49
1869	438,455,894	11.60	1886	663,429,189	11.57
1870	461,132,458	11.97	1887	708,818,478	12.09
1871	573,111,099	14.47	1888	725,411,371	12.11
1872	655,964,699	16.15	1889	770,521,965	12.58
1873	595,248,048	14.27	1890	823,397,726	13.15
1874	562,115,907	13.13	1891	828,320,934	12.96
1875	503,153,936	11.43	1892	840,930,955	12.91
1876	427,347,165	9.47	1893	776,248,924	11.68

TABLE OF UNITED STATES IMPORTS

Year	Imports	Per Capita	Year	Imports	Per Capita
1894	$676,312,941	$9.97	1915	$1,778,596,695	$17.79
1895	801,669,347	11.60	1916	2,391,635,335	23.60
1896	681,579,556	19.66	1917	2,952,467,955	28.73
1897	742,595,229	10.32	1918	3,031,212,710	29.10
1898	634,964,448	8.66	1919	3,904,364,932	38.02
1899	798,967,410	10.68	1920	5,278,481,490	49.60
1900	829,149,714	10.86	1921	2,509,147,570	23.27
1901	880,419,910	11.34	1922	3,112,747,000	28.49
1902	969,316,870	12.30	1923	3,792,065,963	34.27
1903	995,494,327	12.42	1924	3,609,962,579	32.21
1904	1,035,909,199	12.71	1925	4,226,589,000	36.63
1905	1,179,144,550	14.24	1926	4,430,888,000	37.83
1906	1,320,501,572	15.69	1927	4,184,742,000	35.28
1907	1,423,169,820	16.29	1928	4,091,444,000	34.09
1908	1,116,374,087	12.54	1929	4,399,361,000	36.24
1909	1,475,520,724	16.28	1930	3,060,908,000	24.93
1910	1,562,904,151	16.94	1931	2,090,635,000	16.85
1911	1,532,359,160	16.32	1932	1,322,772,000	10.63
1912	1,818,073,055	19.04	1933	1,449,559,000	11.57
1913	1,792,596,480	18.47	1934	1,655,055,000	13.03
1914	1,789,276,001	18.00	1935	2,047,287,000	15.99
			1936	2,390,000,000	18.46

Study the "per capita" column which shows very clearly the great value of these figures in forecasting a panic. At the close of the Civil War the people were importing on a basis of about $10 per capita and this steadily increased to over $16 in 1872. This increase was far above what it should have been, and was therefore naturally followed by the panic, which came the following year, namely, 1873. As is the case with all panic years, the imports immediately dropped off from $16 to about $14 and steadily decreased for about five years.

Beginning with 1879 the imports again increased and property likewise increased until 1882, when they again reached $14.36 per capita. Although this figure was not equal to the previous high figure for 1872, yet the rise was more rapid and it is not surprising that in the latter part of the following year there occurred another panic, namely, the panic of 1883–84. In 1885, or directly after this panic, imports again dropped to a minimum of $10.49, but gradually increased along the normal line until they reached over $13 per capita, at which point they remained constant during 1890, 1891 and 1892. As could readily have been predicted, these high figures were followed by another panic in 1893. During the next year, as invariably the case, imports declined to $9.97.

Since that period, imports have increased at a more or less irregular rate, up to 1907, when they again reached $16, at which figure they stood preceding the great panic of 1873. Then followed a sharp reduction to $12.87, coincident with the panic of 1907–08 and its curtailing of imported luxuries. With the year 1909 imports have again increased to the above figures, therefore showing that the same law has been observed in connection with all panics excepting that of 1903, which, as explained under " New Securities," was chiefly due to one specific cause as stated by Mr. Morgan, namely, " the congestion of undigested securities." Where the figures on 80% of our subjects clearly forecasted all panics excepting said panic of 1903, in only a few tables was the approach of this panic indicated. On the other hand, in these few tables, especially the table for " New Securities Listed " and " New Corporations," the increase was so tremendous, several hundred percent, that they of themselves were a sufficient danger signal, even though the figures on the other subjects appeared normal.

Thus in studying the figures on imports, we see that too great an increase in imports is a dangerous sign. This is due to two reasons: first, it necessitates the exportation of too much gold; and secondly, it signifies too great an extravagance on the part of the American people. As continued exports of gold are usually followed by advanced money rates, so too great an expenditure of money for luxuries and unproductive material, especially when imported, is followed first, by higher commodity prices, and then by a period of economy.

Not only are large figures for imports suggestive of a panic, but small figures, especially when they are increasing at a slow and conservative rate, are suggestive of better times. This latter phase is especially well illustrated in an article which appeared some time ago in the New York *Evening Post*. It began by referring to a Wall Street man who rather facetiously remarked that good times were surely coming for he noticed that people were " wearing their old clothes." This remark, made carelessly, was nevertheless a statement of the tremendously important factor which personal thrift becomes during a period of depression.

In times of abounding prosperity it is easy for people to assume a contemptuous attitude toward petty economies. The talk is of making money, not of saving it. But a panic brings out the economic truth about the relation of savings to new business operations. " It must always be remembered," writes Lord Welby, commenting on an American panic in the *Contemporary Review*, " that the capital required to extend business and to open new fields of trade can only be supplied by the savings of the world. . . . But there is a limit to these accumulations, large as they are. If the passions of the world, the extravagance of the world, and above all the growing needs of the world trench too closely on the accumulations of the world, financial stringency will inevitably be the result." And it is a fact that even the most trivial form of saving becomes a large financial operation when generally practised.

How much can the American nation save should each man wear his clothes two years instead of one? The Census Report of Manufactures shows that the factory product of men's clothing during a good year is valued at about $1,000,000,000. One-third of this, or considerably less than one-third on the basis of retail prices, would more than equal the entire imports into this country in a normally favorable month. There are over $100,000,000 worth of felt hats sold during a good year. By wearing their felt hats 50% longer than they have been accustomed to doing, plain Americans can effect a saving in a year on this one item alone of $50,000,000. The difference between habits of economy and extravagance is great!

Yet it is not always with clothes that people adopt a policy of retrenchment. If, for example, they cut down by only one-third the amount they spend on fresh beef, leaving all other items on the butcher's bill unaltered, the sum would be greater than twice the amount paid over the counters of many a bank, during the long runs faced in crisis. Contract by the same proportion the consumption of all kinds of meat,— and many authorities think this would be well worth while from a hygienic point of view alone, — and a sum equal to the entire Government deficit for the fiscal year 1933 would be saved in about twelve months.

As to the commodities which are classed as real luxuries, the facts are equally striking. Enough cigarettes were "withdrawn for consumption" in 1930 to provide about eleven cigarettes a day for every smoker, on the assumption that one-fourth of the total population, including babes in arms, may fairly be put down in that class. Even for mere purposes of illustration, no one would be cruel enough to suggest treating the cigarettes as the colonists once treated the tea. But in a great emergency the average smoker might consider cutting down his allowance to seven cigarettes a day. That trifling act would make a difference in the country's cigarette bill of more than two hundred millions a year.

Imports of luxuries into the United States during the fiscal year ended June 30, 1909, were valued at $210,872,120, as compared with $173,217,690 in 1908 and $227,661,584 in 1907. This class of imports represented 16% of total imports in 1909, 14% of the total in 1908 and 15% in 1907. The increase of $37,654,430 from 1908 was one indication of the return of prosperous business conditions.

The 1909 value, however, is $16,789,464 below the figures for 1907.

Outside of imports of silk, both manufactured and unmanufactured, which in 1929 reached $471,-000,000, imports of wines and spirits formerly played no small part in United States imports. Champagne imports, amounting to 436,628 dozen quarts, with a value of $6,863,785, were the largest during the same fiscal year (1909) in the history of the country and showed a very perceptible increase over 1907. The increase over 1908 totalled 68,959 dozen quarts, or 18%.

Cut and uncut diamond imports were valued at $51,895,000 in 1929; and the value in 1932 was but $9,339,000, or only 20% of the 1929 value and $662,000 below even the total value for 1908. Total precious stone imports, having a value of $12,918,000 during 1932, were only 16.2% of the value in 1929 and considerably below the total for 1908.

The above suggestions are sufficient to illustrate the reason for tabulating not only annual but also monthly figures on imports, namely, as a barometer of waste or of economy. It is, however, unnecessary that the monthly figures should be tabulated on a per capita basis, as the change in population is so slight.

Merchandise imports are also valuable indicators of the foreign exchange situation. For this purpose they are studied in connection with exports. A considerable balance of exports over imports is favorable to the exchange position of the country holding such balance; conversely, large excess of imports tends toward a rate of exchange against the country having such an excess—provided in either case that sufficient of other items than merchandise are not exchanged to balance the situation.

EXPORTS OF MERCHANDISE FROM THE UNITED STATES

By " exports " is meant the goods shipped from the United States to any foreign port or country. This includes all raw materials, manufactured articles, and in fact anything for which a resident of the United States receives money.

The monetary condition of the country depends on three things:

1st. The amount of money in the country.
2nd. The demand for money.
3rd. The velocity of circulation.

The first item, namely, the amount of money in the country, is very dependent upon the exports of the country. Technically, this is dependent upon the balance of trade, a term explained in the next section of this chapter, but practically it is dependent upon the exports.

Formerly the amount of exports was dependent almost entirely upon the amount of raw material produced; that is, wheat, corn, cotton, live stock, products, etc. The condition of the main crops of wheat, corn, and cotton, as well as that of the smaller crops, such as hay, apples, potatoes, etc., determined the exports. With small crops the exports were very small, while with large crops the exports were large.

This condition, however, has changed during the past thirty years, in which period there has been a very great increase in exports. The total exports of the United States have increased from $800,000,000 to more than $5,000,000,000 and this increase has been much larger in manufactures than in other products. In 1893 the United States was exporting about $677,000,000 in food products and raw materials, which amount increased only to about $946,000,000 for the fiscal year of 1913,— an increase of less than 40 percent. On the other hand, the exports of manufactured products increased from about $177,000,000 in 1893 to more than $1,500,000,000 in 1913,— an increase of more than 747 percent. That trend continued until 1929.

Such a change in the proportions between the agricultural and manufactured exports is important. If exports are to depend upon manufactured articles rather than on raw materials, bread-stuffs, etc., the decline in exports which heretofore has occurred during years of crop failures will tend to be eliminated. Andrew Carnegie once said that the time is coming when the greater part of the raw materials, now forming the bulk of the export figures of this country, will be used here, and their place in export trade will be taken by *manufactured* articles. If so, the American manufacturers must reach the markets of the world and compete therein with all the other industrial and commercial nations.

If this is so, and the figures for the past twenty-odd years seem to prove it, our exports probably will not only continue to increase, but the fluctuations will, as above suggested, be much less marked. This is another reason why we should carefully study the figures on the " balance of trade," rather than the figures on the " exports " or " imports " exclusively.

Many merchants when studying foreign trade, instead of considering exports and imports separately, add them together and call their sum the *volume* of trade. This figure is valuable as a barometer of general business activity. It should not be confused with the balance of trade, which is the difference between exports and imports, and is watched by bankers for its effect upon the money rates and gold supply.

BALANCE AND VOLUME OF TRADE

One of the most important of the subjects that investors and merchants study when analyzing present conditions and forecasting future conditions is the *balance of trade*. When we have sold to foreign merchants raw materials or merchandise greater in value than that which they have sold to us, the balance of trade is said to be " in favor of " the United States as against foreign countries. This naturally results in the shipment to America of gold, to adjust the balance, or the selling in the

United States of " exchange " at a discount, if the
condition is but temporary.   The balance of trade
does not always determine the debtor country, as there
are other factors to be considered.

After the World War, the United States became
for the first time the outstanding creditor nation
of the world.   As the yield of domestic bonds
decreased, the vast amount of money here seeking
an investment outlet was attracted, naturally, by
the higher-yielding foreign bonds.   The recon-
structive phase following such a war must be of
long duration.   Hence, it was to be expected that
the United States investors continued to buy
these bonds in large quantities.

Increasing interest payments thus have to be
made to the United States, necessitating further
receipts of gold or goods from abroad.   As, however, Europe regains her industrial position in the
world's trade, gold shipments tend to be gradually
offset with exports of raw materials and merchandise to the United States.   Incidentally, whenever
there is increasing importation of foreign goods
all of those engaged in our manufacturing and
extractive industries are vitally interested.

*If trade balances were dependent wholly on the ex-
ports and imports of raw material, merchandise, etc.,
it would be unnecessary for merchants and investors
independently to tabulate monthly figures on gold
movements in addition to tabulating monthly figures
on exports and imports.   Owing, however, to these
additional factors —purchase of foreign securities,
payment of interest, expenditures of tourists travelling*

abroad, etc., it is necessary to tabulate figures also on gold movements and these other factors.

Certain merchants when tabulating figures on the balance of trade, which is the difference between the exports and imports, also tabulate figures showing the sum of the exports and imports or what is known as the " volume." This is wholly unnecessary when the imports and exports have been tabulated separately, but rather is of use simply as a short-cut to avoid the necessity of tabulating both imports and exports separately. *Figures, then, on imports, exports and the balance of trade, when tabulated each month serve as a wonderful barometer for discerning present conditions and for forecasting future conditions.*

Although the foreign trade statistics of other countries, when properly compiled for comparative purposes, are of interest to those studying the conditions of the United States, such figures are not conclusive in comparing the trade of two different countries. As there is no uniformity in the classification in the exports and imports of two different countries and as the methods of valuation are also entirely different, it is very dangerous to make comparisons between the various countries.*

GOLD MOVEMENTS

Broadly, the world's gold production originates in South Africa, Australia, and the United States. Africa produces almost half of the world output;

* This matter is discussed very clearly in an article on the " Comparability of Trade Statistics of Various Countries " by Sir A. E. Bateman, C. M. G., published by the American Statistical Association, New Series " 1893," Vol. 3, page 533.

and therefore bankers and merchants tabulate the monthly production of the Transvaal Mines. Most of the stock of the South African and Australian gold mines is held in England. Hence London is the natural market, into which nearly one-half of the world's production of gold comes for distribution. This passage from mines to markets is known as the primary movement, and there is little prospect that it can be reduced by any schemes of international co-operation.

In the United States, New York and Seattle are distributing centers; but there is no bullion market, free or otherwise. The primary movement of gold is from mines to assay offices, where a fixed price is paid. Normally our gold production passed immediately into circulation; and gold was purchasable from the Treasury at a fixed price. On March 3, 1933, however, redemption in gold was discontinued.

Abroad, after gold from the mines has been concentrated in the London market, it is sold virtually to the highest bidder. Its distribution to various European centers constitutes the secondary movement. London as the one free gold bullion market of the world, should not be confused with the so-called gold market maintained by the Bank of England. The final gold movement is its ceaseless flow from one part of the world to another in response to the forces of supply and demand, trade balances and banking reserves.

The importing of gold does not necessarily mean "good times" or even "lower money rates";

nor does the exporting of gold necessarily mean the approach of a crisis. Nevertheless important deductions may be made if monthly figures are systematically collected and tabulated thereon. These deductions may be discussed as follows:

Picture each country as a reservoir, the size of which is proportionate to that country's normal share of the primary gold supply of the world. Assuming the various reservoirs are connected by pipes, all will maintain the same level, altho each will be of different size. A country's normal share of gold depends on its wealth. A nation's metallic money tends to remain in fixed ratio to its other forms of wealth. However, the normal share of gold in each country is influenced by other factors. These include: Volume of trade, established methods of doing business, and the currency system.

In the United States, specie exports and imports have often served as a warning signal of approaching disturbance. Their interpretation, however, cannot be assumed without first examining the trend of fundamental conditions and comparing with other indicators. Excess of gold exports may be construed as cautionary under the following circumstances.

First, when purchases abroad have been made at high prices and gold is required in payment therefor. If such purchases have been made at low prices, exports of gold may not be unfavorable. *Second*, export of gold is distinctly unfavorable when accompanied by scarcity of money and sharp increases in the rate of discount.   *Third*, if not attributable to surplus production, an unusual balance of gold exports is unfavorable if prolonged; a temporary movement of this kind does not necessarily point to instability.   Furthermore, continued withdrawal of gold from circulation and replacement by inconvertible paper, may indicate dangerous expansion of credit.

In localities where gold mining is the leading industry, such as South Africa and parts of Australia, exports of gold may be regarded in a sense as exports of merchandise, — namely, with favorable implications.   On the contrary, in non-producing nations such as England and France, it is imports which give the favorable indication. Sometimes there is noted a tendency toward simultaneous decline of gold reserves in various financial centers.   This may be due to withdrawal for hoarding or circulation outside the banks; or it may represent the transfer of gold to relatively backward countries.

After the World War, gold poured into the Federal Reserve System, swelling reserve ratios and affording the basis of credit expansion.   Gradual exports of gold would have been corrective.   During the war period and after 1919, foreign gold and securities were taken by the United States in payment for the goods we exported.   It was evident that if a free movement of gold was to be resumed, a part of the stocks of gold which we built up would ultimately have to be exported. Such a movement in fact might have been forced upon us in 1933, had we not placed an embargo on gold exports. France suffered an enormous loss of gold from 1935 to 1936. World conditions have not yet improved and stabilized sufficiently to cause a reverse flow of gold from the United States even though we now have lifted the embargo.

FOREIGN MONEY RATES AND FOREIGN EXCHANGE

These two subjects are usually discussed together, first because they are inter-related and secondly, because the subject of foreign money rates of itself is not sufficiently important to be treated independently. All that need be said as regards foreign money rates is that money, like water, seeks its own level, unless artificially held or forced. Therefore, if money rates are low in the United States, but for some time have been high in England, Germany or France, money rates in the United States are sure to increase soon, the increase to be followed possibly by a period of stringency. There are two reasons for this: first, the loans to American bankers by foreign bankers will be called for payment, or else the foreign rate will so be raised that it will be more profitable for the Americans to borrow at home; and secondly, foreign bankers will begin to borrow from America and thus take advantage of the lower American rates. As both of these causes are in operation at the same time, the rates very soon equalize, the foreign rates declining and the American rates increasing. The converse of this principle is also true. When the money rates in America are high, but the foreign rates have been low for some months, the tendency is for the American rates to decline and the foreign rates to advance.

When tabulating foreign rates, investors and merchants usually consider the " rate of discount " of the three leading foreign banks: namely, the Bank of England, the Bank of France and the Bank of Germany. The tabulation and the interpretation of these rates is very simple. The American merchant always keeps in mind, however, that low foreign money rates have their disadvantages as well as their advantages, as very often they signify a low condition of foreign trade which, during certain periods, may be spread to America.

The changes in the Bank of England rate in recent years have been as follows:

June 6, 1901:3½	Jan. 2, 1908:6	May 9, 1912:3	July 13, 1922:3
June 13, 1901:3	Jan. 16, 1908:5	Aug. 29, 1912:4	July 5, 1923:4
Jan. 23, 1902:3½	Jan. 23, 1908:4	Oct. 17, 1912:5	Mar. 5, 1925:5
Feb. 3, 1902:3	Mar. 5, 1908:3½	Apr. 17, 1913:4½	Aug. 6, 1925:4½
Oct. 2, 1902:4	Mar. 19, 1908:3	Oct. 2, 1913:5	Oct. 1, 1925:4
Oct. 31, 1902:4	May 28, 1908:2½	Jan. 7, 1914:4½	Dec. 3, 1925:5
May 24, 1903:3½	Jan. 14, 1909:3	Jan. 22, 1914:4	Apr. 21, 1927:4½
June 18, 1903:3	Apr. 1, 1909:2½	Jan. 29, 1914:3	Feb. 7, 1929:5½
Sept. 3, 1903:4	Oct. 7, 1909:3	July 30, 1914:4	Sept. 26, 1929:6½
Apr. 14, 1904:3½	Oct. 14, 1909:4	July 31, 1914:8	Oct. 31, 1929:6
Apr. 21, 1904:3	Oct. 21, 1909:5	Aug. 1, 1914:10	Nov. 21, 1929:5½
Mar. 9, 1905:2½	Dec. 9, 1909:4½	Aug. 6, 1914:6	Dec. 12, 1929:5
Sept. 7, 1905:3	Jan. 6, 1910:4	Aug. 8, 1914:5	Feb. 6, 1930:4½
Sept. 28, 1905:4	Jan. 20, 1910:3½	July 3, 1916:6	Mar. 6, 1930:4
Apr. 5, 1905:3½	Feb. 10, 1910:3	Jan. 17, 1917:5½	Mar. 20, 1930:3½
May 3, 1906:4	Mar. 17, 1910:4	Apr. 5, 1917:5	May 1, 1930:3
June 21, 1906:3½	June 2, 1910:3½	No change in 1918	May 14, 1931:2½
Sept. 13, 1906:4	June 9, 1910:3	Nov. 5, 1919:6	July 23, 1931:3½
Oct. 11, 1906:5	Sept. 29, 1910:4	Apr. 15, 1920:7	July 30, 1931:4½
Oct. 19, 1906:6	Oct. 20, 1910:5	Apr. 28, 1921:6½	Sept. 21, 1931:6
Jan. 17, 1907:5	Dec. 1, 1910:4½	June 23, 1921:6	Feb. 18, 1932:5
Apr. 11, 1907:4½	Jan. 26, 1911:4	July 21, 1921:5½	Mar. 10, 1932:4
Apr. 25, 1907:4	Feb. 16, 1911:3½	Nov. 3, 1921:5	Mar. 17, 1932:3½
Aug. 15, 1907:4½	Mar. 9, 1911:3	Feb. 16, 1922:4½	Apr. 21, 1932:3
Oct. 31, 1907:5½	Sept. 21, 1911:4	Apr. 13, 1922:4	May 12, 1932:2½
Nov. 4, 1907:6	Feb. 8, 1912:3½	June 15, 1922:3½	June 30, 1932:2
Nov. 7, 1907:7			

Foreign money rates, as affecting American money rates through the transferring of gold, are affected only by the purchase and sale of foreign exchange. Therefore, although merchants usually study only foreign money rates with their common knowledge of foreign exchange, yet theoretically, a study of foreign exchange will in itself suffice.

Foreign exchange is quoted both as to " actual rates " and as to " quoted rates." For a general description of these headings, we quote Howard Irving Smith as follows:

" The quotation ' actual rate ' means the rate at which exchange is sold in large amounts by the dealer; the quotation ' posted rate ' means the preliminary asking **rate** of the day before an actual rate is made, and this is the rate usually exacted for a small amount of exchange by a dealer. The actual and posted rates are the rates at which dealers sell bills of exchange issued by themselves. They do not, as a rule, announce the rates at which they will buy commercial bills of exchange; that is a matter of negotiation and depends on the nature of the bills. The newspapers, however, publish approximate prices for commercial bills.

" Foreign exchange is payable in the money of the country upon which the exchange is drawn, that is, where the exchange is payable. The equivalent of $1.00 in English money is 49.3 pence or four shillings 1.3 pence. When foreign exchange is quoted in the money of the country where it is bought, the unit of the money of the country where payable is figured at so much money of the country where the bill is issued. Thus, when sterling exchange is quoted at $4.8665, £1 in exchange is worth $4.8665.

" When foreign exchange is quoted in money of the country where it is payable (not where it is bought), the unit of money of the country where it is bought is figured at so much in the money of the country where the bill is payable. Thus, when exchange on France is quoted at 21.30 (21 francs, 30 centimes), $1.00 in exchange is worth 21.30 francs.*

" When a bill of exchange is quoted in the money of the country in which it is issued, but is payable (is to be paid) in the money of the country upon which it is drawn (where it is payable), the higher the quotation, or rate, the higher is the cost of such exchange, for the reason that a high rate requires more of the money of the country where the bill is purchased, to buy a given amount of the money of the country where the bill is payable than a low rate requires.

" On the other hand, when a bill of exchange is quoted in the money of the country upon which it is drawn (which is also the money in which it is to be paid), as francs, the higher the quotation the less the cost of such exchange, for the reason that more (in the foreign country's money) can be purchased for $1.00 at a high rate than can be purchased at a low rate.

" Illustration: If exchange for £1 is purchased for $4.89 it costs more than if purchased at $4.84. On the other hand, if exchange for 2130 centimes (21 francs, 30 centimes) is purchased for $1.00 it costs less than if $1.00 is paid for 21 centimes; or, putting it the other way, $1.00 buys more in

* These rates adjusted to early 1937 "apparent par" ratios.

francs* at the high rate than it does at the low rate.

" The amount paid for a time bill depends on the length of time it is to run and the rate of interest prevailing in the country where the bill is payable. A commercial bill payable in London three months after date is bought by a dealer in exchange in New York at a price which is equal to a bill payable on demand, less the three months' interest at the existing rate of interest in London. The London rate of interest serves as the basis in calculating the price of the bill, for the reason that the bill is payable in London and to make it equal to a draft payable on demand it must be discounted in London.

" High cost for exchange ordinarily means that the international balance is against the country where the high cost prevails; conversely, low cost for exchange ordinarily means that the international balance is in favor of the country where the low cost prevails." *However, as all of this may be ascertained by a study of foreign money rates and other tables already mentioned, it is unnecessary for the merchant to collect or tabulate figures on foreign exchange.*

The fact is that financial panics have not always been confined to the United States. Not only in 1931 but in 1907, a crisis occurred in several foreign countries situated in different continents; some of these markets were not directly connected in a financial way with the United States; and the financial collapse occurred in some of them

* These rates adjusted to early 1937 "apparent par" ratios.

before the panic broke out in our country. As early as May, 1907, bank failures, hoarding of money and every general suspension of credit facilities were witnessed in Egypt, and London was hurrying along emergency shipments of gold to Alexandria, exactly as it hurried along the gold shipments to New York about six months later. At nearly the same time, bank failures and panicky conditions on the markets were happening in Japan. In almost every week of our own October crisis, and on yet another continent, the powerful Banco Mobiliario of Valparaiso suspended payments, credit came to a halt in Chile, the currency sank to a low level of depreciation, and the Chilian Government was forced to take measures of relief. Again almost simultaneously with our own crisis, panic broke out in Hamburg, Germany, carrying down two great commercial houses. Leading German financial experts pronounced the crisis the worst Hamburg had witnessed since 1857.

One hardly needs add to this list such other minor crises as the temporary breakdown in credit in Genoa in the middle of 1907, and the panic at Copenhagen, a few months after our own, which compelled the Danish Government to come to the rescue by guaranteeing the assets of banks then subject to a run by depositors. What this part of the history of 1907 conclusively proves is that financiers and historians must look elsewhere than to American legislation and American banking for causes of that year's panic. European economic experts have not found it difficult to assign the cause; it was indeed pointed out by the eminent Paris economist, M. Leroy-Beaulieu, even before the panic came.

" That cause was the exhaustion, in a violent world-wide industrial expansion and an even more world-wide speculation, of the world's accruing capital resources, and a consequent strain on credit which, throughout the financial world, approached the breaking point. With such a tension in the international chain of credit, the break was bound to come, either where the link was weakest or where the strain was greatest. The link was weakest in Chile and Egypt while the strain was incalculably the greatest in the United States, where speculation of an unheard-of rashness and magnitude had been raging for two years.   The severity of the shock in all these localities, and the world-wide liquidation and reaction, in both finance and commerce which followed and which long prevailed, in Europe, Asia, Africa and South America, as well as in this country, were the logical and inevitable outcome." Moreover the greatest economic influences of the World War are still being experienced. Therefore the necessity of studying foreign conditions and not simply conditions in only one country, is apparent. The description of events in 1929–1936, given in the latter part of Chapter VII shows this again in forceful fashion.

PRODUCTION OF GOLD

As to the effect of the production of gold, there is a diversity of opinion.   That it is a subject of great importance when a long period of years is considered is admitted by all; but many deny that it is of such importance when considering a period of only a few years. The theory that as the supply of gold (which is used as a standard of value and a medium of exchange) *increases*, interest rates and commodity prices must *immediately* increase, is actively combated by many authorities. If there were no other possible causes at work affecting interest rates and commodity prices, this theory would be taken more seriously, especially as it would involve a general decline in bonds and all *fixed interest* obligations; but even then it would be obliged to stand the test of experience.

The former editor of the *Engineering and Mining Journal*, Mr. Walter R. Ingalls, claims to have shown by statistics and graphic diagrams, that there has been no correspondence between the fluctuations in the gold supply and those in prices. Going back to the time of the first notable modern increase in gold production, he showed that for some years, beginning with 1851, there was an apparent parallelism, but there was a drop in prices after the crisis of 1857, and then a recovery and increase until 1864, though the production of gold was then falling off. After that prices declined until 1870, while the gold supply fluctuated within narrow limits; but in 1871 prices started up again, with gold production declining. During the fall in prices after 1873, there was an upward turn in the production of gold and by a peculiar perversity, in view of any theory of cause and effect, it fell off again after 1879 as prices began to rise. The decline in gold production continued until 1883 when there was another upward turn followed by a continued increase until 1896. The output was then more than double that of 1884 and the highest ever reached before that time; but during that period there was an almost continual decline in commodity prices, to contrast with the rise which took place, while the annual supply of new gold again doubled. This may not prove that the increased production of gold has had no effect upon its commercial value compared with the general mass of commodities, and consequently upon prices determined by its value as the standard of measurement and computation, but it does very conclusively refute the theory that the two things stand in the *closest* relation of cause and effect. There is certainly no close correspondence between them from year to year and the inevitable inference is that much more potent causes than the volume of gold in monetary use are at work in determining the course of prices.

It is a question whether the demand for the use of gold as a basis of credit and exchange has not kept pace with the supply and prevented any absolute depreciation. Mr. Ingalls forcibly opposes the argument that the cost to capital and labor of producing gold has diminished and that available deposits are on the increase, with cheapening methods of extraction. In connection with the question of increased demand, he took the increasing production of pig-iron as fairly representing the advance made in industries and trade generally and showed both by figures and graphic diagrams that its increase has been relatively greater than that of gold.

The general subject of gold has best been presented in a book entitled " The Story of Gold " by Professor E. S. Meade; while the theory that the rise in commodity prices is due to the increased production of the metal is well described in an old book entitled "Gold Supply and Prosperity," edited by Byron W. Holt of New York City, who was generally recognized as one of the best informed men on this subject. Professor Irving Fisher has also given a great deal of study to this subject, and his book "The Purchasing Power of Money," and "Prices" by Geo. F. Warren and Frank A. Pearson, published by John Wiley & Sons, should be read by all who wish to be well informed concerning this important matter. Another book on this subject is "How to Invest When Prices are Rising," published by G. Lynn Sumner & Co., Scranton, Pa.

Based upon the assumption that gold production was to increase for the next ten years at an average rate of not less than 5%, Mr. Holt arrived at the following fourteen conclusions:

"(1). That the value of gold will depreciate as the quantity increases, though not, perhaps, at the same ratio.

(2). That this depreciation will be measured by the rise in the average price level.

(3). That rising prices will soon lead again to rising and higher interest rates.

(4). That, because of high interest rates, the prices of bonds and most other long-time obligations drawing *fixed* rates of interest, dividends or income will again decline to low levels.

(5). That, because of rising prices and high interest rates, the cost of materials and supplies will tend to decrease the net profits of all concerns the prices of whose products or services either cannot be advanced at all or are not free to advance rapidly.

(6). That, because of rising prices, the net profits of all concerns that own their own sources of materials and supplies will tend to increase.

(7). That, because of rising prices of commodities, the market prices of all tangible property will tend to rise. This includes lands, mines, forests, buildings and improvements.

(8). That, because of rising prices of commodities and property, the prices of the stocks of corporations holding commodities or property will tend to advance.

(9). That, because of rising prices and therefore of cost of living, wages must and will tend to advance.

(10). That, because wages and salaries will not rise as much or as fast as will prices and the cost of living, there will be dissatisfaction and unrest among wage and salary earners.

(11). That, because of rising prices and property, there will be much speculation in commodities, stocks and real estate.

(12). That, because of the great profits that will

result from speculation, honest industry will be discouraged and recklessness and extravagance will be encouraged.

(13). That, because rising prices will decrease the purchasing power of debts, and thus aid debtors at the expense of creditors, they will discourage saving and thrift.

(14). That, then, an increasing output of gold means rising prices, rising wages, high interest rates, the scaling of debts, speculation, unjust distribution of earnings and wealth and general dissatisfaction and discontent."

These conclusions seem to follow each other logically, though their close connection is not wholly evident. The first two conclusions, being the more fundamental and important, Mr. Holt discussed as follows:

" It is almost inconceivable that an increasing supply and output of gold, the standard and measure of values, will not tend to raise prices. It is not asserted that a slight increase in the supply will cause prices to advance. The natural course of prices, especially of manufactured goods, is downwards. To offset this cheapening tendency, due to invention and improvement, an increase of perhaps 2% a year in the supply of gold may be necessary. To offset the growing demand for gold, due to industrial expansion, an increase of perhaps 1% more a year may be necessary.

" An increase of perhaps 3% a year in the world's volume of gold, then, may be necessary to maintain stable prices. This being true, a smaller increase

PRODUCTION OF GOLD 185

than 3% will result in declining prices, and a greater increase will result in advancing prices of commodities. An increase of 5% a year in the supply of gold then would cause prices to rise an average of 2% a year, and an increase of 8% in the supply of gold would cause prices to rise an average of 5% a year."

As to whether Mr. Holt or Mr. Ingalls is correct, the reader must decide for himself. It is very generally admitted that a sudden increase in the supply of gold at certain times gives impetus to business activity, results in the conception of new ventures and indirectly is accompanied by an advance in prices. This rising movement in prices of itself encourages speculation and the extension of credit to a dangerous degree. Large profits lead to waste and extravagance, which conditions are followed by a crisis and a period of depression. Therefore, it seems reasonable to admit that the overproduction of gold is one factor causing increased prices, thus indirectly affecting business conditions; but it is very illogical to point to the production of gold as *the only factor* affecting prices and interest rates. In fact, an increase in credits of any form (that is, bank deposits subject to check), and especially an increase in the velocity of circulation of said moneys and credits, are also important factors. The increase in population, the destruction of natural resources, industrial combination, labor unions, increased cost of agricultural lands and many other factors tend to increase the prices of commodities, rates of interest and investment values.

Gold production is important and careful bankers, manufacturers, and merchants tabulate it monthly. In 1936 it surpassed 34 million ounces. At $35 an ounce, this expands the world monetary supply, in dollars, at a faster annual clip than ever. From the Boer War to date, Transvaal output has increased remarkably. Around the period of the World War, for about 17 years, there were only slight increases, but output and recovery from hoarding old gold increased tremendously in the 'thirties.

Silver is tending to regain its monetary status of about a century ago. Yet the silver purchase program of the U. S. Government may not be fulfilled. In the Americas the silver output is expanding rapidly. A distant possibility is symetallism,— gold and silver in combination as a unit. In any event, output of precious metals is forging ahead, Russian gold production is estimated to be now approximating that of English owned mines. Most nations have re-valued their currencies. Based on quantity of money, therefore, commodity prices could forge ahead to unexplored regions,— cyclical forces are not diminishing.

Without trying to guess the outcome of inflationary policies in the United States, a continued reduction in the world's gold production as we were having meant ultimately a reduction in price of all commodities not artificially supported; an advance in price of bonds; a reduction in rate of interest on mortgages; lower wages in view of the consequent greater purchasing power of gold; and a decline in price of stocks caused by the transference of investments from stocks to bonds. This last development might occur because of the great purchasing power of interest on bonds, the collapse of any inflation movement in stocks, and the investor's preference for a safe investment. But the depression was carried so far that the system snapped, resulting in demands for inflation.

COMMODITY PRICES

One cannot do better, when studying this subject, than to refer to the late Hon. Theodore E. Burton's book entitled " Crises and Depressions," in which, among other things, he states: —

" In the season of activity, which precedes a crisis, prices rise. This rise begins after the worst of the previous depression has been reached. Attention has already been called to the fact that the rise in prices is unequal in different commodities. Iron and steel in their various forms, as well as other commodities required for construction, and those which supply new demands of consumption, show the most striking increases. During a depression, prices of these commodities fall first and most notably. The prices of other commodities do not fall so much or so early. In the preceding season of expansion they do not rise so much, and, in their rise as well as in their fall, they show, for the most part, only a remote effect of the activity or inactivity of the time.

" As is well known, it is the tendency of prices of

iron and steel to reach and pass their maximum some time before the crisis occurs, though if the crisis be precipitated by an unexpected failure, the interval will be short or the high prices may continue until the very outbreak of the crisis.*

" In the United States, prior to the crisis of September 18, 1873, a low price level appeared in almost all grades of iron and steel in January, 1871. This was followed by a rapid and almost unbroken rise, culminating in the months of October and November, 1872. A maximum price of rolled bar iron, $118.72 at Philadelphia, was reached in October, 1872. The price fell, with slight fluctuations, to $80.64 in September, 1873, the month of the crisis.

" In the depression which followed the crisis of 1873, prices of a majority of the varieties of iron and steel fell to a minimum in the latter part of the year 1878, though steel rails and standard sections of iron rails fell to a minimum in the closing months of 1877. The month of November, 1878, may, however, be selected as the turning point. At that date No. 1 anthracite foundry pig iron had fallen to $16.50 per gross ton, less than one-third the price of September, 1872.

" In the expansion which followed 1878, prices reached their maximum in the months of January, February and March, 1880; but the highest figures were maintained only for a very short time. An-

* This is why the price of iron is tabulated each month — as a barometer for forecasting changes in general business; although — as will be seen from a chart in the earlier part of this book — commodity prices do not reach a minimum as a rule until one or two years after the stock market reaches its low point.

thracite foundry pig iron, which had fallen to
$16.50 in November, 1878, rose to $41.00 in February, 1880; rolled bar iron to $85.12 in the same
month; steel rails to $85; cut nails to $5.25 in the
months of February and March.   After the month
of March, 1880, there was a sharp decline, though
interrupted by numerous fluctuations.   A steady
decline began after the closing months of the year
1882, and continued until another minimum was
reached in the summer of 1885.   The crisis of
May, 1884, occurred in the midst of this downward
movement and seems to have exerted but little influence upon the iron market.   Anthracite foundry
pig iron fell to $17.75 in the months of June, July
and August of 1885 and then began to rise.   Rolled
bar iron fell to $40.30 in May of the same year,
and then was quoted at $40.32 for the remaining
months of the year.   Steel rails fell to $26 in the
month of April.

" After the minimum point in 1885, there was an
upward movement continuing until the earlier
months of 1887, the months of February and March
of that year showing maximum prices in most varieties of iron and steel; this maximum was succeeded
by a fall in the prices, which for most varieties
reached a minimum in May and June, 1889.   This
minimum was followed for a short time by rising
prices, which reached a maximum in 1890.   In the
two decades after the maximum prices of 1880, the
trend of prices differed from that in the preceding
decade.   Fluctuations were much more frequent
and for nearly eighteen years the general tendency

was downward, though interrupted by brief revivals in prices in the years 1882, 1886, 1887, 1890 and 1895. The rise in price which occurred in 1887 and other years proved to be greater than the increased demand would sustain. The general statement may be made that during this long period between 1880 and 1897, in fact until 1898, for there was only a slight rise in that year and the average price of several forms was less than in 1897, the demand did not keep pace with the increasing supply, and improvements in production were constantly exerting their influence. The increase in price in the United States in 1887 was greater than in other countries. The reason for the difference may be found in the exceptional demands in the year 1887, in which year occurred the most extensive railway building and the greatest consumption of steel rails. There was an exceptional deficiency in the home supply. There was also a revival of general activity in this country, the effect of which was conspicuous. It should be further noted that the crisis of this decade was much less severe than that of 1873, and the downward movement succeeding it, though long continued, manifested less decline in prices.

" After the high prices of 1890, there was a fall which continued until the month of July, 1897. This fall was more uniform than those after 1880 and 1887. It was interrupted only by a temporary revival beginning after April, 1895, and continuing until the latter part of the year."

Beginning in July, 1897, prices show an upward

tendency, but increases were slight until the beginning of 1899; then there was a very rapid rise until the latter part of the year, which continued, with the exception of a very slight setback in 1903, to the depression of 1907–8.

Again the improved conditions of 1909–10 were *preceded* by a remarkable increase in the price and production of iron, followed later by an increase in the production of copper and other commodities. From the high point of 1909–10, prices of iron and steel declined again to a low point in December, 1911, followed by a rapid advance in 1912.

The depression of 1914 was nipped at about 50% of its progress by the declaration of the World War. At the outset it was believed that the War would soon be over so that commodity prices did not respond immediately. As the destruction of property and war requirements increased and continued for years, commodity prices again advanced as they had during the Napoleonic Wars and the Civil War. Immediately after the War the demand for satisfaction of personal needs which had been held in abeyance for four years, and the concurrent credit inflation for floating government bonds led to peak prices in 1920. Credit liquidation, however, was soon resumed leading to the precipitate decline in the latter half of 1920 and the first half of 1921. A plateau of rather wide fluctuations was established thru 1929,—the long term declining tendency being temporarily checked by extremely active business.

As soon as a shock to the entire inflated security structure took place, the normal forces of lower costs and forced sales of limited international products to the United States, for the purpose of obtaining credit balances for the remittances on debts, caused such commodity prices to go to levels relatively far below those of manufactured products. The decline continued of that nature and was very rapid during the spring of 1932, the final dip taking place in the winter from 1932–1933. An extremely rapid increase took place in international commodities as the United States currency depreciated in terms of currencies still on a gold redemption basis.

In the examination of these price movements several marked tendencies appear:

"(1). The interval between the date of the maximum prices and the succeeding crisis is longer in the later years. This interval continued for a few months prior to the crises of 1825 and 1837, nearly a year prior to that of 1873, and several years prior to the crises of 1884 and 1893. This longer interval may be explained by the greater ability to carry accumulated stocks in expectation of a rise, the larger influence of speculation, and the absorption whenever prices decline, of larger quantities by the market now existing."

These influences explain another tendency, viz.:

"(2). In later years fluctuations are more frequent. In the period after the downward price movement has commenced the market price breaks and then is restored again. It is evident that abundant capital for construction is waiting for investment and even in case of a slight decline, purchases are large and tend to bring prices to the former level.

"(3). Since 1873 the maximum price reached in each upward swing tends to be less than that in the preceding rise. This is due to invention, to the lower cost of manufacturing on a large scale, and improvements of transportation. This tendency to lower prices is a part of the progress of the time and an essential feature in each depression.

"(4). The upward movement of prices continues for a much shorter time than the downward movement. The upward movement preceding the maximum of October and November, 1872, continued for one year and nine months. The succeeding downward movement lasted until November, 1878, or six years and one month. Then an upward movement continued until February, 1880, or one year and three months; the succeeding downward movement lasted approximately five and one-half years, to the summer of 1885, to be followed by a rising movement interrupted in the United States in 1888 and 1889, of four and one-half years, or until January, 1890. It is to be noticed, however, that the rise in most grades of iron and steel for a year after the summer of 1885 was very slight. After January, 1890, the downward movement continued for seven and one-half years, to July, 1897, when prices for a year were almost stationary, to be followed by rising prices, which continued until the end of 1899 or less than a year and a half.

"(5). The rapid rise which precedes a maximum price rarely continues for more than a year. If we take anthracite and Bessemer pig-iron as the best standard, it will be noticed that prior to the maximum price of anthracite, September, 1872, prices rose from $37 in January of that year; prior to the maximum of $41 in February, 1880, prices had risen rapidly from $20.75 in August, 1879, or for six months; prior to the maximum of $19.90 in January, 1890, there was a rise from $17 in May, 1889, or for eight months; prior to the maximum of $25 for Bessemer pig-iron in December, 1899, there was a rapid rise from $11 in January of the same year, or for eleven months. In many respects, the rise in 1899 was the most remarkable of all, because it had been considered by iron manufacturers in the preceding years that the equipment for production was sufficient to properly meet any increase of demand, and yet the rapid rise in that year was unprecedented. The great increase in the price of iron and steel in that year, with the steady increase in production after 1894, proves the more general use of these products for a greater variety of purposes and over an enlarged area."

For a general study of prices, a reliable index should be tabulated or plotted and kept up to date. During that portion of the Major Commodity Swing when the price trend is upward, it will be noticed that the fall after a year of panic, curtailment and depression is usually considerably less than the preceding rise. For this fact there are several reasons:

First. The continuous increase in the amount of active circulating medium. In normal conditions money is valued only as a means of purchasing goods. A certain amount must be kept as " till-money " and for bank reserves. People only hoard money when they become frightened. Hence, an increased supply of money is ordinarily reflected in an increased demand for goods, resulting in higher prices (since there is no corresponding increase in the supply of goods offered).

The output of gold which is being supplied at the rate of over one million dollars per day* is directly responsible for much of the steady increase which has taken place in the world's stock of money. Indirectly, it forms the basis for credit expansion, the effect of which is even more important. The financial history of the past sixty years has been characterized by a great expansion in the use of credit instruments. Bank notes, treasury notes and bank deposits, subject to check, act as a medium of exchange and thus perform the functions of money. Most checking deposits are created by loans made to enable the borrower to purchase goods, and therefore this credit money has the same effect on prices as the same amount of specie.

Second. Another effect in maintaining high prices is the growing pressure of population on the land supply. The best mining and agricultural

---

* See Prof. Irving Fisher's studies on the change in the purchasing power of the gold dollar.

opportunities of the new world have been occupied. The insistent demand for raw material to clothe, feed, house, educate and amuse the steadily increasing population is continually forcing resort to less advantageous sites. These yield their product only at a higher cost per unit.

A given area of land can be made to yield more grain per acre only by the use of more fertilizer or more thorough cultivation. After a certain point is passed, additional product per acre can be obtained only at a disproportionate additional outlay in labor or capital, or both. This will not be undertaken unless the price of the products is sufficient to justify it. The resort to poorer lands, and lands farther from the market will be undertaken only under the same condition.

Broadly speaking, mining, the other great department of extractive industry, is governed by the same general principle. It is true that new and rich ore deposits are discovered from time to time, but the operation of extracting the product from known mines proceeds in a manner practically similar to the method of agriculture. Those deposits are worked first that can be worked at the lowest per-unit cost, and as these are exhausted, it becomes necessary to dig deeper into the ground, to extend operations to less easily accessible territory, or to resort to poorer grade of ore. Increasing demand is thus constantly forcing prices to higher levels.

Third. The maintenance of high prices is in part due to the rise of the standard of living which a period of increasing wealth first produces, and then establishes with a resisting power that even in times of depression resists with a new force any recession in its newly gained advantages.

Fourth. There is a final factor behind existing price levels in the forms of the wastes due to war and the maintenance of great armaments, and in the millions of misdirected capital which have helped to enhance the costs of profitable production.

Therefore, the price of commodities is one of the best of business barometers and all merchants and bankers systematically tabulate each month the "Index Number" compiled by Bradstreet or others, supplemented with figures on the price of iron, copper, cotton, etc. Such figures especially interest bankers since much more money is needed to finance a given volume of business with high prices than with low prices. Therefore, an increase in interest rates usually follows a decided advance in commodity prices.

However, as we brought out in Chapter II, a reversal in the long time trend was started in 1920, and when studying commodity prices since that date this fundamental fact must be kept in mind.

A scientific discussion of prices may be found in Prof. Irving Fisher's book, entitled " The Purchasing Power of Money," published by Macmillan & Co., New York, also in "Prices" by Messrs. Warren and Pearson, as above mentioned in the chapter on Gold.

CHAPTER VI

STOCKS, NEW SECURITIES, CROPS AND OTHER PRODUCTION, RAILROAD EARNINGS, POLITICAL AND SOCIAL FACTORS.

THERE are three features in connection with the New York Stock Exchange which are of value in forecasting business conditions. They are as follows:

1. The Quotations.
2. The Transactions.
3. The New Securities listed. (See section entitled " New Securities," page 203.)

QUOTATIONS

When studying the quotations, only a long period of time showing the general tendency should be considered. The fluctuations from day to day are of no value whatever, nor are the swings covering only a period of a few weeks. A study of the general tendency of the market, however, is of considerable value in forecasting business conditions.

If the highest point of each successive swing is higher than the high point of the preceding swing, and if the low point of each successive swing is not so low as that of the preceding swing, then the tendency of the market is upward. If the last high point and the last low point are lower than the high points and low points of earlier periods, then the tendency of the market is downward.

In order to study this matter intelligently, a plot should be made of the average prices of the leading railroad and industrial stocks. For many years

the rails were the leading stocks in the market and
their fluctuations best indicated the market trend.

The *Wall Street Journal* publishes averages which
are widely used as indicating the trend of the market. This list now contains the following 30
industrial stocks, 20 railroad stocks, and 20 public utility stocks.

Industrials. — Allied Chemical; Am. Can.; Am. Smelting;
Amer. Tobacco B; Bethlehem Steel; Chrysler; Corn Prod-
ucts; DuPont de Nemours; Eastman Kodak; General Elec-
tric; General Foods; General Motors; Goodyear; Interna-
tional Business M.; Internat'l Harvester; Int'l Nickel; Johns
Manville; Loew's Inc.; Nash-Kelvinator; National Distillers;
National Steel; Procter & Gamble; Sears Roebuck; Standard
Oil of Cal.; Standard Oil of N. J.; Texas Corp; Union Carbide;
U. S. Steel; Westinghouse Electric; Woolworth.

Railroads. — Atchison; Atlantic Coast Line; Balt. & Ohio;
Canadian Pacific; Ches. & Ohio; Del. & Hudson; Del. Lac. &
W.; Erie; Great Northern Pfd.; Illinois Central; Louisville
& Nashville; N. Y. Central; N. Y., Chic. & St. L.; New
Haven; Norfolk & W.; Northern Pacific; Pennsylvania;
Southern Pacific; Southern Rwy.; Union Pacific.

Public Utilities—Am. & Foreign Power Co., Inc.; Am.
Gas & Elec.; Am. Pr. & Light; Am. Tel. & Tel.; Am. Water
W.; Brooklyn Union; Columbia Gas; Com. & South'n Corp.;
Cons. Edison; Electric P. & L.; Engineers P. S.; Inter. Tel. &
Tel.; Nat'l P. & L.; Niagara Hudson; North American; Pacific
Gas & E.; Public Service N. J.; So. Cal. Edison; Standard
Gas; Western Union.

As an aid in determining the tendency of the
market, merchants make a dot at the center of
each movement, or midway between the high point
and the low point of each main swing. These dots
are then connected with a line and this line shows
at a glance the tendency of the market.

When two or three plots are made, it is interesting to compare a railroad plot with one for industrials. Up until about 1911 or 1912 the railroad

quotations almost always preceded the industrials either up or down. Since that time, however, the reverse has been true. Space does not permit a detailed account of the reasons for the change, so it must suffice to state that a change in conditions may sometimes be discerned more quickly by having the two plots, one for railroads and the other for industrials, than if both are averaged together on the one plot.

A chart of bond prices is essential to obtain a correct perspective of financial conditions in the very important field of long-term interest rates, the supply of loanable funds for long term, the margin of profit in industry, and other economic considerations. The curve on the Babsonchart, consisting of 60 high and medium-grade bonds is plotted by means of an inverted scale for the yield of these bonds. This results in a curve which swings as would a curve of bond prices, but still permits reading the figures on the basis of interest yield Low prices or high yields indicate the scarcity of funds to be lent for a long period of time such as for construction and relatively permanent capital expenditures. The interest rate for short-term funds, such as call money on the New York Stock Exchange or loans from banks for a short term may at times be very different from the rate for long-term loans as represented by bonds.

Usually, a change in the bond market precedes a change in the stock market. The *New York Times* publishes a useful average of the prices of 50 stocks and 40 bonds.

If considered in a conservative manner, the tendency of the stock market is very interesting to merchants when endeavoring to forecast business conditions. This is due to the fact that a change in the stock market is often the first *visible* sign of a change in general business conditions. Railroad earnings are absolutely dependent upon business conditions, and stock market quotations are dependent upon anticipated earnings. But a very large surplus of money seeking investment may hold the stock market for many months at a level resulting in yields out of line with the risk involved. However, a rising market over a certain period of time means that the majority of operators believe that fundamental conditions are more sound, while a falling market means that these operators believe that fundamental conditions are unsound and unsatisfactory. This is the reason why the stock market often tends to go down while railroad earnings are increasing, and often tends to go up while railroad earnings are still decreasing. Therefore, the one who makes the most is not only the one who guesses right, *but the one who makes the right guess first*. Hence stock market movements usually have been the first *public* sign of a change in fundamental business conditions. *All plots of prices should, however, be supplemented by a plot of what the given stocks yield in order to allow for the changes in dividend rates.*

TRANSACTIONS

A study of " Quotations," without due consideration of " Transactions," is of little value, because a rising market, during which only a few shares change hands, means very little, as such a market may be the result of manipulation. In the same way a falling market, when only a few shares change hands, may mean very little. In order to reach a correct conclusion, the "quotations" should be considered in connection with the "volume."

The volume of transactions is usually largest at about the culmination of a long-swing bull movement, and during severe liquidation. Between these points, however, the variations in volume are less significant. It is believed by many market traders that, in the trading from day to day, when the volume of transactions diminishes as prices fall off, and then increases as prices rise, that this shows the real trend of the market to be upward. On the other hand, when the volume is heaviest on the down grade and lighter on the rallies, a general decline may be expected.

There is probably some truth in this idea, but such matters are subject to manipulation to such an extent that one can never safely trust to such surface indications. Manipulation is always present, and there are always pools and individual operators trying to put the market up or down as suits their interest. Certain of these are said at times to control the market. Though hard to prove, this is probably true as regards many of the minor movements and short swings.

Yet no pool or group of operators, however strong, can hold up a market indefinitely, when fundamental conditions are against them, nor can they prevent a rise (though they may delay it) when fundamentals are right for a real improvement. Of course those operators who foresee aright and who conduct their operations in harmony with fundamental conditions reap great profits, and in the popular gossip are often credited with causing the movement. The merchant or investor, or the conservative speculator, basing his purchases and sales on a careful study of fundamental statistics, had better not worry himself trying to solve the mysteries of manipulation.

NEW SECURITIES

The reason for studying the subject of " New Listings " may be understood by a review of the three following laws of economics:

1. *During a Period of Over-expansion, as the number of new companies, new promotions and new securities listed increases, the danger of a reaction increases and the time between said Period of Over-expansion and a future Period of Depression decreases.*

2. *When the number of new promotions, new companies and new listings is at a minimum, financial depression is sure to be reaching an end.*

3. *As the number of new companies, new promotions and new listings increases from a minimum, the gradual increase is a sign of improved conditions until the normal number of new companies, new promotions and new listings is reached, after which an increase again becomes a source of danger.*

Out of the entire list of fundamental statistical tables of which this book treats, this particular one, "The Number of New Companies and New Promotions" is the one by which it was most clearly possible to forecast the panic of 1903. For this reason this panic was said to be due to "undigested securities" and was known as "The Rich Man's Panic."

Of course one cannot rely upon the study of this one subject, as many panics have taken place when the figure for "New Securities" has been normal and the change in conditions could only have been forecasted by a study of the other subjects. In fact, the difficulty in studying this subject is that the figures remain very constant for a long period of time, and it is only the great movements up or down which are of any use.

Under normal conditions a study of this subject is of little value, but it is most useful under abnormal circumstances. If we are in a period of depression and we reach a period where no new companies are incorporated and there are absolutely no new promotions or listings, we may be sure of better conditions in the near future. Conversely, if we are in a period of prosperity and there are an abnormally large number of promotions, an abnormally large number of new corporations being formed and new securities being listed, we may be sure that trouble will come. This usually comes first in the form of tight money, followed immediately by a decline in the bond and stock markets, and later by a period of business depression.

The following figures on corporate securities clearly show this, particularly in connection with the panic of 1929:

Year	Stocks: Total Value Including New Capital, Old and Refunding Issues	Year	Bonds: Total Value Including New Capital, Old and Refunding Issues
1885	$56,913,116	1885	$197,259,000
1886	329,469,350	1886	238,097,690
1887	270,053,550	1887	343,477,321
1888	248,228,275	1888	511,002,218
1889	259,649,774	1889	389,720,000
1890	437,992,330	1890	684,867,879
1891	188,914,954	1891	287,645,700
1892	237,036,105	1892	317,861,500
1893	198,245,261	1893	288,803,400
1894	251,193,003	1894	309,804,600
1895	143,373,970	1895	257,275,400
1896	590,732,215	1896	582,286,700
1897	502,974,891	1897	357,415,902
1898	528,153,996	1898	700,064,680
1899	704,172,605	1899	525,384,240
1900	620,935,000	1900	443,713,000
1901	1,642,013,715	1901	923,010,100
1902	784,032,595	1902	533,519,300
1903	426,890,295	1903	581,288,800
1904	175,866,800	1904	535,079,600
1905	533,434,900	1905	980,026,650
1906	662,769,450	1906	571,898,500
1907	576,032,050	1907	420,813,000
1908	513,927,450	1908	872,958,000
1909	1,325,526,485	1909	1,098,956,500
1910	1,239,501,545	1910	808,162,500
1911	643,614,830	1911	580,834,400
1912	1,161,030,790	1912	654,977,750
1913	611,993,230	1913	648,066,100
1914	571,796,360	1914	488,993,000
1915	939,326,240	1915	541,192,300
1916	967,161,758	1916	862,706,000
1917	1,481,285,345	1917	990,834,000
1918	312,024,647	1918	227,634,700
1919	1,573,100,000	1919	1,166,400,000
1920	1,100,300,000	1920	1,865,900,000
1921	290,000,000	1921	2,100,700,000
1922	673,400,000	1922	2,390,800,000
1923	735,900,000	1923	2,496,800,000
1924	866,400,000	1924	2,972,300,000

Note:—This table does not include government bonds.

Year	Stocks: Total Value Including New Capital, Old and Refunding Issues	Year	Bonds: Total Value Including New Capital, Old and Refunding Issues
1925	$1,310,900,000	1925	$3,427,200,000
1926	1,317,700,000	1926	3,981,600,000
1927	1,773,400,000	1927	5,546,000,000
1928	3,626,200,000	1928	4,191,500,000
1929	6,921,500,000	1929	3,104,900,000
1930	1,567,200,000	1930	3,904,900,000
1931	343,131,373	1931	1,840,773,800
1932	24,035,045	1932	405,844,800
1933	152,605,624	1933	138,491,500
1934	34,601,349	1934	287,038,100
1935	150,830,990	1935	2,066,058,650
1936	567,904,081	1936	4,001,271,600

AGRICULTURAL PRODUCTION AND MARKETINGS

In studying agricultural production and marketings, it is important to distinguish between the physical volume of the output and the value thereof in dollars. History shows that sometimes in a year of crop failure, farm income in total has been larger than in years of bountiful harvests. The price factor is often of dominating importance in the farmers' financial returns.

This subject does not now hold the same relative importance in the study of Fundamental Statistics that it once held when statistics on other topics were less carefully compiled. But the condition of the standing crops will always be interesting and valuable as a barometer inasmuch as the full annual harvest of the grains and cotton is one of the factors at the bottom of American business prosperity. Of all subjects studied by the merchant and investor it is the only one which the government attempts to forecast. Figures on banking conditions, labor conditions, imports and exports are accumulated by the government and are valuable as a matter of history; but for none of these subjects is there any official attempt to use the figures for forecasting conditions.

But in the subject of crops, not only does the government publish a report on their amount and condition in various stages from planting to the beginning of harvest, but it makes a prediction for the benefit of business interests of what the total crop is likely to be. It has been well proved that this forecast made by the government is better than any forecast which at the present time can be made by any association of merchants or bankers independently.

For this reason the method of compiling and distributing these forecasts should be clearly understood and the following is a detailed explanation thereof:

The title of the Bureau in charge of the preparation of crop reports is the "Bureau of Agricultural Economics." This Bureau has been formed by a consolidation of three former branches of the Department of Agriculture: The Bureau of Markets; the Bureau of Crop Estimates; and the offices of Farm Management. The former Bureau of Crop Estimates is now the Division of Crop and Livestock Estimates and continues the work of preparing the Government crop and livestock reports with, as formerly, a field force to collect information and an office force of tabulators and computers.

Statistical information concerning crop production and livestock that is collected by the slow and exact methods of a census is generally not given

to the public until after the crops enumerated are
harvested and marketed and the immediate interest in it has passed away.   Prices of agricultural
products are primarily governed by the law of
supply and demand; therefore early information
concerning the supply is of value to all.   Those
who produce and those who consume are vitally
interested as well as the dealer who stands between
them.   The relations and mutual interests of agriculture, manufacture, and commerce demand that
there should be published at brief intervals during
the crop season reliable information on the condition, acreage, production, and value of the principal crops, by States and agricultural areas.

As commerce consists largely in an exchange of
the products of agriculture and manufacture among
their respective producers, commerce thrives as
the farmer and the factory operative prospers.
Some individuals, however, do not always regard
the common welfare, and injurious commercial
speculations occur when ignorance prevails concerning the condition of our crops and the true relations of supply and demand.   At such times the
farmer often does not obtain just prices, while the
consumer derives no benefit and business is inju-
riously affected.   The consequences of false reports concerning the condition and prospective
yield of the cotton crop alone may be very injurious.
If there were no adequate government crop-reporting service, and by misleading reports speculators
should depress the price a single cent per pound, the
growers might lose $70,000,000 or more; if the

prices were improperly increased, the manufacturers and allied interests would be affected to a proportionate degree. All interests therefore demand that the true condition of crops should be made known promptly, and harmful speculation discouraged.

The Bureau of Agricultural Economics issues each month detailed reports relating to agricultural conditions throughout the United States, the data upon which these facts are based being obtained through a special field service, and through a large body of voluntary correspondents composed of the following classes: county correspondents, township correspondents, field aids, individual farmers, and special cotton correspondents.

The field service relating to crop reporting has forty offices in different parts of the country with an agricultural statistician in charge of each. It has also a number of assistant agricultural statisticians, livestock statisticians and investigators, truck crop specialists, etc. These officials are especially qualified by statistical training and practical knowledge of crops. They systematically travel over their territories, carefully note the development of each crop, keep in touch with the best informed opinion, and render written and telegraphic reports monthly and at such other times as required. Each statistician has a large number of crop reporters in his state or territory who report to him monthly or oftener on crop conditions, etc.

There are approximately 2,800 counties of ag-

ricultural importance in the United States. In
each of these counties the Department has a principal county correspondent who maintains an
organization of several assistants. These county
correspondents are selected with special reference
to their qualifications and constitute an efficient
branch of the crop-reporting service. They make
the county the geographical unit of their reports,
and after obtaining data each month from their
assistants and supplementing these with information obtained from their own observation and
knowledge, report directly to the Department at
Washington.

In the townships and voting precincts of the
United States in which farming operations are
extensively carried on, the Department has township correspondents who make the township or
precinct the geographical basis of reports, which
they also send directly to the Bureau of Crop
Estimates each month. Finally, at the end of the
growing season, a large number of individual
farmers and planters report on the results of their
own individual farming operations during the year;
and valuable data are also secured from about
30,000 mills and elevators.

With regard to cotton, all the information
secured from the foregoing sources is supplemented
by that furnished by special cotton correspondents,
embracing a large number of persons intimately
concerned in the cotton industry, and, in addition,
inquiries in relation to acreage and yield per acre
of cotton are addressed to the list of cotton ginners

through the courtesy of the Bureau of the Census.

Eleven monthly reports on the principal crops are received yearly from each of the agricultural statisticians, crop specialists, county correspondents, and township correspondents, and one report relating to the acreage and production of general crops is received during the year from individual farmers.

Six special cotton reports are received during the growing season from the cotton crop specialists, agricultural statisticians, the county correspondents, and from township correspondents. The first and last of these reports relate to the acreage and production from individual farmers, special correspondents, and cotton ginners.

The general reports for January and February are combined on one schedule and relate to the number and value of farm animals.

The general report for March relates to the stock of grain in farmers' hands. The percentages of the last year's crops of corn, wheat, oats and barley remaining on the farms and shipped out of the county where grown and the percent of the last year's corn crop that was of merchantable quality.

Reports on the condition of the crops of the year begin with the April report, when the condition of winter wheat and rye is dealt with, the number of breeding sows and the supply of farm labor, and the condition of pastures.

The report for May comes at a time when few of the crops are sufficiently advanced for their condition to be reported upon; consequently the inquiries relative to condition apply only to winter wheat, rye, meadow mowing lands, and spring pasture. This schedule also deals with the portion of the original acreage sown to winter wheat, if for any reason, any has been or will be abandoned, the percentage spring plowing and planting and sowing done, and contains inquiries with regard to the mortality and condition of livestock.

The schedule for June deals with the acreage of five crops, the most important of which is spring wheat. It also covers the condition of wheat, oats, barley, rye, all hay, alfalfa, clover, spring pastures, apples, peaches, pears, berries, field peas and beans, cabbages, onions, melons and sugar beets.

The July schedule deals with the acreage of corn, potatoes, tobacco, and timothy, flax, rice and sorghum cane for syrup; the stocks of wheat in farmers' hands; the average condition of all the principal crops, fruits, vegetables and spring pastures, and the average weight of wool per fleece.

The August schedule deals with the average yield of winter wheat, rye and clover hay per acre, acreage of buckwheat and hay, the condition of the principal crops, vegetables and fruits, the quality of clover hay, and the stocks of oats and barley in farmers' hands.

The September schedule deals with the condition when harvested, of spring wheat, oats and barley; the acreage of clover seed; the production and quality of peaches; the average yield per acre of hay (tame, wild, timothy and alfalfa), the condition of the principal crops, fruits and vegetables and the number and condition of stock hogs on hand for fattening.

The October schedule deals with the average yield per acre of spring wheat, oats, barley, alfalfa seed, field beans, cabbages, onions and broom corn, the quality of spring wheat, oats and barley, the condition at time of harvest of buckwheat, tobacco, rice, flaxseed and clover seed, the condition of the principal growing crops including corn, buckwheat, grain sorghum, sorghum cane for syrup, peanuts, apples, pears and grapes.

The November schedule deals with the average yield per acre of corn for grain, corn for silos, buckwheat, potatoes, tobacco, flaxseed; clover and grain sorghum, cranberries and peanuts, the percent of the corn crop that was of merchantable quality and the percent of the last year's corn crop remaining on the farms; the quality of buckwheat, potatoes, tobacco, flaxseed, apples, grapes, pears, cranberries and peanuts; the per cent of potatoes grown for market; the total production of apples, grapes, pears and cranberries in a percent of a full crop and the percent of plowing done for spring crops in a percent of the usual. The average weight per measured bushel of wheat, oats and barley is also dealt with.

The December schedule deals with the production and farm prices of all the principal crops, and the acreage of winter wheat and rye sown for the crop of the following year, and also with the condition of winter wheat and rye. It also deals with the percent of the apple crop that has been shipped; of the county where grown; the yield per acre of the various straws; the percent of all farm lands plowed in the fall; the wage of male farm labor; the average number of cords of firewood cut on the farm during the year and the average number of cords burned on the farm.

In addition to the foregoing, the reports during the past few years have been extended to include condition figures of many small fruits, vegetables and minor products. Information in regard to such products has been urgently requested, and as a basis for comparison has now been satisfactorily established, the reports are received with interest and favorable comment.

Previous to the preparation and issuance of the Bureau's reports each month, the correspondents of the several classes send their reports separately and independently to the Department at Washington.

In order to prevent any possible access to reports which relate to speculative crops, and to render it absolutely impossible for premature information to be derived from them, all of the reports from the aforesaid agricultural statisticians are sent to the Secretary of Agriculture in specially prepared envelopes addressed in red ink with the letter " A " plainly marked on the ends. By an arrangement with the postal authorities these envelopes are delivered to the Secretary of Agriculture in sealed mail pouches. These pouches are opened only by the Secretary or Assistant Secretary, and the reports, with seals unbroken, are immediately placed in the safe in the Secretary's office, where they remain sealed until the morning of the day on which the reports are issued, when they are delivered to the Statistician by the Secretary or the Assistant Secretary. The combination for opening the safe in which such documents are kept is known only to the Secretary and the Assistant Secretary of Agriculture. Reports from those agricultural statisticians residing at points more than 500 miles from Washington are sent by telegraph, in cipher. Those in regard to speculative crops are addressed to the Secretary of Agriculture.

Reports from the field service in relation to non-speculative crops are sent in similar envelopes marked " B," which go to the Bureau of Crop Estimates, and are kept securely in a safe until the data contained in them are required by the Statistician in computing estimates regarding the crops to which they relate. The reports from the county correspondents, township correspondents and other voluntary agents are sent to the Chief of the Bureau of Crop Estimates by mail in sealed envelopes.

The plan of intrusting the final preparation of reports to a Crop Reporting Board has been continued, and after years of trial it has been demonstrated that such is a satisfactory method. It relieves one man of the strain and responsibility, and secures the benefits of consultation and a consensus of judgment of men who have been on the ground.

The Crop Reporting Board is composed of the

Chief of Bureau as chairman, and four other members, whose services are brought into requisition each crop-reporting day from among the statisticians and officials of the Bureau, and the agricultural statisticians who are called to Washington for the purpose.

The board's personnel is changed somewhat each month. Meetings are held in the office of the Statistician, which is kept locked during sessions, no one being allowed to enter or leave the room or the Bureau, and all telephones being disconnected.

When the board has assembled, reports and telegrams regarding speculative crops from the agricultural statisticians which have been placed unopened in a safe in the office of the Secretary of Agriculture are delivered by the Secretary, opened and tabulated. The reports, by States, from the several classes of correspondents and agents relating to all crops dealt with are brought together in convenient parallel columns on final tabulation slips. The board is thus provided with several separate estimates covering each State and each separate crop, made independently by the respective classes of correspondents and agents of the Bureau, each reporting for a territory or geographical unit with which he is thoroughly familiar.

Abstracts of the weather condition reports in relation to the different crops, by States, are also prepared from the weekly bulletins of the Weather Bureau. With all these data before the board, each individual member computes independently, on a separate sheet or final computation slip, his own estimate of the acreage, condition, or yield of each crop, or of the number, condition, etc., of farm animals for each State separately. These results are then compared and discussed by the board under the supervision of the chairman, and the final figures for each State are decided upon. It has been interesting to note how often the reports of the different classes of correspondents and statisticians are nearly identical and how closely the figures arrived at independently by the individual members of the board agree. The estimates by States as finally determined by the board are weighted by the acreage figures for the respective States, the result for the United States being a true weighted average for each subject.

Reports in relation to cotton, after being prepared by the Crop Reporting Board, and personally approved by the Secretary of Agriculture, are issued on the seventh or eighth day of each month during the growing season, and the reports relating to the principal farm crops and livestock are prepared and made public on the ninth or tenth day of each month. In order that the information contained in these reports may be made available simultaneously throughout the entire United States, they are handed, at an announced hour on report days, to all applicants and to the Western Union Telegraph Company and the Postal Telegraph Cable Company, who have branch offices in the Department of Agriculture, for transmission to the exchange and to the press. These companies have reserved their lines at the designated time, and forward immediately the figures of most interest. A mimeograph or multigraph statement also containing such estimates of condition or actual production together with the corresponding estimates of former years for comparative purposes, is prepared and sent immediately to exchanges, newspaper publications and individuals. The same afternoon data concerning principal crops in each State and totals for the United States are telegraphed to the Weather Bureau Station director in each State, and the information is printed and issued immediately to all the local papers of the State, thus insuring wide publicity to the crop reports within a few hours of their issuance at the Washington office.

Promptly after the issuing of the report, it, together with other statistical information of value to the farmer and the country at large, is published in "Crops and Markets," a publication of the Bureau of Agricultural Economics, under the authority of the Secretary of Agriculture. An edition of many thousand copies is distributed to the correspondents and other interested parties throughout the United States each month. Thus the information is spread broadcast.

As the United States has always been rich in agricultural resources, receipts of cattle, hogs, sheep, wheat, corn, oats and wool, as well as cotton into sight are important business barometers. Grain and cotton are in demand all over the world, as well as in the domestic market. Vast areas in

the great West and South are dependent for their
buying power on the returns from the shipping of
their agricultural products.

Many industries are absolutely dependent on
the crops; and a large group of commodity prices
are directly affected thereby. The importance of
agricultural marketings may be realized from the
estimate of 1925, 1932 and 1934 gross income of
farm products, as tabulated below in millions of
dollars:

	1925	1932	1934
Cattle	1,003.0	498.6	717.4
Hogs	1,666.0	548.4	613.2
Sheep	152.6	76.0	106.5
Milk	6,758.8	1,260.4	1,421.3
Wheat	804.2	203.1	303.3
Corn	386.5	171.4	137.3
Oats	150.4	34.8	30.3
Barley	55.4	16.9	26.9

A large part of the income of the railroad lines is
derived from the shipments of grain, produce and
cotton. A total of 115,000,000 tons of agricultural
products was given to the roads from their own
territory in the year 1929. Some idea of the great
volume of this agricultural product appears in the
realization of the fact that it represents over 8%
by weight of the total freight originating along the
line of the railroads. The entire coal tonnage originating on these traffic lines, which is expected to be
very large, is only 440,000,000 tons, or about 33%
of the total freight. Total tonnage in 1929 was
1,340,000,000.

It is, therefore, not to be wondered at, that in
times that are dull in the manufacturing world, or

in the general trade, great wealth may be brought
to the railroads, and through them to the nation,
by the moving of successful crops. Years of very
large harvests, such as 1906 and 1914 and 1926, may
increase enormously the revenue of every railroad
in the country.

If the good years have such an effect on the
general prosperity of the United States, it is not
surprising to see the tide turned in the opposite
direction by a yield below the average. Crop values
can reach more than $10,000,000,000, and a fluctua-
tion of $1,000,000,000, or over, in this great total
has in every way a wide-spreading effect on the
business of the country. Even partial crop failures
may result at once in a depression, and bumper
crops may boom a stock market as no other influence has power to do. This influence operates
especially through its effect on railroad earnings
and on the export trade. Full crops yield a surplus
for export and help pay a nation's debt; they may
create a credit and turn an adverse gold movement
into a favorable balance and increased imports of
gold. Viewed from every angle, the progress of the
crops and the study of crop statistics should be
regarded as of the utmost importance.

The profits, and therefore the stocks of railroad
companies, which operate through the grain and
cotton sections, are affected in the most direct and
powerful manner by the promise of generous or
stunted crops. Investors need to keep in touch
with the crop outlook. Wall Street usually discounts the future and rarely waits for earnings to

be affected actually before adjusting prices to what it sees coming.

A slackening in the investment business comes during a great boom and precedes every financial crisis; and every investor should be as alert to detect the signs of a coming change of importance as are the bankers, brokers and stock operators, who are continually watching the crops as well as the Babsonchart.

It is axiomatic that most railroads are affected directly and seriously by crop conditions. Many industrial concerns are also directly affected. "Crops" is one subject which requires constant attention, and never more so than when a boom or reaction has run on for a number of months or years. *Conservative merchants and investors therefore tabulate each month as published, the government estimate of the wheat, corn, and cotton crops, then in the ground, together with the annual figures when the crops have been harvested.*

PRODUCTION OF COMMODITIES

As the government crop statistics are necessary and valuable as business barometers so figures showing the production of leading commodities are of intense interest. In fact, as the country becomes more and more industrialized, the relative importance of the production of the basic materials increases. Huge amounts of coal, copper, lumber, petroleum, pig iron, etc., are required to supply our growing industries. Values for some of these products for 1925 are as follows:—Coal (Bituminous

and Anthracite), $1,400,000,000; Copper, $300,-
000,000; Lumber, $1,200,000,000; Petroleum, $1,-
200,000,000 and Pig Iron, $800,000,000.

Until recent years, relatively few data were
available indicating manufacturing activity. Business men have always realized the importance of
watching the course of manufacturing for it has
had a growing effect on the purchasing power of
the country both through the rapidly rising standard of living of industrial workers and the need for
increasing amounts of raw and partly fabricated
materials. The biggest impetus to industrial
development began with the World War. Along
with this, additional industrial production data
became available, furnishing the business man with
more tools for charting the course of business.

Some industries are so basic in their effect on
business activity that every wise business man
recognizes the necessity of following the trend of
the statistics concerning them. Some idea of the
dominating position of basic industries may be
obtained from the following United States Census
estimates of value for 1929 (latest available):

	1929
Food and Kindred Products.....	$12,023,589,000
Textiles and their Products......	9,243,303,000
Iron and Steel and their Products (not including machinery).....	7,137,928,000
Lumber and Allied Products.....	3,591,765,000

The production of iron, for example, reported
by the two leading weeklies on the subject, is a
very important factor in determining present conditions and forecasting future conditions. This was

especially true before the United States Steel Corporation was formed and to a large extent is also true today. Figures regarding pork, copper, wool, coffee, rubber, sugar and other commodities are also of interest. A decrease in the production of commodities is always accompanied by a decrease in activity, which means that men and capital are idle. This reduced activity, if pressed beyond a certain point, will result in a crisis followed by a period of depression.

RAILROAD EARNINGS

Railroad earnings are of interest for two reasons: *first*, in forecasting the conditions of the railroads, upon which the prices of securities are directly dependent; *second*, in determining and forecasting the condition of general business.

Although stocks of roads barely earning their operating expenses and interest charges are of some nominal value simply on account of their voting power (and this value is generally considered in the vicinity of about $10 per share, par value $100), yet railroad stocks as a rule are worth very little unless the roads are earning money. But whether or not a stock pays a dividend, it is self-evident that the prices must vary with the earning power. Increased earnings forecast increased values for the securities, and reduced earnings forecast lower values. Manipulation may temporarily force stocks far above or far below their true investment value, but neither high prices nor low prices can artificially be maintained for long.

In the end the prices must adjust themselves according to earnings. As all industries are either directly or indirectly dependent upon railroads, railroad earnings are of great importance to the investor.

For the purpose of forecasting general business conditions, railroad earnings are also of interest. As statistics they are so important for this purpose that many merchants consider railroad earnings second only to check transactions in making a study of actual business conditions. There are several reasons for this choice, of which the two following are especially well founded:

(1) Because nearly all bills are paid in checks, check transactions serve as a barometer of the total amount of sales; but railroad earnings likewise serve as a similar barometer, because practically all goods purchased or sold are shipped on the railroads. If the freight earnings of the United States show an increase, it is very evident that manufacturing and commerce are increasing; and the same is true conversely, if the freight earnings are decreasing. Therefore the earnings of the railroads may be considered in the same manner as the clearings of the banks, especially when " tonnage," rather than cash receipts is considered.

(2) Another important reason is that not only are railroad conditions a barometer of trade conditions, but to a large extent they are the *basis* of general trade conditions. This is due to the fact that the railroads employ so large a proportion of the working class population of the United States,

and that so many industries are absolutely dependent on the railroads for their business. The railroads are the best purchasers of contractors' supplies and contract labor; of iron and steel for rails and bridges; of lumber for ties and stations; of coal for motive power and heating; of oil for fuel and for lubricating; of printers' supplies for time-tables, tickets, etc., etc. In fact this list might be indefinitely extended to show that the prosperity of the country is inseparably connected with the prosperity of the railroads.

Therefore, for the above two reasons, the wise investor and merchant very carefully watches railroad earnings, both for determining the present conditions and for forecasting future conditions. In this connection the history of railroad earnings during three serious depressions may be of interest. During the reaction of 1873 the high level of gross earnings was reached in the same calendar year as the panic itself, but the recession from this high point was fairly evenly spread over the next four years. The recovery, on the contrary, was strikingly rapid. In 1879, only two years after gross earnings had been at their worst, they had nearly regained their former high level, and this was steadily raised.

By reducing " maintenance charges," the net earnings increased for a year after the reaction began, the gain between 1873 and 1874 having been more than three percent. Thereafter net earnings declined along with the gross, to their low level in 1877. In the following two years they recovered even more rapidly than gross earnings, making up most of their lost ground in one year. The re-action between the top and bottom levels in net earnings was practically 10%, but between the years in which the gross receipts sank from top to bottom levels, the difference in net was considerably less. Moreover, this decrease was accompanied by an increase in mileage of nearly 12%.

While the panic of 1873 severely checked rail-road construction, it by no means checked such development altogether. This crisis followed one of the most pronounced waves of railroad construc-tion ever witnessed. In two years (1870–72) pre-ceding the panic, operated mileage increased by about 13,250 miles, or 25%, which of course is always a distinct danger signal.

The depression of 1884–5 differed from other depressions in the relation of operating expenses to volume of business. In 1894 the percentage decline in net earnings was a trifle less than that of gross; but in the '80's the lessening volume of traffic was not accompanied by a proportionate reduction in earnings. The comparison of top and bottom levels in this depression follows:

	Mileage	Gross	Net
1883	121,422	$817,317,000	$295,737,000
1885	128,320	765,493,000	266,616,000
Decrease	*6,898	51,884,000	29,121,000
Per cent	5.7	6.3	9.8

" In so serious a crisis as that of the '90's, the maximum reaction in railroad earnings was not more than 12%. However, aggregate figures cover-

* Increase.

ing so many railroads of such wide diversity of
location and condition tend to obscure the facts as
they apply to individual undertaking. Constant
addition of new mileage tends to reduce the record
of damage sustained by the old roads. The reduction of the figure to a mileage basis would still be
an inaccurate test, because the earning power of new
and additional mileage is naturally low. Furthermore, construction of new roads frequently takes
away business from those roads already in existence, and thus tends to lower the average earnings
per mile without any actual decrease in the amount
of business. A comparison between fat and lean
years could best be made by using figures for identical mileage."

Aggregate railroad earnings reached a new high
level in 1893 and again acted as a distinct danger
signal, for the crisis itself took place in the second
half of that calendar year. The reaction in general
business came the next year, when both gross and
net immediately reached the low level of that
movement. The recovery, though slow, was fairly
continuous throughout five or six succeeding years.
Note extent of reactions from top levels to bottom:

	Mileage	Gross	Net (1)
1893.........	169,780	$1,221,000,000	$392,831,000
1894.........	175,691	1,073,000,000	341,947,000
Decrease......	*5,911	148,000,000	50,884,000
Per cent.......	*3.5	12.1	13.0

Figures below taken from Railway Statistics of U. S., 1933.

	Mileage	Gross	Net (1)
1929..........	253,679	$6,386,368,889	$1,801,362,776
1933..........	248,755	3,140,690,446	746,069,017
Decrease......	4,924	3,245,678,443	1,055,293,759
Per cent......	1.9	50.8	58.6

(1) From operations before fixed charges and taxes.   * Increase.

We insert herewith a chart of railroad traffic compiled by the Research Department of Babson's Reports Incorporated. The study is thorough inasmuch as it extends back to 1866.

It is therefore advisable for merchants and investors to watch carefully the reports of the Interstate Commerce Commission. These reports include nearly all the railroads in the United States and give mileage, gross and net earnings. These statistics are published monthly and from them the gross and net earnings per mile may be computed.

REVENUE FREIGHT CAR LOADINGS

Revenue Freight Car Loadings figures are of even more direct interest in forecasting business conditions than are figures on "Railroad Earnings." In fact, they bear the same relation to railroad earnings that the Government crop estimates bear to the final figures compiled after the crop has been gathered.

The car loadings data are collected by the American Railway Association which receives every week from the officials of each railroad the reports of revenue freight cars loaded, divided as grain, livestock, coal, coke, forest products, ore, merchandise in less than carload lots, and miscellaneous loadings. Not only are the loadings for the different classes of freight available as given below, but the data by territorial divisions are also given. Car loadings often continue heavy after new orders for goods have begun to fall off and vice versa.

In other words, car loading figures represent the movement of goods which have been manufactured during the two or three months preceding.

These reports on revenue freight cars loaded are especially valuable because of the prompt indication given by changing conditions. They are available seven days after the close of each week. It may be two or three months after a car is taken from the siding for loading before the earnings appear in the monthly statement of the railroads.

The following table gives the average weekly loadings for recent years.

CAR LOADINGS (U. S.) (Average Weekly)

	Grain and Grain Products	Live Stock	Coal and Coke	Forest Products	Ore	Merchandise L. C. L. and Miscellaneous	Total
1922							
January....	50,460	32,568	166,075	48,960	4,410	421,722	734,442
February....	51,199	29,113	195,982	50,124	4,151	486,143	768,741
March......	41,184	18,092	204,517	52,734	5,250	495,258	827,400
April.......	32,874	27,114	76,080	56,052	9,654	521,106	727,488
May........	42,186	29,550	91,272	60,714	18,384	540,546	782,670
June........	39,614	29,201	103,574	62,621	54,054	563,043	851,700
July........	50,229	26,656	83,731	54,892	63,364	545,585	825,018
August......	56,111	29,633	109,009	58,563	66,002	557,241	876,517
September...	51,670	34,603	180,060	57,116	53,769	560,896	934,387
October.....	52,160	40,404	202,338	59,525	46,819	587,702	992,470
November...	53,602	39,671	204,181	61,964	33,565	569,774	968,331
December....	50,537	33,764	198,823	57,383	9,659	487,525	839,784
1923							
January.....	47,890	34,049	207,049	66,238	10,596	477,952	843,491
February....	40,345	31,500	200,656	65,570	9,578	492,697	840,400
March......	41,363	30,748	201,410	74,490	13,051	554,111	916,235
April.......	38,411	31,010	192,417	77,188	19,426	581,867	941,067
May........	33,599	30,625	194,284	75,445	61,627	588,955	975,379
June........	34,847	29,712	201,269	77,960	79,562	577,274	1,011,901
July........	42,498	30,014	198,073	69,899	82,675	561,025	985,184
August......	52,223	33,646	206,767	76,393	80,458	582,848	1,041,844
September...	50,249	39,114	190,435	72,599	73,288	597,986	1,036,946
October.....	49,624	42,500	205,856	73,818	61,368	643,954	1,078,163
November...	48,520	39,630	187,247	72,498	35,657	614,131	977,900
December....	45,431	35,916	172,372	58,916	10,445	545,519	826,681

CAR LOADINGS (Average Weekly)—*Continued*

	Grain and Grain Products	Live Stock	Coal and Coke	Forest Products	Ore	Merchandise L. C. L. and Miscellaneous	Total
1924							
January.....	43,118	36,216	207,724	63,661	8,243	482,523	840,534
February....	49,414	33,135	201,864	79,494	9,392	528,025	904,358
March......	42,240	30,914	177,472	81,155	11,369	573,179	921,541
April.......	37,024	29,328	134,633	76,244	17,561	580,486	874,803
May........	39,327	30,893	140,655	72,801	51,120	560,171	894,950
June........	37,994	30,044	149,234	68,292	59,357	561,948	906,368
July........	43,584	29,493	182,345	59,677	55,176	509,295	881,625
August......	60,993	30,520	130,858	68,367	51,142	597,048	968,681
September...	67,433	36,772	187,581	67,068	47,082	628,724	1,036,601
October.....	69,047	41,560	200,797	70,541	44,223	667,454	1,095,037
November...	56,291	39,745	192,972	69,231	21,457	615,792	994,478
December....	46,826	36,931	188,057	63,214	9,818	523,753	867,918
1925							
January.....	49,035	36,025	214,302	67,905	9,704	514,419	891,390
February....	42,233	30,769	183,526	79,891	11,257	558,085	905,762
March......	37,668	27,616	161,963	81,134	11,828	605,394	925,603
April.......	32,857	27,659	150,454	78,100	22,700	619,936	931,707
May........	36,641	27,226	162,624	75,428	61,964	606,793	970,676
June........	36,450	26,519	166,475	73,513	63,019	625,491	991,468
July........	53,937	33,233	217,533	82,424	78,579	767,017	1,232,724
August......	43,933	24,252	166,612	57,355	50,234	521,803	864,189
September...	52,415	32,797	182,793	69,731	57,603	679,024	1,074,363
October.....	46,392	42,327	199,182	70,343	49,698	699,540	1,107,482
November...	48,691	35,067	199,771	66,349	33,069	640,794	1,023,742
December....	51,377	32,806	189,294	64,387	11,942	574,859	924,665
1926							
January.....	45,249	32,516	199,614	62,451	9,796	536,777	886,402
February....	42,775	28,299	192,519	74,666	10,483	570,369	919,112
March......	39,839	28,432	195,862	76,740	10,891	617,521	969,285
April.......	37,438	26,001	176,299	74,998	13,768	620,455	948,959
May........	39,599	28,553	179,615	76,681	48,637	655,491	1,028,576
June........	40,229	26,875	183,598	73,985	67,861	635,488	1,028,037
July........	55,900	26,900	187,700	67,000	73,000	638,600	1,049,000
August......	57,000	29,300	202,400	70,600	77,600	667,500	1,104,000
September...	50,400	37,200	216,200	70,700	77,500	698,700	1,148,000
October.....	54,200	40,500	240,800	72,300	66,700	730,600	1,205,000
November...	45,100	34,600	247,800	65,800	31,800	642,900	1,068,000
December....	44,100	29,100	226,000	54,400	9,600	540,700	904,000
1927							
January.....	44,700	32,300	234,900	64,300	9,500	553,400	939,100
February....	43,400	27,700	225,600	68,900	10,700	574,200	950,500
March......	39,200	27,200	216,500	70,500	10,800	704,000	997,600
April.......	37,100	27,600	165,800	68,400	25,500	644,500	883,400
May........	39,700	28,800	172,300	71,000	59,900	655,300	1,029,600
June........	40,200	27,000	161,400	67,700	64,700	638,200	999,400
July........	46,500	25,500	153,900	63,300	63,000	626,200	978,400
August......	55,100	28,100	183,700	69,000	62,200	664,500	1,062,500
September...	58,800	31,700	192,800	67,600	55,900	690,700	1,097,600
October.....	54,800	39,600	200,100	67,200	48,000	706,500	1,116,200
November...	45,600	33,600	178,300	61,100	19,300	617,700	955,700
December....	44,400	28,900	174,000	52,000	8,400	528,000	835,100

CAR LOADINGS (Average Weekly)—*Continued*

	Grain and Grain Products	Live Stock	Coal and Coke	Forest Products	Ore	Merchandise L. C. L. and Miscellaneous	Total
1928							
January.....	46,800	31,900	188,200	58,300	7,900	528,800	861,900
February....	46,800	32,500	181,600	67,700	7,800	561,000	897,400
March......	47,500	28,700	173,900	68,800	8,600	623,100	950,400
April........	39,800	26,300	155,200	64,300	10,300	638,700	934,600
May........	40,800	26,700	167,700	67,400	41,300	657,600	1,001,500
June........	34,800	25,200	154,700	66,000	65,600	638,700	984,700
July........	51,800	22,700	151,700	59,900	62,500	637,000	985,700
August......	57,800	24,700	171,600	66,500	63,300	673,800	1,057,700
September...	59,200	32,900	190,500	64,500	63,900	706,200	1,117,300
October.....	54,800	38,700	217,300	66,500	60,200	737,700	1,175,200
November...	52,400	44,500	208,100	65,000	37,900	664,400	1,061,300
December....	48,400	27,800	186,500	55,000	10,400	553,000	882,800
1929							
January.....	45,492	29,500	214,387	54,662	8,918	539,787	892,744
February....	47,161	26,421	225,308	60,259	9,243	573,547	941,940
March......	42,598	24,221	171,443	67,096	11,423	644,808	961,589
April........	35,936	26,724	160,810	69,704	27,670	675,153	995,994
May........	38,136	26,460	172,505	69,329	70,951	674,046	1,051,427
June........	43,121	23,349	168,511	69,583	75,963	671,588	1,052,114
July........	61,674	22,992	161,179	61,259	76,241	654,960	1,038,305
August......	63,114	24,257	183,243	68,690	75,712	703,155	1,118,171
September...	49,842	30,911	202,770	62,932	68,650	719,540	1,134,644
October	46,420	37,275	219,394	63,589	60,041	742,624	1,169,344
November...	38,395	31,378	200,399	55,042	29,215	623,940	978,369
December...	39,919	25,450	204,147	45,452	8,219	512,061	835,248
1930							
January.....	39,200	27,000	207,100	45,500	8,400	510,200	837,000
February....	43,700	25,700	199,500	54,300	8,400	544,900	876,000
March......	40,200	23,600	147,100	88,800	9,000	604,200	883,000
April........	39,150	24,500	146,100	57,400	16,600	628,800	912,000
May........	37,300	22,800	145,200	51,900	56,600	600,200	914,000
June........	41,500	21,600	145,100	49,700	62,500	609,900	930,000
July........	59,200	19,600	140,300	40,200	60,500	574,900	895,000
August......	60,300	22,000	156,000	41,500	56,700	599,100	938,000
September...	47,300	26,900	159,500	40,400	48,800	608,400	931,000
October	41,400	32,300	183,600	39,400	39,800	616,000	950,000
November...	36,500	26,900	166,800	34,000	14,200	519,700	798,000
December....	35,100	22,900	158,000	29,000	5,500	429,300	680,000
1931							
January......	40,700	25,700	166,400	33,100	5,200	447,700	719,000
February....	41,200	22,000	145,900	34,600	5,600	459,700	709,000
March......	38,300	19,800	138,900	34,400	5,800	497,700	735,000
April........	37,500	21,800	123,200	32,800	8,000	528,900	752,000
May........	35,900	20,500	120,400	32,900	17,300	513,400	740,000
June........	35,000	18,600	116,100	31,300	29,800	517,100	748,000
July........	54,100	18,100	115,300	26,700	34,800	488,600	738,000
August......	44,400	21,700	123,200	27,700	35,000	495,500	747,000
September....	37,300	24,800	132,800	26,000	29,800	486,500	737,000
October......	38,700	29,400	151,800	24,300	18,600	496,100	759,000
November....	36,200	25,900	126,700	21,900	6,300	438,000	655,000
December....	27,100	21,000	121,200	17,000	3,500	365,500	555,000

CAR LOADINGS (Average Weekly)—*Continued*

	Grain and Grain Products	Live Stock	Coal and Coke	Forest Products	Ore	Merchandise L. C. L. and Miscellaneous	Total
1932							
January......	31,000	22,100	120,800	18,400	2,900	372,200	567,000
February.....	34,300	19,000	121,200	19,300	2,700	364,900	561,000
March.......	28,900	16,500	121,700	19,900	2,600	375,600	565,000
April........	31,200	19,300	95,400	19,800	3,700	387,500	557,000
May.........	29,200	17,100	77,800	18,700	2,600	376,500	522,000
June........	26,300	14,700	69,700	16,000	3,900	360,000	491,000
July........	38,600	14,600	76,000	14,300	6,400	333,400	483,000
August......	38,900	17,400	91,400	15,700	6,900	354,700	525,000
September....	36,800	21,300	113,400	17,800	6,100	381,400	577,000
October......	33,500	23,700	141,500	18,900	6,500	410,000	634,000
November...	28,600	19,300	127,400	16,200	2,700	354,500	549,000
December....	25,200	15,700	131,900	12,400	1,800	297,900	485,000
1933							
January.....	26,600	17,200	112,300	13,700	1,800	306,000	478,000
February....	25,300	15,400	129,300	13,700	1,800	303,900	489,000
March.......	27,600	13,400	95,000	15,100	2,100	313,900	467,000
April........	35,800	16,900	80,700	17,300	3,400	348,500	503,000
May........	36,400	16,300	83,300	21,200	7,900	362,100	527,000
June........	39,600	15,500	104,500	26,400	13,300	398,400	598,000
July........	44,700	14,900	118,500	26,400	23,200	390,900	617,000
August......	30,300	17,000	133,600	26,800	35,400	390,800	634,000
September....	30,800	20,700	128,000	24,500	35,900	394,500	634,000
October.....	29,800	23,200	131,600	24,400	27,800	414,600	651,000
November...	30,000	19,200	127,300	22,900	6,500	366,500	572,000
December....	25,800	15,200	123,800	17,500	2,900	332,300	518,000
1934							
January.....	29,800	17,100	138,500	18,700	3,000	341,200	548,000
February....	29,500	14,900	160,400	22,100	3,200	357,200	587,000
March.......	29,700	13,300	151,400	24,200	4,000	391,100	614,000
April........	26,500	16,300	106,000	24,200	7,400	403,300	584,000
May........	28,100	16,200	113,600	25,100	20,700	406,600	610,000
June........	34,900	15,400	107,100	24,600	33,100	400,500	616,000
July........	42,700	22,200	97,600	20,800	31,300	371,900	587,000
August......	40,000	30,900	100,000	22,300	29,000	382,700	613,000
September....	34,800	34,100	121,400	22,000	24,400	345,200	624,000
October.....	30,600	28,500	126,600	22,400	17,100	407,700	629,000
November...	27,800	22,500	129,000	21,200	6,500	381,400	557,000
December....	25,100	16,300	128,900	18,300	3,100	326,700	526,000
1935							
January.....	24,250	14,500	145,000	18,750	3,250	336,500	542,250
February....	25,500	12,500	152,250	25,000	3,250	363,250	581,450
March.......	27,000	11,600	143,200	25,200	3,600	392,200	603,000
April........	27,000	13,000	100,500	25,500	8,750	401,250	575,750
May........	25,500	13,000	104,250	25,000	2,550	388,500	581,750
June........	25,400	10,200	130,200	26,200	3,180	383,200	607,000
July........	30,000	9,750	84,250	26,500	3,275	373,750	557,250
August......	42,200	12,800	103,400	30,400	3,420	397,400	620,400
September....	40,500	17,250	118,000	31,000	3,375	417,500	658,000
October.....	37,000	21,750	143,500	31,500	3,250	454,250	720,500
November...	31,400	16,800	132,200	27,400	1,340	414,400	635,800
December....	27,250	12,750	138,750	26,000	520	369,500	579,750

*CAR LOADINGS (Average Weekly)—*Continued*

	Grain and Grain Products	Live Stock	Coal and Coke	Forest Products	Ore	Merchandise L. C. L. and Miscellaneous	Total
1936							
January.....	32,100	12,800	162,000	26,600	5,600	357,700	595,000
February....	30,100	10,300	193,600	26,400	5,700	362,200	623,000
March......	34,000	11,900	112,500	30,500	6,000	409,800	605,000
April.......	31,100	13,000	120,000	30,700	10,600	437,900	643,000
May........	30,700	11,600	117,500	32,400	42,300	435,600	670,000
June........	34,900	11,800	114,900	34,700	50,500	450,000	697,000
July.........	52,600	13,400	120,500	33,300	52,500	442,300	715,000
August......	41,400	15,400	128,700	36,200	55,200	461,400	738,000
September...	31,800	18,600	147,800	34,700	56,300	468,500	776,000
October.....	32,300	22,200	168,600	35,900	51,600	508,500	819,000
November...	32,800	19,200	167,400	34,000	28,300	471,600	753,000
December....	32,500	14,750	167,400	33,000	8,250	437,750	694,000

* Readers desiring to bring this compilation up to date may obtain data by addressing Babson's Reports Incorporated, Wellesley Hills, Mass.

The car loadings are available by weeks since 1918. Prior to that one must study data on idle cars. These figures also are reported weekly to the American Railway Association. They give for each railroad district and for principal roads the surplus and the shortage of cars of different types requisitioned during the week.

In interpreting idle car figures, therefore, an increase in the number of idle cars naturally indicates a slackening in business, while a decrease in the number of cars available signifies improvement in business. Likewise when there is a shortage of cars, a further increase in the shortage indicates greater demand for transportation; a decrease in shortage indicates a lessening in demands of business and better transportation service. In interpreting the figures two factors must always be kept in mind: first, the seasonal tendency. The heaviest demand usually comes during the fall months, while the lightest demand is found during the spring. Second, the additions to railroad equipment which, of course, make a difference in the relation of car supplies to the demands of business.

POLITICAL FACTORS

Some of the most successful merchants of the old school maintained that the three greatest factors which influence business conditions are crops, money and politics, and that of these the most important is the last named, politics. Certainly this statement appears reasonable to some, but it is probable that political as well as social changes are largely governed and influenced by other fundamental business conditions. For instance, at a time of great expansion of business when commodity prices are rising, the common people gradually get disgruntled and wish a change in administration. On the other hand, at a time of depression the political party in power is likely to suffer from the liquidation in wages and customary hard times. In fact, once in every little while the populace assumes control, institutes a few improvements, but soon becomes divided by contentions, and again capital and the conservatives are given the reins. Nevertheless a study of politics as reflecting the underlying conditions of the country is quite necessary. That portion of American history with which these pages are most concerned, from 1860 up to the present time, is most admirably described by Alex. Dana Noyes in his "Forty Years of American Finance."

There has always been a most delicate relation between politics and the state of trade. Almost every period of depression and period of prosperity, although not actually due to political conditions, has been greatly augmented by them. Among those various political factors may be mentioned the following: —

The " Embargo Act " in the early part of the century and the war of 1812.

The establishment of the United States Bank.

The discontinuance of the United States Bank.

The beginning of " state rights " discussions.

The slavery discussion and the Civil War.

The " Reconstruction Acts."

The inflation of the currency.

The " Resumption Act."

The silver coinage law.

The resumption of specie payments.

The circulation of silver certificates.

The radical measures under President Arthur, followed by the panic of 1884.

The campaign and the election of the Republican Party in 1888, coincident with the period of prosperity.

The silver purchase act and the great gold exportations followed by the panic of 1893.

The tariff legislation of the '90's followed by the prosperous conditions of 1900.

The various Bryan scares.

Theodore Roosevelt's campaigns against trusts.

Continuation of campaigns against trusts under President Taft's administration.

The organization of a national Progressive Party, and the victory of the Democratic Party in 1912.

Anti-trust legislation and the tariff, income tax and currency laws of 1913.

Federal Reserve system inaugurated in 1914.

Stock Dividend Decision.

Fordney McCumber tariff.

Cancellation of War Debts.

War Veteran Bonuses.

Agricultural Credit Act.

National Recovery Act, etc.

Of all these various acts, by far the most influential were those affecting the currency and the tariff. Both of these are extremely sensitive questions. Any change in the money standard or banking system, especially if it disturbs either foreign or domestic confidence, is very destructive to the commercial prosperity of the country. Even when banking questions or the money standard are discussed in Congress, there seems to be an immediate division of interests between the producer or the manufacturer and the banker or the investor. The legislation desired by the producer seems to be opposed by the investor and vice versa. The reason for this is very evident, for anything which tends to make money easier to the producer, depreciates the value of money in the hands of the bankers and investors who possess it. On the other hand, legislation which strengthens the importance of the banker and investor, tends to handicap the producer and manufacturer.

Any legislation designed to reorganize the bank-

ing system of the United States on anything but a
gold basis, like that upon which the banking systems of England and other countries were founded,
always retards trade. Any legislation which gives
any additional importance to gold is always greeted
with approval by all classes of manufacturers,
merchants and investors. All other legislation,
especially that recognizing as a standard, silver or
anything other than gold, is always a dangerous
sign, often causing bankers and investors to call
loans and raise rates. Such conditions usually
precede a general crisis.

As to the propriety of high or low duties on
foreign goods, this is an open question. Although
nearly all bankers are in favor of protection, yet
most economists (on whose advice the bankers depend regarding many matters) are almost without
exception against heavy protection; but whether
high tariff for protection or low tariff for revenue
only is best for the country, the fact remains that
whenever the subject is discussed and whenever
there is to be a change in classifications or duties,
this discussion and legislation have always affected
business conditions. Moreover, although the adoption of certain tariff legislation may give a great
impetus to prosperity, yet the previous discussion
of the subject has always tended to disturb confidence, promote a feeling of uncertainty and seriously check business.

This was very well described by Henry Hall as
follows: —

"In the United States the business world has

become accustomed to the protective principle
and even the prospect of reduced duties has always
chilled the spirit of enterprise, while the reality
has always given a setback to business, sooner or
later.   On the other hand, enactment of protective
tariff, in lieu of one for revenue only, has always
proved exciting and has quickened into intense
activity the looms, forges and machinery of the
entire country.

"The backward state of American industry
prior to the Civil War is held to have been due in
large measure to the relaxation of protection under
the tariff laws of 1842 and 1857.   There can be no
question that the twenty or more tariff enact-
ments from 1861, when the Morrill protective tariff
went into operation, to 1872 when the system had
been fairly adjusted to the requirements of home
industry, aided materially in developing the mines,
sustaining the factories against foreign competition, supplying the railroads with an immense and
profitable traffic, and promoting the farming interest of every section of the States."

The lower duties of 1883 on many manufactures,
added to the force of other evil influences, ended
in the crisis of 1884.   The crisis of 1893 rose
in a distinct measure from the agitation in the
then Democratic Congress for a tariff for revenue only, which eventuated in the Wilson bill.
The prosperity which the States subsequently
enjoyed must be attributed in a marked degree
to the protective tariff enacted under President
McKinley, while recent international problems
were accentuated by high tariffs.

All writers on crises agree in giving great weight to tariff changes. An investor should therefore at all times be fully informed with regard to such actual or possible revolutions in political control at Washington as are likely to have a bearing on the tariff laws. As a further illustration of this subject the setback given business during the tariff discussion from July, 1929 to 1930, and the continued business depression which followed upon the passing of the bill is of suggestive interest.

Therefore successful bankers, merchants and investors always carefully watch political conditions and if possible reduce them to a decimal or barometer index number.

SOCIAL CONDITIONS AND MISCELLANEOUS STATISTICS

The condition of public opinion in the country as a whole, and the stand taken by any large number of people, or a representative body of people, with regard to social or religious questions, exerts a constant influence upon business conditions. Not only in politics and the larger field of government as shown in election or municipal reforms, but in all religious or social movements, the feeling of the people should be watched closely. Most investors and merchants look upon crops, money and politics as the three most important topics to study in order to form a clear idea of the present state of business and a sound judgment of what is to be expected. They would also do well to look into the field of social and religious tendencies, because they will find there material of great use in determining the trend of business.

From time immemorial, periods of prosperity have been accompanied by a decline in religious interests and by a laxness in moral and social customs. Conversely, a period of hard times and business depression always brings men back to religious thoughts and worship. A striking illustration of this is found in the panic of 1857. " It was in October of this year (1857) that Mr. Lamphier, a missionary of the Dutch Reformed Church, thought in his own heart that an hour of daily prayer would bring consolation to afflicted business men! "* In a few weeks those holding meetings were astonished to find crowds growing too large for the buildings. The Methodist Church on John Street and the Dutch Reformed Church on Fulton Street were opened daily. Next Burton's Theatre was hired, and throughout the winter, noonday prayer meetings were held at numerous places in the city. " Even the firemen and policemen held their prayer meetings, so that we may feel perfectly assured of the truth of what the writer says when he adds, ' It is doubtful whether under heaven was seen such a sight as went on in the city of New York in the winter and spring of the year 1857–1858.' From New York as a centre, the mysterious influence spread abroad till it penetrated all New England in the East, southward as far as Virginia and even beyond, westward to Buffalo, Cincinnati, Chicago, St. Louis."

* Ross' " Social Psychology," page 78.

The American Civil War was followed by great financial and social corruption, and even General Grant, although himself incorruptible, could not save his country from the effect of greed and wrongdoing. The famous election which followed was noted for the frauds which characterized both parties. These frauds were so gigantic that to this day it is uncertain whether Tilden or Hayes was actually elected President of the United States. As is the case during all such periods of personal, commercial and civic corruption, this period was followed by the great business depression beginning about 1873.

Immediately following this depression a period of religious and civic revivals swept over the nation. The additions to churches, the great temperance movement, and other similar movements for righteousness received an unprecedented impetus during these years following the panic of 1873. This return to righteousness was again followed by a return to over-expansion in the early '80's.

The nation, however, soon forgot whence these blessings came and religious interest again declined. This lack of interest in religious matters culminated in the panic of 1884. Once more the reign of ungodliness was checked and the country recuperated from the depression of 1884, and again enjoyed several years of wonderful prosperity. It, however, took the nation only a few years to forget again, and once more civic corruption, social immorality and intemperance began to increase. From 1890 to 1893 religious and similar organizations showed very little

growth.   Consequently the era of expansion began
to wane, and culminated in the panic of 1893.

The panic of 1893 again brought people to think
upon serious matters, and during the following few
years there was a great revival of righteousness
throughout America.   In fact, the additions to
churches and the growth of other religious movements even exceeded that during the period following the panic of 1873.   The people again cast aside
luxuries, municipal and state governments were
purified, evil doers were replaced by men of high in-
tegrity, and great interest in all religious and moral
undertakings developed in all parts of the country.

People again lived in a more decent and honest
manner in accordance with what their station per-
mitted.   Commercial houses forsook the careless
and questionable methods used during former
times and the old-fashioned " drummer " was replaced by the modern high grade salesman.   It was
on this foundation that the new period of improvement started and it was due to this revival of righteousness, that the country was able to enjoy many
years of sound prosperity which began simultaneously with the close of the Spanish War in 1898
and 1899.

Unfortunately, however, the nation again forgot
and was still unable to stand the temptations of a
period of prosperity.   Therefore again religious
interest declined, political corruption re-opened
and social immorality increased.   Referring to
these conditions Dr. Lyman Abbott once stated
as follows:

"Popular rumor attributed to Mr. McKinley's managers, although not to him, wholesale corruption in securing his first nomination and his first election. This corruption has not been confined to any one locality or to any one party. It has been equally appalling in its dimensions in New York, Boston, Philadelphia, Cincinnati, Chicago, St. Louis, Minneapolis, Denver and San Francisco. It has included not only Boards of Aldermen but Legislatures, and it has crept into both the administrative and legislative departments of the Federal Government. Two United States Senators and three United States Representatives have subjected themselves to criminal prosecution for participation in frauds. Nor has this corruption been confined to political circles. Insurance companies, banks, trust companies, manufacturers and trade unions have all been implicated. More than one financial magnate is now serving a sentence for fraud. Others are under sentence and are awaiting the decision on appeal. Even judges have not been wholly free from suspicion of obligation for their election to the plutocracy."

This is a description of the conditions from 1902 to 1906, when the exposures commenced. Like all preceding periods of unrighteousness, this was followed by the panic of 1907, and the succeeding years of depression. The scandals and corruption of the '20's are too recent to demand review.

Of course some writers, although admitting that a business depression revives interest in religious matters and that, during the boom times, men do not have the time or inclination to give religious matters any thought, claim that the religious state of the nation does not affect the business conditions as here represented. Whether or not this is true, is debatable; but certainly a study of the history of the United States *and every other nation*, seems to point to a definite relation between the two interests. Moreover, all economists agree that the religious condition of the country is distinctly worthy of study,—although they may disagree as to its relative importance compared with other subjects.

Thus Ex-President Taft said: " The hum of prosperity and the ecstasy of great profits are likely to dull our interest in these reforms and to lead us back again to the old abuses, unless we insist upon legislation which shall clinch and enforce those standards by positive law."

Surely this happened as ex-President Taft foretold. Following the World War came the election of Harding and a riotous era of expansion and speculation. The Roosevelt "New Deal" was simply a reaction from the "hum of prosperity."

Or to quote a higher authority:

" Beware lest . . . thou say in thine heart, ' My power and the might of mine hand hath gotten me this wealth.' But thou shalt remember the Lord thy God, for it is He that giveth thee power to get wealth." Deut. 8 : 11, 17, 18.

STATISTICS SHOWING INCREASE IN THE MEM-
BERSHIP OF CONGREGATIONAL CHURCHES
IN THE UNITED STATES BY PROFESSION

(This denomination is chosen as an illustration owing to
its complete reports; but it is believed that the same changes
from one year to another would be true of an average of the
figures of all denominations.)

Year	No. of Churches	Add. Members by Confession	Total New Members	Business Conditions	Additions by Confession per 100,000 Population
1860	2,585	7,468	14,821	Decline.........	24 Persons
1861	2,555	5,522	12,151	Depression......	17 "
1862	2,580	6,196	12,629	"	19 "
1863	2,652	7,765	14,378	Over-expansion...	23 "
1864	2,667	9,032	15,809	Decline.........	27 "
1865	2,723	11,030	18,442	Depression......	32 "
1866	2,780	11,249	19,994	Improvement....	32 "
1867	2,810	19,127	30,210	"	53 "
1868	2,951	16,432	28,246	Over-expansion...	45 "
1869	3,043	15,167	27,373	" ...	40 "
1870	3,121	13,501	25,137	Decline.........	35 "
1871	3,202	13,271	23,343	"	34 "
1872	3,263	13,945	25,394	"	34 "
1873	3,325	13,216	24,620	"	32 "
1874	3,403	15,279	27,300	Depression......	36 "
1875	3,437	17,306	29,645	"	39 "
1876	3,509	20,844	33,294	"	46 "
1877	3,564	24,138	35,111	"	52 "
1878	3,620	20,498	31,735	Improvement....	43 "
1879	3,674	16,689	27,506	"	34 "
1880	3,745	12,230	22,749	Over-expansion...	24 "
1881	3,855	11,311	22,646	" ...	22 "
1882	3,936	13,539	25,895	Decline.........	26 "
1883	4,010	14,800	28,377	Depression......	28 "
1884	4,092	17,923	32,055	"	33 "
1885	4,170	21,729	37,135	"	39 "
1886	4,477	27,166	43,185	Improvement....	47 "
1887	4,404	41,156	67,530	"	70 "
1888	4,569	25,994	45,036	Over-expansion...	43 "
1889	4,689	29,286	49,859	"	48 "
1890	4,817	27,592	47,782	"	44 "
1891	4,985	30,614	52,086	Decline.........	48 "
1892	5,140	31,582	54,576	"	49 "
1893	5,236	34,444	57,561	Depression......	52 "

Year	No. of Churches	Add. Members by Confession	Total New Members	Business Conditions	Additions by Confession per 100,000 Population
1894	5,346	38,853	62,946	Depression 58	Persons
1895	5,486	35,327	57,932	" 51	"
1896	5,546	32,147	54,640	Improvement.... 46	"
1897	5,614	31,090	52,211	" 44	"
1898	5,620	25,189	44,492	Over-expansion... 35	"
1899	5,604	24,514	44,185	" ... 33	"
1900	5,650	27,101	48,602	" ... 36	"
1901	5,753	28,398	49,879	" ... 37	"
1902	5,821	29,195	51,627	Decline......... 38	"
1903	5,900	29,403	51,521	Depression...... 36	"
1904	5,919	30,193	58,198	Improvement.... 37	"
1905	5,931	34,881	57,722	Over-expansion... 42	"
1906	5,923	32,890	56,543	Improvement.... 38	"
1907	5,977	34,642	59,346	Decline......... 40	"
1908	6,006	35,100	59,792	Depression...... 40	"
1909	5,991	34,245	62,461	Improvement.... 38	"
1910	6,033	30,582	57,689	Over-expansion... 33	"
1911	6,048	30,319	57,667	Depression 32	"
1912	6,064	30,776	57,662	Over-expansion... 32	"
1913	6,096	34,294	61,430	Decline......... 36	"
1914	6,093	40,787	68,467	Depression...... 42	"
1915	6,103	43,172	70,026	Improvement... 43	"
1916	6,089	42,081	68,259	Over-expansion... 42	"
1917	6,050	39,624	65,734	" ... 38	"
1918	6,019	29,467	51,372	" ... 28	"
1919	5,959	33,852	59,922	" ... 32	"
1920	5,924	39,922	71,857	Decline......... 37	"
1921	5,873	45,875	78,365	Depression...... 42	"
1922	5,826	44,175	73,030	Improvement.... 40	"
1923	5,716	37,305	63,680	Over-expansion... 34	"
1924	5,680	44,132	74,339	Depression....... 39	"
1925	5,636	45,722	74,930	Expansion....... 40	"
1926	5,608	42,091	72,724	Over-expansion... 36	"
1927	5,548	39,811	72,487	" ... 34	"
1928	5,497	36,748	65,469	" ... 30	"
1929	5,419	34,294	62,724	" ... 28	"
1930	5,381	34,719	60,353	Decline......... 28	"
1931	6,434	37,251	61,739	Depression...... 30	"
1932	6,379	34,115	58,170	" 27	"
1933	6,368	34,669	56,816	" 28	"
1934	6,282	33,332	55,002	" 26	"
1935	6,209	33,035	58,833	" 26	"

MISCELLANEOUS STATISTICS

Among those miscellaneous statistics which are tabulated by some bankers and merchants may be mentioned the following:

Statistics on Losses and Wastes.
Statistics on Changed Conditions.
Absorption of Capital.
Results of Invention.
Economies due to Improved Methods.
Statistics on Frauds and Lack of Credit.
The Abuse of Credit.
The Contraction of Circulating Mediums.
Commodity Stocks.
Psychological Tendencies.
Military Armament.
Income Taxes.
Excise and Internal Revenues.
Associated Charity Reports.

All of the above have some distant bearing either for diagnosing present conditions or for forecasting future conditions; but none are sufficient in themselves, and when studying any one, due weight must be given to all of the others. The figures on any one of these subjects are of value only in their relation to the other figures which we have previously considered. *As, however, none of these miscellaneous subjects are of sufficient importance to the merchant or investor for him to collect and tabulate figures, no extended reference need be given to them here.*

CHAPTER VII

CONDITIONS AND EVENTS SINCE 1860

1860

THOUGH this year ended in a panic, the comparatively favorable conditions existing during the first six or eight months account for the fact that many of its figures are about normal. New railroad construction amounted to 1,846 miles; while 821,223 tons of pig-iron were produced at an average price of $22.70 per ton. Bank clearings amounted to more than $7,231,143,000. The number of failures was 3,676 with total liabilities of $79,807,000. Wages in general were high; and 133,143 immigrants entered the country.

With money rates high throughout the year, conditions became particularly strained in November, when for the first time in the history of the country, clearing house certificates were issued. The total volume of foreign trade amounted to more than $681,000,000 with a considerable unfavorable balance. The index of English commodity prices for the year was 2,713.

On the stock exchange, prices were generally low. Certain conservative stocks rose from 59 in the spring to 93 in the summer. The production of wheat amounted to about 173,104,000 bushels at $1.37 per bushel; that of corn amounted to about 838,700,000 bushels at 73 cents per bushel; and that of cotton amounted to 3,849,000 bales at 11 cents per lb.   Panic conditions began in November with the election of Lincoln to the Presidency and the subsequent action of the Southern States towards secession.

1861

The depression existing at the end of 1860 continued through the first six months of this year. Only 651 miles of new railroad were constructed; and only 653,164 tons of pig-iron were produced at an average price of $20.26 per ton.   Bank clearings decreased to the very low figure of $5,915,-742,000.   Failures amounted to 6,993 in number, with liabilities of $207,210,000.   Wages continued high, while 142,877 immigrants came into the country.

Money conditions were marked by high rates which dropped somewhat with the improving conditions of the last six months of the year, by a further issue of clearing house certificates, and by a suspension of specie payments.   The total volume of foreign trade decreased to about $500,000,000. The index of English prices for the year was 2,751.

Prices on the stock market were low throughout the year.   Certain stocks, selling at 84 early in the year dropped to 62 in the fall.   The production of wheat and corn decreased considerably.   The number of bales of cotton amounted to 4,500,000. Wheat sold at $1.30, corn at $.60 a bushel, and cotton at 13 cents.   In March the Morrill Tariff Act was passed, levying heavier duties and giving an impetus to industry.   Thus, in spite of the beginning of the Civil War, conditions improved steadily after the middle of the year.

1862

This year shows a marked improvement over 1861. While only 834 miles of new railroad were constructed, 703,270 tons of pig-iron were produced at an increased price of $23.92. Bank clearings rose to $6,871,443,000. Failures were only 1,652 in number, with $23,049,000 of liabilities. 72,183 immigrants entered the country.

In money matters, currency was considerably inflated by paper issues and money rates were lower. The progress toward improved conditions was marked by a low volume of foreign trade amounting to about $380,000,000. The index of English commodity prices was 2,878.

Transactions in the stock market increased and prices rose steadily. Certain stocks sold for 71 in the spring and for 107 in the fall. Railroads prospered. Among the crops, cotton production amounted to 1,600,000 bales at $.31 per lb.; while wheat sold at $1.28 a bushel and corn at $.60 a bushel. The most significant political feature of the year was the development of the policy of a heavy war tariff for revenue purposes.

1863

This was a year of expansion. There were 1,050 miles of new railroad constructed, and 846,000 tons of iron produced at about $35 per ton. The bank clearings increased to $14,867,597,000, and failures decreased to 495, with liabilities of only $7,900,000. Immigration amounted to 132,925.

Money conditions were temporarily aided by measures of Congress providing for a further currency inflation, and gold exportation was increased considerably. Foreign trade increased to over $447,000,000. The English index of prices was 3,492 as against 2,878 for the preceding year.

On the stock exchange a fever of speculation brought about a considerable increase in transactions and an advance in prices. Certain stocks rose from 106 in the spring to 153 in the fall. Wheat sold for $1.16 and corn for $.84; 450,000 bales of cotton were produced at an average price of $.67 per lb. Railroad earnings increased and the first horse car line was constructed in New York. Congress passed the Internal Revenue Act to increase the war revenue. In general the Northern troops were successful.

1864

Inflation was at full height in the beginning of the year, but showed marked evidences of instability in the last months. Only 738 miles of new road were constructed, while pig-iron production amounted to 1,014,282 tons, and the price rose to the phenomenal point of $59 per ton. Bank clearings nearly doubled those of the preceding year amounting to more than $24,000,000,000. Failures increased slightly to 520 in number with liabilities of $8,579,000, while immigration totalled 191,114.

Inflation of currency and exportations of gold continued to an abnormal degree and money rates rose. Foreign trade increased to over $475,000,000. The index of English prices was 3,787.

Before the end of the year, prospects as indicated by these abnormal figures and conditions strained by the corner in connection with the stock of the Harlem River R.R., appeared so unsatisfactory that many began to sell their stocks. Average prices of securities for the year were higher than in 1863. Rail stocks, selling at about 150 in January, rose to 177 in April, fell to 141 in October and rose again to 155 in December. Cotton production amounted to about 300,000 bales selling at the extraordinary price of $1.00 per lb. Wheat sold at $2.00 per bushel and corn at $1.44 per bushel. The general condition of inflation was marked further by high wages and increased dividend payments by railroads. In politics, Lincoln was re-elected to the Presidency.

1865

Conditions were unstable and unsatisfactory during this year. While 1,177 miles of new road were constructed, the production of pig-iron decreased sharply to 831,770 tons, selling at $46 a ton. Bank clearings increased slightly to $26,000,000,000. Failures numbered 530 with liabilities of $17,625,000. The number of immigrants decreased to 180,339.

Money rates remained high, but did not increase. Paper money issues were somewhat contracted and

reserves were increased. Foreign trade fell off to
about $400,000,000, and the index of English com-
modity prices dropped to 3,575.

On the stock exchange, the price of several stocks
fell from about 160 in the spring to 125 later in the
year. The production of cotton jumped up to
2,269,316 bales, selling at $.83 per lb.; while wheat
and corn were at $2.04 and $1.26 per bushel respectively. Conditions steadily declining during
the first of the year improved somewhat with the
surrender of Lee, but became unsteady again with
the death of Lincoln. The year was, on the whole,
one of panic.

1866

Depression followed the panic of the previous
year. 1,716 miles of new railroad were constructed,
while 1,205,663 tons of pig-iron were produced at a
price of $46.84 per ton. Bank clearings increased
slightly to $28,717,000,000. Business failures in-
creased 200% amounting to 1,505 in number, with
liabilities of $53,783,000. Immigrants coming to
the country amounted to 332,577.

Banking conditions were rather more settled, and
money became easier with the close of the war and
the slight improvement in fundamental conditions.
Foreign trade increased to more than $780,000,000
and exports of gold somewhat decreased. Commodity prices in general were low. The English
index figure was 3,564.

In the stock market, the decline in prices of the
preceding year continued. The average for certain

stocks went as low as 99 and as high as 128. The first official crop report of the national government gave a production of 152,000,000 bushels of wheat sold at $2.20; 867,946,000 bushels of corn sold at $.90 per bushel, and 2,097,254 bales of cotton sold at $.43 per lb. Though, as shown by these figures, fundamental conditions appeared to be somewhat improving, still the surface conditions especially evident in the action of the stock market were decidedly depressed.

1867

During this year, though depression still existed improvement was plainly visible. There were 2,449 miles of new railroad constructed, and 1,305,-023 tons of pig-iron produced at $44 per ton. Bank clearings amounted to $28,675,159,000 and failures increased to 2,780 with liabilities of $96,-666,000. Immigrant aliens numbered 303,104.

Monetary conditions showed a slight improvement over those of the previous year. Gold exportations decreased and rates were somewhat lower. Foreign trade amounted to $681,615,000 in volume with a balance of $61,337,308 of imports. The English commodity price index was 3,024.

On the stock market, the price of the seven stocks ranged from 98 to 122. Railroad earnings improved. 2,519,554 bales of cotton sold at $.32 per lb.; 768,320,000 bushels of corn sold at $1.21 per bushel; and 212,441,400 bushels of wheat, a considerable increase over the previous year, sold at $3.33 per bushel. Confidence was strengthened

by the purchase of Alaska and by the opening of
new territories in anticipation of the coming prosperity.

1868

This was a year of marked expansion. New
railroad construction increased to 2,979 miles; and
1,431,250 tons of iron were produced at $39.25 per
ton. Bank clearings amounted to $28,484,288,000.
The number of failures decreased to 2,608 with
total liabilities of $63,694,000; and the number of
immigrants decreased to 138,840.

Money rates were slightly higher. The excess
of gold exports amounted to $51,217,027, or almost
five millions more than that of the previous year.
The volume of foreign trade amounted to $649,-
328,000, with a balance in favor of imports amounting to $87,000,000. The English commodity price
index was 2,582.

The market became active. Certain stocks rose
from 108 to 144. While the cotton crop was much
the same as that of the previous year, the wheat
crop increased to 224,036,000 bushels selling at
$2.43 per bushel; and the corn crop increased to
906,527,000 bushels selling at $1.23 per bushel.
While general conditions were thus improving, the
prices of stocks and the conditions of the stock
market were rendered uncertain by the great con-
test being waged between Drew and Vanderbilt for
control of the Erie, in which the former won virtually by loading an issue of convertible bonds
upon the Erie, and then immediately converting

the bonds.   This and certain other unfortunate incidents left the fundamental conditions of the stock market at the end of the year quite unsatisfactory.

1869

This was the year of the " Black Friday " panic, a panic of the stock market which, in spite of prosperity in other branches of business, served to render conditions unsound.   Miles of new railroad amounted to 4,615, and 1,711,287 tons of pig-iron were produced at $40.61 per ton.   Bank clearings increased to $37,407,028,000.   Failures numbered 2,799 with liabilities increased to $75,054,000. The number of immigrants increased to 352,768.

The money market was affected somewhat by the manipulations of the stock market.   Money rates though firm were high.   The excess of gold exportations decreased to only $17,990,000, while the balance of trade in favor of imports increased to $101,079,906.   The English commodity price index was 2,666.

On the market, the stocks, at 144 in the early summer, fell to 114 in the fall.   The Union Pacific was completed and railroad earnings in general were good.   In crops there were 3,000,000 bales of cotton at $.29 per lb.; 874,000,000 bushels of corn at $1.03 and 260,146,900 bushels of wheat at $1.50.   With the general conditions of expansion came a great westward movement.   As was the case, however, with the Harlem corner in 1864, the " Black Friday " panic of this year seemed to create a wound that would not heal, so that although business continued to increase and surface conditions appeared to be more favorable, fundamental conditions grew more and more unsatisfactory every day. The leading bankers and merchants who were studying these underlying conditions and watching the relation between actual and normal figures, disposed of their securities and reduced their merchandise.

1870

Expansion continued through this year in spite of the unsatisfactory monetary conditions at the close of 1869. There were 6,070 miles of new road constructed, and 1,665,000 tons of iron produced at $33.23 per ton. Bank clearings, to be sure, declined to $27,804,000,000; and failures increased in number to 3,546; but wages were high and immigration amounted to 387,000.

In the money market, rates remained firm, although money was easier than it had been in the preceding year. The excess of gold exports amounted to $42,673,184, while the excess of imports of merchandise decreased to $57,546,000, and the volume of foreign trade was $864,718,000. The English commodity price index was 2,689.

The stock market, though steady, dropped during the year, so that the stocks selling for 120 in the first part of the year were selling at about 102 later. Wheat was somewhat decreased in both price and production as compared with 1869; but a phenomenal corn crop, amounting to 1,094,255,000 bushels, sold at $1.02; and the cotton crop in-

creased to 4,352,317 bales, selling at $.24 per lb.
The year as a whole was looked upon by the business men as prosperous.

1871

In this year the miles of new railroad amounted
to 7,379, while 1,706,793 tons of iron were produced
at $35 a ton.   Bank clearings rose to $29,300,000,-
000.   The number of failures fell to only 2,915,
with liabilities of $85,000,000.   The number of
immigrants during the year was 321,350.

Monetary matters showed the effects of the
weakening underlying conditions.   Money was not
as easy as in the preceding year.   The excess of
gold exports amounted to $39,074,000; while the
volume of foreign trade amounted to $1,033,463,-
000, with an excess of imports of $112,759,000.
The English commodity price index for the year
was 2,590.

On the stock exchange, stocks rose during the
year from 103 to 117.   Railroad gross earnings
per mile were $9,040, an unusually high figure.
Crops were not as good as those of the preceding
year.   Cotton amounted to less than 3,000,000
bales selling at $.17 per lb., corn to 991,898,000
bushels selling at $.77, and wheat to 230,722,400
bushels selling at $1.60.   Added to the decline in
crops were other factors which hastened panic
conditions which were soon to follow.   The Chicago fire, coming in this year, shook confidence and
helped to increase money rates.   In political

circles much corruption sprang up; and the Tweed
Ring exposures produced a still further disquietude
and lack of confidence.

1872

The general decline which had begun in 1871 was
in this year somewhat checked by a number of
causes. New construction declined to the more
nearly normal figure of 5,878 miles; and the production of iron increased to 2,549,000 tons selling
at about $49. This great increase of iron produc-
tion was probably due to the perfection of commercial methods of making Bessemer and open
hearth steel, greatly increasing the demand for all
grades of pig-iron, but especially the lower grades.
Bank clearings increased to $33,844,000,000. Fail-
ures numbered 4,069 with $121,000,000 of liabilities;
404,806 immigrants came to this country.

Money conditions were not altogether satisfactory. The banks were carrying a very small surplus reserve. The excess of exports of gold increased to more than $57,000,000. The volume of
foreign trade amounted to $1,124,802,000, with an
excess of imports amounting to $187,000,000.
The English commodity price index was 2,835.

Speculation was active on the stock exchange.
Certain stocks dropped from about 110 to about 97.
Gross railroad earnings per mile fell to $8,116.
Crops were rather better than in the preceding
year, but money rates were higher. Money was
not easy, wages were high and strikes were disturbing confidence. In politics a revision of the

tariff and a presidential election made conditions still more uncertain. Although this was a year of apparent prosperity, students of fundamental statistics, who had not already done so, now saw that the area of over-expansion was practically consumed, and immediately liquidated.

1873

The Boston Fire of November, 1872, precipitated the panic which overwhelmed the business world in this year. New construction declined to 4,097 miles, though iron production increased slightly to 2,560,000 tons and sold at $42.79 a ton. Bank clearings rose to $35,461,052,000. Business failures increased to 5,183 with liabilities over $100,000,000 more than those of the year before. 459,803 immigrants came into the country.

Monetary matters were so unsatisfactory, and bank failures were so serious that clearing house certificates had to be issued. The excess of gold exports decreased from $57,000,000 to less than $5,000,000; while in volume foreign trade increased to $1,163,000,000 and in excess of imports it decreased to $27,000,000. The English commodity price index rose to 2,947.

On the stock exchange panic conditions were even more evident than elsewhere. Stocks fell as low as 75. Gross railroad earnings declined to $7,947 per mile. Crops were fair. The cotton production amounted to 4,000,000 bales and sold at $.20 per lb. Corn production amounted to 932,-

000,000 bushels, and wheat to 281,000,000 bushels; and sold at $.63 and $1.76 respectively. Money rates were very high, being 7% in New York for time loans. The Pacific Railroads, opened in the year 1869, were largely owned in New England and the promoters of both State Street and Wall Street had been borrowing money heavily of the insurance companies. These loans the insurance companies were now obliged to call. Moreover, the preceding year was the culmination of the Erie tragedy when James Fiske was shot and Erie stocks were struck from the New York Stock Exchange. Money had been very tight in 1872 and men of affairs clearly saw at the beginning of 1873 that it would be impossible to continue business under existing conditions and that a house cleaning would be necessary. Consequently, when crop reports continued to point to small harvests, which later turned out to be about 100,000,000 bushels less than the preceding year, and when the number of failures showed a distinct increase, things were allowed to seek their own level. That is, the large bankers and merchants withdrew their support and business began to decrease immediately.

Conditions at this time are interesting to study as they show clearly the three steps in the progress of a decline and the precipitation of a crisis: *first*, the large bankers and merchants sell their securities and reduce their merchandise, while the public is very optimistic; *second*, after some special event has taken place, in this case the Boston fire, which convinces these bankers and great merchants that the time has come for a house cleaning, they withdraw their support, although the people are still bullish and the ordinary store-keeper is borrowing money to buy goods; and *third* comes the panic itself, which in the case of the great panic of 1873 caused the failure of Jay Cooke & Co., and many other firms. This panic made imperative the closing of the New York Stock Exchange from September 18th to the 30th. This third step is the beginning of the decline in the eyes of the ordinary merchant, manufacturer and laborer. And in reality, until this third phase comes, there is no decline in surface conditions, although fundamental conditions have been unsatisfactory for a year or more, during which time bankers and merchants who study fundamental conditions have been preparing for the depression.

1874

In this year panic passed into depression. New railroad construction declined to 2,117 miles; and the production of pig-iron fell off somewhat, to 2,400,000 tons selling at only $30. Bank clearings declined to $22,900,000,000. Failures increased in number to 5,830; and immigration declined to 313,339 persons.

Surplus reserves in the banks increased. Gold exports showed an excess of $35,700,000 over imports; and of a total volume of foreign trade amounting to $1,131,988,000, exports exceeded imports by $7,756,000. The English index figure for commodity prices was 2,891.

Conservative stocks rose from the 75 of the preceding year to 100 in the summer of this year, only to fall back to 93 in December. Gross railroad earnings per mile fell off to $7,513. Many roads were in the hands of receivers, and railway affairs were shaken by adverse legislation. Crops declined to a total for corn and wheat of 1,158,251,-200 bushels. Granger laws, political investigations and the prosecution of certain prominent promoters, intended to place a check on the growth of public confidence.

1875

Depression continued throughout this year, and in fact through the succeeding three years. Only 1,711 miles of railroad were constructed, the smallest number in ten years; and iron production dropped to 2,000,000 tons with the price at $26 a ton. Bank clearings showed a slight increase, amounting to $25,000,000,000. Failures, however, increased in number to 7,740 and in liabilities to $201,000,000. Immigration declined still further to 227,498.

In monetary matters, the excess of gold exports was $39,000,000; the balance of trade was again "in our favor" to the amount of $7,784,000 though the volume of trade had declined to $1,014,-110,000. The index figure for English commodity prices was 2,778.

On the stock exchange stocks were irregular and declining in price. Stocks averaged 100 high and 87 low. Gross railroad earnings amounted to $7,010 per mile, showing a considerable falling off, and both the Erie and the Wabash defaulted interest on their bonds. Money continued high and confidence was greatly upset. The crops, however, were much better than in the preceding year. Cotton production amounted to 4,632,313 bales at $.154 per lb. Corn amounted to 1,321,-069,000 bushels at $.84; and wheat amounted to 292,136,000 bushels at $1.33. This fact of better crops together with the business depression, relieved the money market somewhat, and rates gradually decreased.

1876

In this year the depression reached its low ebb. Liquidation was very thorough. New construction, to be sure, rose somewhat to 2,712 miles; but iron production decreased to 1,869,000 tons selling at $20.75 per ton. Bank clearings declined to only $21,597,000,000. Failures rose to 9,092 in number with liabilities of $191,117,786; and immigration declined to 169,986.

Owing to the thorough liquidation, money was becoming easier. Only $7,555,000 of gold was exported in excess of imports; and in foreign trade the decline in volume to $1,018,000,000 was due to a decline in imports which raised the excess of exports to $163,319,000. The English commodity price index was 2,711.

The tendency of the stock market was downward. Stocks, selling at 100 in the spring, dropped to 62 in the winter. Railroad earnings continued their decline to a gross per mile of $6,764. Crops were about the same as the year before in yield, with prices slightly lower. Money rates in New York on time loans had declined to 5%; and abroad, to $3\frac{1}{4}\%$. In politics the Presidential election and the Hayes-Tilden dispute disturbed confidence. In fact, the public had become very much discouraged. All who had been connected with stocks had lost their money, prominent bankers and merchants had failed, railroads were carrying traffic at a loss, mills and factories were idle. Money rates were less than at any time since 1860.

These facts showed that the pendulum had swung too far. But knowing that business conditions are like the pendulum which, after wide swings in either direction, tends to resume a normal position in response to the laws of gravity, investors and merchants who were studying the conditions and comparing figures saw clearly that this was the year in which to buy stocks, make plans for further extensions, and prepare for the period of improved conditions which was bound to come. In fact, the stocks which these investors sold at an average of 144 a share in 1869, many now purchased at an average of 73 a share, while others who waited until the beginning of the following year purchased at an average price of 54.

1877

Though the depression continued, improvement in underlying conditions was well under way. New railroad construction amounted to 2,280 miles; and pig-iron production increased to 2,067,000 tons, selling at $19.25. Failures remained about the same in number as in the preceding year. Strikes were common owing to reductions in wages, and immigration continued its decline in numbers to 141,857.

In monetary matters the excess of gold exports decreased to $7,352,000; while the volume of foreign trade increased slightly, and the excess of exports decreased to $140,000,000. Commodity prices, as indicated by the Economist's index figure, declined to 2,715.

On the stock exchange, stocks dropped during the spring and summer to 54, but began to rise in the fall, selling at 75 in December. Gross railroad earnings per mile declined to $6,380; and net per mile to $2,307. Crops were good: 4,773,865 bales of cotton sold at $.118 per lb.; 1,342,558,000 bushels of corn sold at $.59 per bushel; and 364,194,000 bushels of wheat sold at $1.63 per bushel. In politics, the silver agitation, as usual with all currency disputes, tended to retard improvement. But though the country was in extreme depression at the beginning of the year, still, with the good crops, railroad earnings and confidence improved, and money rates gradually decreasing, Christmas, 1877, was a time of thanksgiving for many who had escaped being crushed during the preceding five years.

1878

In spite of the signs of improvement in the year preceding, this year, though continuing the improvement, was still in depression. New construction increased to 2,629 miles; and iron production rose to 2,301,000 tons with the price per ton at $17.00. Bank clearings increased to $27,814,000,-000. Failures increased in number to 10,478, and in liabilities to $234,000,000. Immigration declined still further to the low point of 138,469.

Monetary affairs reflected the improvement which was under way. The volume of foreign trade remained the same as in the preceding year; but the excess of exports increased to $305,000,000, and the gold movements showed an excess of imports amounting to $1,822,000. The London Economist's commodity figure of 2,554 indicated the general tendency of commodity prices to remain low.

The stock market was still unsteady and inactive. Only 39,875,000 shares were traded on the New York Exchange. Stocks rose from 69 in the spring to 104 in the fall. Net railroad earnings per mile, however, increased to $2,375. The crops of corn and cotton were about the same as those of the preceding year; while the wheat crop increased to 420,000,000 bushels and dropped in price to $1.24 per bushel. In politics, the silver dispute was continued over the Bland-Allison bill; and certain changes were made in the Bankruptcy Law. On the whole, the confidence of the public and of the business world was returning.

1879

During this year, depression passed into over-expansion. New construction jumped to 4,746 miles;

and iron production increased to 2,742,000 tons, selling at $22.82. Bank clearings increased to $39,000,000,000. Failures decreased remarkably to 6,658 in number, and only $98,149,000 in liabilities. Immigration increased somewhat to 177,800 in number.

The volume of foreign trade increased to $1,278,-762,000, the excess of exports amounted to $251,-557,000 and the excess of gold imports to $74,652,-000. Commodity prices were still low. The English index figure for the year was 2,225.

On the stock market, the stocks rallied from 69 to 104, and transactions nearly doubled. Net railroad earnings increased to $2,610 per mile. Crops were as follows: cotton, 5,755,000 bales selling at $.108 per lb.; corn, 1,548,000,000 bushels selling at $.47 per bushel; and wheat 449,000,000 bushels selling at $1.24 per bushel. In New York, time loan money rates were at 5%, and in Europe, at $2\frac{3}{4}\%$. In accordance with the Specie Payments Act of 1875, specie payments were again resumed in this year. In fact, the entire year witnessed an improvement so marked that at the end of the twelve months, mills were in full operation, all labor was employed, and the entire country was in a very prosperous condition.

1880

This was the first of a series of three years of marked prosperity. New railroad construction increased to 6,876 miles, and pig-iron production

amounted to 3,835,000 tons selling at $30 a ton.
Bank clearings jumped to $50,000,000,000. Fail-
ures decreased still further to only 4,735 in number
or .63 of 1% of all the firms in business, with one
exception the lowest point on record. The number of immigrant arrivals increased to 457,000.

The volume of foreign trade increased to $1,586,-
490,000, and the balance " in favor of " the United
States amounted to $192,876,000. Excess of gold
imports amounted to $70,582,000. Commodity
prices improved as illustrated by the English index figure of 2,577. The average surplus reserve
of the New York banks declined from $6,800,000
in 1879 to $6,100,000 in this year.

On the New York Stock Exchange, transactions
increased from 72,000,000 to almost 98,000,000
shares. The stocks rose from 99 to 123. Net railroad earnings increased to $3,029 per mile. Crops
were excellent; 6,606,000 bales of cotton selling at
$.115 per lb.; 1,717,434,000 bushels of corn selling
at $.55 per bushel and 499,000,000 bushels of wheat
selling at $1.30 per bushel. Confidence reigned
throughout the country; consolidations were in
progress; new industries were started; new railroads were projected; and every one was elated
over the fact that the country was once more prosperous. Moreover, Garfield, the candidate for the
Republican party, always representative of business interests, was elected President in November.
Money was constantly in more demand, and the
rates were gradually increasing.

1881

Although the general public considered this year one of great prosperity, there were certain events which caused the barometers of fundamental conditions to begin to decline, and before the year closed, said fundamental conditions were unsatisfactory. Thus, a new construction rose to the abnormal figure of 9,778 miles; while production of pig-iron increased slightly and the price declined. Clearings jumped to more than $63,000,000,000. Failures increased in number to 5,582. The number of immigrant arrivals amounted to 669,431.

Money conditions, too, were not altogether satisfactory. The volume of foreign trade decreased slightly, and the balance "in favor of" this country decreased as did the excess of gold imports. In the New York banks the surplus reserve fell to $4,500,000. Commodity prices were somewhat lower as indicated by the English index figure of 2,376.

Transactions on the New York Stock Exchange amounted to more than 114,000,000 shares. Stocks selling at an average price of 125 in January, rose to 134 in June, and fell again to 121 in December. Railroad net earnings declined slightly to $2,928 per mile, being due in part to the Trunk Line Rate War. Money rates abroad increased to 4% and at home to 5¼% on time loans. The crops decreased considerably in yield, wheat and corn together amounting to less than 1,600,000,000 bushels. Tremendous stock issues were being floated, and large stock dividends were being de-

clared.   While to outsiders everything appeared to
be very prosperous, yet to the careful student it
was plain that conditions were not what they
should be, and needed only some sudden disturbing
event to start disaster, such an event as the Harlem
corner in 1864 and the Boston fire in 1872.   This
sudden event turned out to be the shooting of
President Garfield on July 2, 1881, after which
event, the bankers and merchants who kept careful watch of conditions decided to sell.

1882

Fortunately for those who had not already liquidated, prosperous conditions continued in many
of the important lines during this year and the
next.   New railroad construction amounted to
11,599 miles, or next to the largest new mileage
for any year in the history of the country; and
iron production was correspondingly inflated to
4,623,323 tons, selling at $25.77 per ton.   Bank
clearings decreased slightly to $61,000,000,000.
Failures numbered 6,738, with liabilities of $101,-
547,564.   Immigration rose to the abnormal figure
of 788,992.

Monetary matters were also uncertain.   Gold
movements showed a return of excess of exports
amounting to more than $25,000,000; while the
volume of foreign trade increased to $1,520,000,000
and the excess of exports declined to $15,138,000.
The surplus reserve of the New York banks declined still lower than in 1881, to $3,500,000.   The

London Economist's commodity price figure for the year was 2,435.

On the New York Stock Exchange, transactions increased to 116,300,000 shares. Nine stocks fell to a low point of 113 in the early summer and rose again to 126 in August. Railroad earnings decreased to a net per mile of $2,670. Crops, however, the real redeeming feature of the year, were better than in 1881. The cotton crop of 6,950,-000 bales sold at $.115 per lb. Corn amounting to 1,617,000,000 bushels, sold at $.77 and wheat, amounting to 504,000,000 bushels, sold at $1.32 per bushel. Owing chiefly to these crops, although a decline had set in, it was not perceived by the general public. As mentioned in the account of the year 1873, there are three steps in every decline; and the second, that in which the leaders withdraw their support, had not come, for this was the year in which Jay Gould made his famous exhibit of securities. As will be seen by referring to the newspapers of that day, it was clearly understood by students of conditions that a distinct decline had begun, and Gould probably knew this as well as any man. Therefore, although he was preaching that the conditions were perfectly sound and that still greater prosperity was ahead, he himself was doubtless unloading and liquidating with all possible speed in preparation for the public withdrawal of his support later. Moreover, the banks were aiding their directors by keeping down money rates although the demand for money was very great. Students of fundamental statistics, however, could not be misled, and knowing that the area of over-expansion was rapidly being consumed, prepared for trouble.

1883

Though nominally considered a year of prosperity, this was in truth a year of decline and instability of underlying conditions. New construction fell off to 6,818 miles, and iron production to 4,595,000 tons. Bank clearings in this year, for the first time published for the whole country instead of for New York alone, amounted to $51,731,472,000. Failures increased in number to 9,184 and in liabilities to $172,800,000. Immigration also showed a decline.

Money conditions were supported by a volume of foreign trade amounting to $1,482,275,000. The balance in favor of this country increased to $108,000,000, and excess of gold imports due to gold purchases from abroad amounted to $16,-000,000. The New York bank reserves were still low, being about $4,200,000. The English commodity price index fell to 2,343.

The stock market held up remarkably well, although the high prices were maintained only through manipulation and in order to allow the insiders the opportunity to liquidate. Stocks fell from 119 to 109. Railroad earnings increased slightly both in gross and net. Money rates in New York averaged $5\frac{1}{4}\%$ and in Europe, $3\frac{1}{2}\%$. Crops, too, were poorer than in the preceding year, the yield of wheat and corn combined amounting to less than 2,000,000,000 bushels.   On the whole, these facts, added to agitation over tariff and internal revenue questions, rendered business conditions abnormal and unsound, and clearly foretold the panic about to follow.

1884

The unsound conditions of the preceding year were reduced, in this year, to *panic* conditions by the great Ward and Grant failure on May 6, together with the failures of Henry Villard and James R. Keene.   New construction declined to 3,973 miles, and iron production was reduced by about 500,000 tons.   Bank clearings decreased to $44,-000,000,000.   Failures rose to 10,968 in number, with $226,000,000 of liabilities.   Immigration also declined to 500,000 in number.

In foreign trade, both exports and imports decreased.   The balance " in favor of " this country was $120,000,000; but gold movements showed an excess of exports amounting to $12,990,000.   The New York banks held a large surplus reserve of $20,800,000.   Commodity prices fell as illustrated by the English index figure of 2,195.

On the stock market, artificial support being removed from money conditions, stock prices fell rapidly.   Stocks sold at 113 in February, and 85 in the winter months.   Net railroad earnings declined to $2,318 per mile.   Crops, however, were again good, corn and wheat amounting to over 2,300,000,000 bushels.   If it had not been for the good crop reports during this year, probably stocks would have declined very much further. As it was, even the election of Grover Cleveland by the Democrats in November did not seem to break the market very severely.

1885

Depression, as usual, followed the panic, in this year. Only 3,131 miles of new railroad were constructed; and iron production declined to 4,044,000 tons, selling at $18. Bank clearings declined to the low figure of $41,474,000,000. Failures were slightly lower than in 1884 both in number and in liabilities. Immigration figures declined to 395,-346.

In monetary matters, the volume of foreign trade decreased to $1,276,118,000 and the balance " in favor of " the country decreased to $100,000,000. Gold movements showed an excess of imports of $12,200,000. The average surplus reserves in the New York banks rose to the enormous sum of $48,000,000. The English commodity price index was 2,023.

The stock market was comparatively active. Stocks rose from 86 to 111. There was a considerable issue of new stocks and bonds amounting together to $567,500,000. Railroad earnings dropped to the low figure of $2,185 net per mile. Money rates in New York dropped from 4% to 3% on time loans. The crops were rather better than in the preceding year, but prices were considerably lower. In politics, the silver agitation rather increased the general weight of depression which existed throughout the year.

1886

General depression continued in this year, though improvement was well under way before its close. New construction jumped up to 8,128 miles; while iron production increased to 5,683,000 tons, selling at $18.70. Bank clearings, too, increased to $49,-000,000,000 and failures decreased somewhat both in number and in liabilities. Immigration decreased slightly to 334,203.

In the monetary field money was easier. The volume of foreign trade remained about the same; but the balance between exports and imports of both gold and commodities was much reduced. The abnormal average surplus reserve of the New York banks in 1885 was in this year reduced to $14,200,000. Commodity prices in general were the same as indicated by the English index figure of 2,023.

The New York Stock Exchange was active during this year. Transactions amounted to more than 100,000,000 shares, and stocks rose from 106 to 118. Money rates in New York rose to $4\frac{3}{4}\%$ and the banks began pretty generally to buy bonds. Railroad earnings improved both in gross and net; and crops were about the same as in the preceding year in yield, but somewhat lower in prices. Cotton sold for $.092 per lb., corn for $.52 per bushel and wheat for $.89 per bushel. A period of improvement had commenced, and although many small merchants were only beginning to feel the effects of the great depression, true conditions were distinctly more than normal and the pendulum

was swinging too far the other way. In view of
this, stocks began to rally and plans for extensions
and large undertakings were again discussed.
Moreover, the defeat of the various bills which were
introduced into Congress for the reduction of the
tariff caused a special increase of confidence among
manufacturers, wholesalers and bankers. Money
rates also, remaining normal, greatly encouraged
new enterprises.

1887

This year ushered in a new period of expansion.
New railroad construction amounted to 12,983
miles, the largest figure in the history of the country; while pig-iron production increased to 6,417,-
148 tons selling at $21 a ton. Bank clearings rose
to $51,000,000,000, and failures amounted in num-
ber to 9,634 or .90 of 1% of all the firms in business.
Impelled by the tide of expansion, immigration
increased to 490,000.

The volume of foreign trade also showed a
marked increase due chiefly to an increase in imports, as is generally the case in a period of expansion. Consequently the balance of trade favoring
exports decreased to $6,000,000; but the excess of
gold imports increased to $35,700,000. Surplus
reserves were still further reduced, and prices began
to rise. The London Economist's commodity index for the year was 2,087.

The stock market was rather less active than in
the preceding year, and the prices of stocks fell
from 125 to 112 in the summer and fall, owing

probably in part to the approaching presidential election and the doubt and hesitation which is always reflected in business circles with the approach of this process in politics. But railroad earnings improved, the net per mile being $2,444, and money rates were normal. Moreover, while the yields of corn and wheat together amounted to less than 2,000,000,000 bushels, the cotton yield increased from 6,500,000 bales of the year before, to 7,000,000 in this year. In politics, government control of railroads was inaugurated in this year by the passing of the Interstate Commerce Act.

1888

Owing to satisfactory fundamental conditions, all business made rapid progress in this year in spite of the fact that it was a " presidential year." New construction amounted to 7,066 miles, and iron production increased slightly to 6,489,000 tons. Bank clearings were about normal at $49,541,000,-000; and failures, though increased in numbers, were decreased in total liabilities. The number of immigrant arrivals increased to 546,000.

Monetary conditions were interesting. While exports decreased, imports increased and the total volume of foreign trade decreased to $1,417,000,000. Consequently there was at the end of the year a balance of trade " unfavorable " to the United States amounting to $33,600,000 and a resulting excess exportation of gold amounting to $23,500,-000. Domestic money rates remained at 5%, but surplus reserves in New York banks increased to an average reserve of $17,000,000. The English index figure for commodity prices rose to 2,458.

The inactivity of the stock market during this year can probably, as in the fall of 1887, be ascribed largely to the approaching presidential election. Early in the year, stocks stood at a low point of 113; after the election they bounded up to 126 in December. In fact, with the election of the Republican candidate, General Harrison, business in general showed a marked improvement. The net railroad earnings for the year amounted to $2,045 per mile, a low figure. Total crops, too, showed no great increase, though the total wheat and corn crops amounted to 2,400,000,000 bushels.

1889

This was a year of prosperity. New railroad construction was normal at 5,695 miles; while iron production increased to 7,600,000 tons selling at $17.79 a ton. Bank clearings rose to $56,000,000,000, and failures increased somewhat. Immigration declined to 444,000.

The volume of trade was only slightly larger than in the preceding year with an unfavorable balance again amounting to an excess of imports equal to $56,584,000. Exportations of gold, however, continued to exceed imports, in this year, by $38,900,000. Surplus reserves of the banks were somewhat below normal. As indicated by the index figure of the London Economist, which was 2,362 for this year, commodity prices had somewhat dropped.

On the stock exchange, transactions showed an increase. Stocks rose from 123 in the spring to 136 in the fall. Domestic time loan rates continued at 5%, while those abroad were at 3%. The net earnings of railroads still remained low. Crops, however, were excellent, especially those of corn and cotton, which were the largest in the history of the country thus far. The cotton crop of 7,472,511 bales sold at $.106 per lb.; the corn crop of 2,112,892,000 bushels sold at $.44 per bushel; and the wheat crop of 490,560,000 bushels sold at $.91.

1890

In this year, sound prosperity changed to an "uncertain prosperity," which was to continue for two years longer, during which time, while surface conditions looked satisfactory, fundamental conditions were far from sound. New construction amounted to 5,656 miles, and pig-iron production increased to 9,000,000 tons, selling at $18. Bank clearings also rose to $60,800,000,000, and failures increased only slightly. Immigration showed little change.

In monetary matters, the volume of foreign trade increased to $1,680,000,000 and the excess of exports amounted to $34,000,000. Exports of gold exceeded imports by only $3,700,000. Surplus reserves in the New York banks fell to the low average figure of $3,700,000. The English commodity price index figure, 2,247, shows a still further drop in prices.

The stock market conditions were peculiar. Railroad earnings rose to a net per mile of $2,162. The cotton crop was unusually large, amounting to 8,600,000 bales; but the wheat and corn crops fell off considerably, amounting together to only 1,900,-000,000 bushels. Money rates in this country rose to 6% and abroad to 4%. Ten stocks which remained above 130 until the fall, suddenly dropped then to 118. This drop marked what may be called a " surface panic," brought on by the great Baring Failure at which time clearing house certificates were issued to relieve the pressure on the banks. Public confidence and courage, greatly agitated by this panic, was still further disturbed during the year by the political discussions which ended in the passing of the McKinley Tariff Act and the Silver Purchase Act.

1891

In spite of the generally favorable surface conditions of this year, confidence was not fully restored. New railroad construction decreased to 4,620 miles and pig-iron production fell off nearly a million tons. Bank clearings also declined to $56,700,000,000; and failures increased to 12,273 in number with liabilities of $189,868,000. Immigration increased to 560,319.

Foreign trade continued to develop, amounting in volume to $1,798,830,000 with a balance of $142,000,000 in favor of the United States. Gold exports increased correspondingly to an excess over imports of $34,000,000. Surplus reserves in the

New York banks rose to $11,000,000. The English index figure of commodity prices declined to 2,207.

The listing of new securities, which had amounted to the large figure of $1,122,800,000 in 1890, declined in this year to $476,500,000. The Exchange was dull. Ten stocks sold around 115 until the late summer, when they rose to 128. Railroad earnings remained much the same as in the year preceding. Crops, however, were phenomenally large. The cotton crop of 9,000,000 bales sold at $.086 per lb. The corn crop of 2,000,000,000 bushels sold at $.67 per bushel. The wheat crop of 612,000,000 bushels sold at $1.05 per bushel. These fine crops caused the newspapers to be especially bullish, and enabled bankers and merchants to keep money rates from advancing further and to bolster up the market in order to unload their securities and merchandise. In fact, most people believed this a very satisfactory year. Students of fundamental statistics, however, clearly saw that the area of expansion was about consumed and prepared for trouble.

1892

The prosperity of this year, so-called, was largely due to artificial causes. New construction amounted to only 4,584 miles, while the production of pig-iron rose to more than 9,000,000 tons and its price fell off to $12.74 per ton. Bank clearings increased to $62,011,000,000; failures declined in number to 10,344 and in liabilities to $114,000,000, and immigration figures rose to 623,000.

Although the commodity exports exceeded imports by $97,000,000, still there was a net exportation of gold amounting to $58,000,000. The New York banks' average surplus reserve amounted to $15,600,000. Commodity prices in this country, as indicated by Bradstreet's index figure of $7.78 which began in this year, were fairly high, while in England the index figure of 2,107 indicates that there they were low.

On the New York Stock Exchange, transactions increased to 86,000,000 shares. Ten stocks fluctuated between 126 and 135, beginning and ending the year at about 130. Net railroad earnings per mile declined to $2,068. Crops were much smaller than in the preceding year, corn and wheat together amounting to less than 2,150,000,000 bushels. In short, it was clearly evident to students of fundamental statistics that the area of expansion was more than consumed, and those who had not already liquidated, sold securities, merchandise and everything else possible in preparation for a period of depression.

1893

Questionable prosperity passed readily into panic with the great failure of the National Cordage Co. on the 4th of May. The collapse was complete. New construction dropped to 2,789 miles; and iron production amounted to only 7,000,000 tons. Bank clearings in like manner fell off to $54,143,-000,000; failures increased to 15,000 in number with liabilities of more than $347,000,000; and immigration, though not so quickly affected as these other subjects, declined to 502,917.

In monetary affairs, both exports and imports of commodities declined; and while the excess of exports increased slightly to $99,600,000, the excess of gold exports declined to $6,700,000. The average surplus reserve of the New York banks increased to $21,600,000. Bradstreet's index figure of American prices dropped to $7.53, while the English figure rose slightly to 2,113.

The stock exchange was dull and, of course, declining. Ten stocks dropped from 135 to 102. Railroad earnings showed no particular change from the year before; but commercial paper rates in New York averaged 7%. Unfavorable crop reports, which had increased the collapsing tendency during the year, were fully substantiated by the final reports. To be sure, cotton was a little better than in the preceding year, and corn showed only a slight decline, but wheat had dropped off from 516,000,000 bushels to 396,000,000 bushels, selling at the decreased price of $.74 a bushel. In fact, support of all kinds had been withdrawn, and every commodity, including money, was allowed to seek its own level.

1894

In this year the inevitable period of depression following a severe panic began in earnest. New railroad construction declined to only 2,264 miles, and the production of iron amounted to only 6,700,000 tons. In like fashion bank clearings declined to $45,460,000,000; failures were still high at 13,885 in number, though liabilities decreased to $173,000,000; and immigration declined to 314,467.

Monetary matters showed the same depression. The volume of foreign trade declined to $1,501,415,-000 while the excess of exports increased (through a decided decrease in imports) to $149,000,000. Excess of gold exports jumped up to $80,000,000 and bank reserves in the New York banks increased to $45,900,000. Commodity index prices dropped in America to $6.68 and in England to 2,002.

On the New York Stock Exchange only 49,000,-000 shares were traded. The ten stocks rose to 115 in the spring and fell back again to about 106 in the winter. Railroad earnings fell to $1,803 per mile, net, the lowest figure on record. Crops, too, were exceptionally poor. Cotton, to be sure, amounted to 9,900,000 bales in yield, but it sold at the low price of $.07 per lb.; and corn and wheat together yielded less than 1,673,000,000 bushels. In reality this year witnessed the greatest crop failure in the history of the country. The crops had fallen below 1,600,000,000 bushels during the '70s, yet a very much smaller area was then under cultivation and conditions were entirely different. As figures clearly show, a small increase or decrease in crops does not affect business excepting sentimentally; but a great failure such as was witnessed in 1894 gives the country a shock from which it may take several years to recover. In addition to the crop failures, the Pullman strike occurred in this year, and the Wilson bill affecting the tariff was also passed; in fact, 1894 was apparently the worst year since the Civil War.

1895

This year began in great gloom. The depression of the preceding two years, during which so many bankers and merchants had failed and one-third of the total railroad mileage of the United States had fallen into the hands of receivers, began to have its effects upon all labor and even upon the most humble storekeeper. Mills were shut down, great poverty existed in the cities, and distress was everywhere felt. New railroad construction declined to 1,938 miles. Iron production, however, had improved both in yield and in price, amounting to 9,000,000 tons and selling at $10.86 a ton. Bank clearings, too, showed a gain to $53,000,000,000; and failures decreased slightly in number. Only 279,948 immigrants entered the country.

The total volume of foreign trade showed a slight increase over the preceding year, but the balance " in favor of " the United States declined to $23,-000,000. Still, the gold exports continued in large amounts, exceeding the imports by $70,600,000; and the surplus reserves, though reduced from the figures of the year before, were still high. Commodity prices were slightly lower than in 1894 in this country, and dropped somewhat in England.

The stock market was rather more active; but again the ten stocks rose from 105 in March to about 121 in September only to fall back to about

108 in the winter.   Railroad earnings were $1,804
per mile net, or practically the same as in 1894.
But crops were somewhat improved.   The cotton
yield of 7,000,000 bales sold at $.074 per lb.; the
corn crop of 2,000,000,000 bushels sold at $.48 per
bushel; and the wheat crop of 467,000,000 bushels
sold at $.67 per bushel.   And, added to the fair
crops, there was the low domestic money rate of
4% to lend aid to an improvement.   In fact, conditions would doubtless have taken a turn for the
better had it not been for the very unfortunate
condition of finance, and the great exportation of
gold.   Although President Cleveland did everything within his power to uphold the gold standard
and the credit of the United States, the drain was
too heavy, especially after his famous Venezuela
message, and the threatened possibility of war
with our greatest foreign creditor, England.

1896

This year business was still depressed from the
panic of 1893 and the heavy gold exportations of
1894–5.   Railroad mileage increased to 2,067 miles,
129 miles above the low figure for 1895; and
iron production declined to 8,600,000 tons selling
at $10.29 a ton.   Bank clearings decreased to $51,-
000,000,000.   Failures increased considerably to
15,000 in number with total liabilities of more than
$226,000,000.   Immigration amounted to 343,267.

In monetary matters, the volume of foreign trade
increased to $1,687,000,000 and the excess of ex-
ports jumped up to $324,000,000.   In gold move-

ments, imports exceeded exports $46,400,000. The American index of commodity prices dropped to the low point of $5.91.

The New York Stock Exchange was dull in transactions, but listed more than $1,000,000,000 of new securities about equally divided between bonds and stocks. The ten stocks once more fluctuated between 113 and 99 in August. Railroad earnings increased to $1,840 per mile net. Money rates on time loans in New York, owing to the currency troubles of the preceding year and the spring of this year, rose from 4% to 6%. Though the wheat crop itself declined somewhat, the total of corn and wheat amounted to more than 2,700,000,000 bushels and cotton yielded 8,522,000 bales. Therefore, although there were no signs of better times in surface conditions, fundamental conditions were becoming much sounder. Had it not been for the alarm felt at the Democratic nomination of Bryan in June, this would have been from its very beginning a year of distinct improvement; and when the election of McKinley in the fall of 1896 had removed this cause of distrust, bankers and merchants who were studying the situation became convinced that a change for the better was imminent. In fact, it was evident from a study of fundamental statistics that the area of depression was about consumed, and a period of over-expansion due. They therefore purchased securities and merchandise in large quantities, and later made great profits thereby, as the major bear movement commencing in 1892 was at an end.

1897

Distinct improvement characterized this year. New railroad construction increased to 2,161 miles and the production of pig-iron amounted to 9,600,-000 tons. Bank clearings increased to $57,000,-000,000 and failures decreased in number from 1.31% of all the firms in business to 1.26%. Immigration amounted to 230,832.

Monetary matters were more sound. The foreign trade increased to $1,842,000,000; and the excess of exports to $357,000,000. Gold exports again exceeded imports but only to the small amount of $253,000. Surplus reserves in the New York banks averaged the high figure of $38,500,-000. Commodity prices in this country rose as shown by Bradstreet's index figure of $6.12.

The stock market was more active, but the ten stocks continued much the same range of fluctuations they had passed through in the last three years. Domestic money rates returned to the 4% of 1895, and railroad earnings continued to improve. Crops, too, remained strong. Though corn showed a decrease, wheat increased to 530,-000,000 bushels and cotton increased to 11,000,000 bales. The three sold respectively at $.319, $.954 and $.07. When the Dingley Tariff Act had brought an end to anxiety in that field, it was discovered that the country was well on the road to prosperity.

1898

Everywhere prosperity reigned. New construction amounted to 3,199 miles, while iron production increased to 11,700,000 tons selling at $9.46. Bank clearings jumped up to $68,827,000,000; failures decreased to 12,000 in number; and 230,000 immigrants entered the country.

In monetary affairs, the volume of foreign trade still showed an increase due to the great increase in exports in spite of the fact that imports had somewhat declined. Exports which had amounted to only $824,000,000 in 1895 had increased steadily with the improving crops until in this year they amounted to $1,255,000,000 or rather more than two-thirds of the total volume. Imports of gold increased correspondingly to the immense figure of $120,391,674. Surplus reserves showed a decline from the abnormally high figures of the preceding year. American commodity prices continued to rise as indicated by Bradstreet's index figure of $6.57.

The New York Stock Exchange reported transactions amounting to 113,000,000 shares, and new securities listed amounting to $1,228,000,000 of which $700,000,000 were bonds. The ten stocks rose from a low point of 115 to a high point of 127 in June. Net railroad earnings jumped up to $2,111 per mile. Once more money rates were normal, time loans in New York averaging 4½%. The crops, too, kept pace with the advancing prosperity, for cotton amounted to 11,200,000 bales, corn to 1,900,000,000 bushels, and wheat to 675,-000,000 bushels. Although the Spanish War temporarily disarranged business, it was so short that it acted in the end as a great stimulus to trade.

1899

Conditions, already prosperous, continued to improve throughout this year. New mileage amounted to 4,592 miles; iron production advanced to 13,600,000 tons. Bank clearings showed a phenomenal growth to $94,000,000,000, while failures decreased to 9,337 in number or only .81 of 1% of all the firms in business. The number of immigrants increased to 311,715.

Monetary conditions showed a similar strength. The volume of foreign trade amounted to more than $2,000,000,000 and the balance sheets showed an excess of exports amounting to $476,000,000. Money rates at home and abroad were 4%, and the excess of importation of gold amounted to only $6,000,000. Commodity prices in this country and in England showed an increase as indicated by Bradstreet's index figure of $7.21 and the Economist's figure of 1,972.

On the New York Stock Exchange, transactions increased to 176,000,000 shares, while the listing of new securities amounted again to nearly $1,230,-000,000. The ten stocks continued their rise from 126 to 144. Net railroad earnings increased to $2,272 per mile. Though the cotton and wheat crops showed a decline, corn increased so that the total bushels of corn and wheat together again amounted to more than 2,600,000,000 in number. Industry in all lines was again firmly on its feet. In reaction against the cut-throat competition which had existed all through the depression just ended, and had thoroughly exasperated business interests, a great movement towards consolidation in industries and towards "integrating trusts" began in earnest with this burst of expansion. In fact, this year saw the beginning of many of our largest trusts and monopolies in their present form of organization.

1900

With the opening of this year, over-expansion was in full swing. To be sure some of the figures in the fundamental subjects showed a slight decline as compared with those of 1899, but this was rather a hopeful sign than otherwise for the prospects of the continuation of good times. Thus new railway construction declined to 4,157 miles while pig-iron production remained high at 13,789,000 tons selling at $17 a ton. Bank clearings, too, declined to $86,000,000,000, but this was still more than $15,-000,000,000 greater than the clearings of two years before. Failures numbered 10,774 with liabilities of $138,495,000. Immigration increased to 448,570 in number.

While the total volume of trade advanced to $2,300,000,000, the balance "in favor of" this country reached to $648,800,000, the largest balance of this kind in the history of the country. Imports of gold exceeded exports by $12,600,000. Bank reserves were normal. In commodity prices, Bradstreet's figure rose to $7.88 and the Economist's to 2,178.

The stock market continued active in transactions but a smaller amount of new securities were

listed. Though suffering the usual spring slump of
this period, the ten stocks rose from a low point of
132 to a high point of 155. Net railroad earnings
advanced to $2,519 per mile. Domestic money
rates strengthened to 5% on time loans. Crops
were again firm both in yield and in price. Corn
and wheat together amounted to 2,627,000,000
bushels and sold respectively at $.80 and $.45 per
bushel. The reëlection of McKinley and the enactment of the " Gold Standard " bill gave additional impetus to business. Everywhere consolidation was the rule, especially in the railroads,
where " community of interests " was becoming
common.

1901

Prosperity was running riot. New construction
increased to 4,912 miles, while iron production advanced to 15,878,000 tons selling at $14. Bank
clearings bounded up to $118,410,000,000 and
failures remained about the same as in 1900.
Immigrants increased somewhat to 487,900.

A slight increase came in the total volume of
foreign trade, but the excess of exports decreased
somewhat. The latter fact was due to an increase
in imports, and the excess of gold exports which
came in this year amounted to $3,000,000. Bank
reserves were still about normal, though tending to
decline. Commodity prices both in this country
and in England declined as indicated by the respective index figures of $7.57 and 2,014.

The activity of the stock market was extreme.

On the New York Exchange more than 266,000,000 shares were traded, and more than $2,565,000,000 of new securities were issued, of which the majority were stocks. This was the year when a partial panic in the market was caused by the Northern Pacific stock corner, and most stocks suffered from artificial manipulation. The ten stocks, which we have used heretofore, rose from 154 to 172 between January and November, 1900, but more active stocks continued the sharp advance begun in 1900, to May of 1901. Net railroad earnings continued their increase to $2,668 per mile. To be sure the corn crop decreased somewhat, but the wheat crop increased from 500,000,000 to 748,000,000 bushels.

1902

This was a year when the average business man and manufacturer were very optimistic; when the daily papers were prophesying still higher prices and still greater activity, and when the surface conditions were apparently more satisfactory than ever before. If it had not been for gigantic crops, a severe depression would probably have set in at once. In mercantile conditions, new railroad construction amounted to 5,076 miles while iron production increased to 17,800,000 tons, selling at the advanced price of $20 a ton. Bank clearings remained at about $118,000,000,000 while failures remained abnormally low at 11,615 in number or only .93 of 1% of all the firms in business. Immigration increased to 648,743.

Monetary conditions showed a slight decrease in the total volume of trade; also a decrease to $391,000,000 in the balance of exports, due, again, entirely to an increase in imports. Gold imports exceeded exports by $8,000,000. Bank reserves were abnormally low, those of the New York banks averaging only $10,700,000. American commodity prices showed a distinct gain indicated by Bradstreet's index figure of $7.87, but English prices were falling.

The New York Stock Market, though not so active as in 1901, still reported transactions amounting to 188,000,000 shares, and new securities listed amounting to $1,317,000,000. Thus in two years new securities had amounted to almost $4,000,000,000. Men who recognized the meaning of this tremendous increase in new securities issued, knew that a day of reckoning must come soon. Meanwhile, the ten stocks continued to rise from 170 to 190, but fell again to about 170 in December. Net railroad earnings continued to increase to $2,830 per mile. A slightly decreased wheat crop was reinforced by an increase in corn amounting to 1,000,000,000 bushels, so that the total crop of wheat and corn amounted to more than 3,150,000,-000 bushels. Cotton production increased 2,000,-000 bales over the previous year. But even these excellent figures could not save the unsound conditions of the money and stock markets. Furthermore, confidence was unsettled by severe anti-trust agitation and certain government prosecutions of trusts. These facts, together with a study of the

Babsonchart, clearly warned students of the situation that the area of over-expansion was about consumed, and another depression was again imminent, although it was generally believed that this " area " represented only a minor movement, and that the major movement, beginning in 1897, was still upward.

1903

Shaken confidence and unstable stock market conditions resulted in the so-called " Undigested Securities Panic " of this year, in which few figures of fundamental subjects were radically altered except those directly related to the stock market. Thus new railroad construction advanced to 4,675 miles, and the production of pig-iron to 18,000,000 tons.   Bank clearings declined to $109,000,000,000. Failures increased in number to 12,069 or .94 of 1% of all the firms in business.   Immigration advanced to 857,000.

In monetary matters the volume of foreign trade advanced to $2,480,000,000 and the balance " in favor of " this country amounted to $489,000,000. Excess of gold imports increased to $20,900,000. Bank reserves increased somewhat.   American prices remained strong at $7.94 and English prices strengthened.

On the New York Stock Exchange, transactions declined to 161,000,000 shares, but the issue of new securities continued to be large at $1,008,000,000. In the past six years more than $8,000,000,000 of new securities had been turned loose on the market.

The ten stocks fell during the year from 180 to
146. Net railroad earnings per mile continued
their steady increase to $2,887. Crops declined to
no great extent from those of 1902. In justice to
those statisticians who found no signs forecasting a
depression in this year, it must be said that these
figures were not extremely unsatisfactory. In fact,
had it not been for the very great increase in
securities, there probably would have been no depression of 1903. However, owing to the stock
market troubles, labor troubles, and certain other
conditions, this year was one of depression.

1904

That the panic of 1903, like that of 1890, was not
fundamental in its effects is pretty clearly shown by
the fact that expansion, not depression, followed
immediately in 1904. New railroad construction
continued to increase to 5,003 miles, though iron
production declined to 16,497,000 tons selling at
$12.73 a ton. Total bank clearings also increased
to $112,600,000,000; and failures increased slightly
in actual numbers, and also in percentage of firms
in business to .92 of 1%. Immigration almost held
its own at 812,870.

Monetary matters showed firm banking conditions. The volume of foreign trade again increased
and owing to a marked increase in imports and a
slight decrease in exports, the balance " in favor of "
this country decreased to $415,000,000. Once
more gold exports exceeded imports, in this year, by
$36,000,000. The average surplus reserve of the

New York banks rose from $12,000,000 to $28,000,-
000.   Commodity prices remained much the same
as in 1903.

The stock market was again active, though the
issue of new securities on the New York Exchange
declined to $710,900,000 of which more than $500,-
000,000 was bonds.   The forty stocks* rose again
after their sharp decline in 1903.   Net railroad
earnings increased to $2,989 per mile.   Time loan
rates dropped to 5% in this country and 3½%
abroad.   In crops, cotton amounted to the largest
yield on record of 13,451,000 bales, selling at $.117
per lb.;   corn amounted to 2,467,000,000 bushels,
selling at $.594 per bushel; and wheat amounted to
552,000,000 bushels, selling at $1.11 per bushel.   In
this year, Roosevelt's administration was continued
by his election to the office of Presidency, and the
attention of the whole world was attracted to the
Russo-Japanese War.

1905

Boom times continued in increasing and unparalleled measure.   New railroad construction
amounted to 5,050 miles, and pig-iron production
jumped to 22,990,000 tons selling at $15.57 a ton.
Bank clearings advanced to $143,800,000,000 while
failures declined in number to 11,520.   Immigration increased greatly to 1,026,000 persons.

Both volume of foreign trade and excess of exports showed an advance, and $3,498,000   were

* Beginning 1904, the forty stocks (twenty rails and twenty industrials)
have been used in place of the ten stocks previously mentioned.

imported in excess of gold exports. The average surplus reserve of the New York banks declined to only $10,200,000. The American index figure of commodity prices advanced to $8.09.

The stock market was very active. On the New York Exchange, transactions amounted to 263,-000,000 shares, and new securities listed amounted to a billion and a half dollars, of which nearly a billion were in bonds. The forty stocks in this year had an unprecedented rise from 82 to 100. Net railroad earnings advanced to $3,135 per mile. Though the cotton crop declined 3,000,000 bales, the wheat and corn crops were both larger than in 1904, amounting together to more than 3,400,000,-000 bushels. Though surface conditions appeared wonderfully prosperous, confidence was badly shaken by the Life Insurance and Traction Company exposures of this year.

1906

Business continued on an inflated basis. New construction in this year amounted to 5,643 miles, and iron production advanced to 25,000,000 tons selling at $16.70. Bank clearings were at the second high point on record, increasing to $160,000,-000,000, while failures declined in number to only 10,682 or .77 of 1% of all the firms in business. Immigration amounted to 1,100,000.

The volume of foreign trade amounted to $3,-118,000,000. The balance " in favor of " this country increased to $477,000,000; while the excess of gold imports, aided by artificial importation,

amounted to $109,000,000. The average surplus
reserve of the New York banks dropped to only
$7,300,000. Commodity prices advanced as shown
by the American index figure of $8.42.

On the stock exchange, transactions increased,
and prices continued abnormally high. The forty
conservative stocks dropped from the high of 114 in
January to a low point of 100 in the winter. Railroad net earnings advanced to $3,580 per mile.
Crops were tremendous. Cotton yielded 13,000,-
000 bales at $.115; corn yielded 2,927,000,000
bushels at $.56; and wheat yielded 735,000,000
bushels at $.865. Such satisfactory crop condi-
tions, however, only served to increase the mad pace
which prosperity had assumed, and students of
fundamentals were not satisfied. Liquidation,
therefore, commenced, securities and merchandise
were sold, and stocks of all classes declined in price.
The money situation was especially strained, as the
depression of 1903 was not severe enough to liquidate many accounts which should have been cleared
up. In fact, conditions were far from satisfactory
at the end of the year. The San Francisco Earth-
quake proved to be another factor which unsettled
business.

1907

In this year prosperity, carried to an extreme
point, collapsed in panic. But, as is usual, the
change in conditions was not foreseen except by
those students of fundamental statistics who clearly
saw by means of a Babsonchart that the area of

over-expansion was well advanced, and that we
were entering upon a period of liquidation which
might last for many months. New construction
decreased to 5,499 miles, while the iron production
amounted to 25,000,000 tons selling at an average
price of $23. Bank clearings, however, declined
to $145,000,000,000, and failures increased in
number to 11,725. Immigration advanced to
1,285,000.

In monetary affairs, the total volume of foreign
trade continued its increase to the unparalleled
figure of $3,346,000,000; the balance from excess of
exports increased to $500,256,000; and in gold
movements the excess of imports declined to $88,-
000,000. The bank reserves were everywhere
extremely low, those in New York averaging under
$400,000. This together with high commodity
prices, as illustrated by Bradstreet's index figure
of $8.90, showed money conditions to be highly
unsatisfactory.

The stock market, always a sensitive barometer
of all changes, declined decidedly from the beginning of the panic in March. On the New York Exchange, transactions amounted to only 196,000,000
shares, and new securities, to only $997,000,000.
The forty stocks which had temporarily recovered
from their severe decline in 1906, dropped again
from a high point of 113 in December, 1906, to a
low point of 58. Railroad net earnings continued
their increase to the high point of $3,699 per mile,
held up by crops and the volume of trade. Crops
declined somewhat from the bumper crop of 1906,

but were still excellent. Wheat and corn together amounted to more than 3,200,000,000 bushels and sold at $.963 and $.64 respectively. Domestic rates on time loans advanced to 6½%, while rates abroad advanced to 4¾%. Legislation adverse to trusts and railroads added to the general consternation in business circles, and before the end of the year, the country had dropped from over-active prosperity into dull depression.

1908

Depression had, in this year, extended from the stock market to other lines of business. New building was at a very low ebb. Although 3,654 miles of new railroad were constructed, only 15,-900,000 tons of pig-iron were produced, and there was little new building. Pig-iron sold at about $15.54 per ton, Bank clearings declined to $132,-408,000,000 and failures increased in number to 15,690. The lack of demand for labor is shown by the fact that only 782,870 immigrants entered the country, although wages still held up.

As has been universally true in the past, such a period of depression is accompanied by low money rates. The surplus reserves held by the banks were very large throughout the entire year and the percentage of cash was high. Not only were rates low in the United States but also throughout Europe. The volume of foreign trade amounted to $2,869,-209,000 and the balance of trade " in favor of " the United States amounted to $636,461,000, while gold movements showed an excess of exports amounting to $30,939,163. The demand for money was still further lessened by a distinct decrease in commodity prices, the Bradstreet Index declining to $7.72 in June.

The stock market remained almost as depressed as in 1907 both in transactions and new stocks listed, but by November the prices began to show a distinct rise. Thus the forty stocks, which had remained under 80 all during the spring, rose in December to 92. Railroad net earnings declined to $3,144 per mile. Fortunately, crops remained good. Cotton, yielding 13,086,000 bales, sold at $.106 per lb.; corn yielding 2,668,000,000 bushels sold at $.786; and wheat yielding 664,000,000 bushels sold at $1.05. In politics a temporary currency bill was passed to meet the depressed conditions; while Mr. Taft's election to the Presidency secured the continuation of the Republican administration and policy. The depression had passed the low point, giving place to marked improvement. In fact, by the spring of the next year, the area of depression was completed.

1909

Though still suffering from the depressing business conditions following the panic of 1907, this was a year of considerable improvement. New railroad construction decreased to more than 3,476 miles, and the production of pig-iron showed a decided advance to 25,800,000 tons selling at $16.12. Bank clearings also advanced to $165,838,000,000, and failures decreased in number to 12,924. Immigration continued low at 751,786 new arrivals.

In monetary affairs, money rates continued at a low level, as is usual in depressions following a panic. But the volume of foreign trade advanced to more than $3,000,000,000, due entirely to an increase in imports, while the excess of exports decreased to $252,677,000. Once more gold exportations exceeded imports, reaching in this year the high point of $88,793,000. Bank reserves declined from the high figures of 1908 to more normal figures. Bradstreet's index figure of commodity prices advanced to $8.51.

The stock exchange was again thoroughly active. In New York, transactions amounted to more than 214,000,000 shares, while new securities listed increased to $2,424,000,000, almost equally divided between stocks and bonds. The forty stocks rose from 86 to 105. Railroad earnings increased slightly in the gross, while the net was $3,912 per mile as a result of economies introduced during the depression. Though crop reports in the early part of the year were unsatisfactory, the final figures showed a decline only in cotton, while wheat and corn were good. Cotton yielded more than 10,-000,000 bales selling at $.126 per lb.; corn yielded 2,772,000,000 bushels selling at $.767 a bushel; and wheat reached the high point of 737,000,000 bushels selling at $1.26 per bushel. These figures signify that the country enjoyed a temporary improvement, as would be expected after the conditions of 1907 and 1908.

1910

During the first few months of this year mercantile conditions forged ahead in a fashion that bade fair to precipitate a premature period of forced liquidation. Only the slowing up of business, as general conditions became increasingly unsound, saved the situation. Iron production, which averaged 2,500,000 tons for the first four months of the year, averaged only 2,100,000 tons for the remaining months, while the price fell from $16.12 to $15.16 before the end of the year. Bank clearings declined slightly to about $164,095,000,000, and liabilities in failures increased by an average of $4,000,000 a month over those of 1909. The number of immigrants increased to over 1,000,000.

The fundamental figures in monetary conditions showed most clearly the unsound condition of the country, which could not have withstood the strain of a continued advance in mercantile affairs. Thus, money rates were forced up from their low level of 1909, marking a strained money market fully a month earlier than the usual rise due to crop movements. The loans of the New York Clearing House banks averaged per month more than the deposits for the twelve months of the year. These facts, together with a yearly figure for Bradstreet's index of commodity prices amounting to about $9.00, showed clearly that the country's money market was strained and unsound.

Investment conditions reflected this unsatisfactory state of affairs most faithfully. Transactions on the New York Exchange declined to less than

165,000,000 shares, the lowest figure since 1903; but new securities listed, amounted to $2,047,664,-045, a considerable amount of which was due to the abolishment of the unlisted section of the Exchange. The forty stocks dropped from 104 to 83. Although gross earnings of the railroads showed an increase over the year before, the unfavorable increase in the ratio of operating expenses caused net earnings to show a marked and most unsatisfactory decline. Optimism based on the crop reports was well justified by the actual returns. Wheat production declined somewhat, but cotton was better, and corn yielded a bumper crop of more than 2,800,000,000 bushels. The prices of all three, however, declined respectively to $1.12 a bushel, $.151 a pound and $.66 a bushel. Uncertainty was the keynote of the year. " Insurgency," Democratic success at the polls, and governmental delay in trust and railroad rate questions, had their share in causing hesitation.

1911

Mercantile conditions became less favorable. Total bank clearings declined slightly. Under conditions of normal growth along the X-Y Line, clearings for the country, excluding New York, should have been increased greatly instead of remaining so nearly on a level. There was a larger number of failures, and liabilities were about 5% lighter. A marked decline of more than 15% was shown in immigration reports. Average per mile earnings of the railroads reporting to the Interstate

Commerce Commission declined. Commodity prices declined, and this slackening was followed by an advance in food-stuffs, which checked the decline of Bradstreet's index of commodity prices.

Money rates were much easier, but students of fundamental conditions did not feel that the loans of the banks had been sufficiently liquidated to render the situation satisfactory. In January and March the National Banks reported a percentage of loans to deposits, with the exception of the call of September 1, 1910, higher than at any time since 1908. The net deposits also increased, the figure $6,689,018,000 on June 7 being the highest on record, with the per cent of reserve at 22.10% compared with a previous high of 23.94% in 1908. Imports declined, and exports of general merchandise increased about 12%.

Investment conditions during 1911 were very unsatisfactory. Dullness was at times exceedingly marked. On the New York Stock Exchange the number of shares traded was very small, 127,-207,258, compared with 164,051,061 in 1910. Bond sales increased, and fewer new securities were listed, but the amount of actual issues was nearly 15% greater. Gold production continued to increase. A severe drought reduced the yield in some of the crops; wheat, oats, hay, and potatoes were below the average; corn was only fair, while the largest acreage of cotton ever known produced over 15,000,000 bales. Investment conditions were adversely affected by the Supreme Court decisions and reorganization of large corporations under the

Sherman Law, the consequent discussion and uncertainty reacting unfavorably on the market and
business in general.

1912

With the activity attendant upon satisfactory
crops, business remained for the most part above
the line of normal growth. Nevertheless failures
numbered even more than in the preceding year.
Bank clearings, although responding in the late
fall to the crop influence, remained nearly at a
level for the first three quarters of the year. Commodity prices advanced sharply throughout the
year. Pig-iron production increased to more than
29,000,000 tons. Railroad earnings as reported to
the Interstate Commerce Commission showed a
gain; both gross and net earnings of the roads
increased. Only 838,172 immigrants came to
this country, 5% less than in 1911.

Money rates were high. Circulation increased.
Surplus reserves of the New York clearing house
banks (excluding the trust companies) reported at
$44,000,000 in February, was reduced in July to
a deficit of more than $200,000. Imports gained
about 19% for the year, giving the largest total in
the history of the trade. The balance in favor of
the United States was $581,144,938 compared with
a previous high of $636,461,360 in 1908. Gold ex-
ports gained about 27% over 1911, with gold
imports remaining about the same, thus resulting
in a rather less favorable balance.

Investment conditions were not satisfactory.

Prices of forty representative stocks fluctuated
from a winter low of 89 to a high of 100 in August.
Bond sales fell off and prices were lower than in
any recent year since 1908.   The crops were large,
but cotton made a small showing as compared with
the big crop of 1911.   Tariff discussion, corporation
investigation, and other unsettling influences, dis-
turbed the market and business in general.   Labor
troubles were particularly in evidence and exerted
a most adverse effect.   Students of fundamental
conditions saw in Mr. Wilson's election the fulfillment of the great law, that whenever there is deep
social and economic unrest and dissatisfaction, the
people seek a new administration in hope of relief.

1913

The decline in business which started early
continued throughout the year, but the decline was
rather hastened by unusual events, notably the
Ohio flood in March and the financial strain
caused by the Balkan War, which ended during
the year.   Failures again increased in number
from 15,452 to 16,037, and in liabilities from
$203,117,391 to $272,672,288.   The average liabilities per failure were somewhat greater.   Commodity prices declined throughout the year,
indicating that the turning point had been reached
in 1912.   Pig-iron production during the first of
the year was the heaviest in history, but after the
first few months declined rapidly.

Monetary stringency and contraction of credit
were characteristic throughout the entire year.

Rates for prime commercial paper averaged over 5½% and rates of the banks of England, France and Germany averaged nearly 5%, the highest since 1875 and probably for many years before that. Much of the strain was caused by the financing of the Balkan War, which ended during the year. If foreign monetary affairs had not been so serious, the heavy balance of exports would have been favorable. As it was, Europe settled the balance by returning United States securities. Two direct results of the monetary stringency were, a steady contraction in business, and the speedy enactment of a new currency law.

Security prices declined steadily from the first of the year, and on June 11 broke sharply in a near panic. The forty stocks which averaged 95 in January, dropped to 70, and the twenty bonds fell from 95 to 91. The summer market picked up considerably, but another drop occurred in December, when many issues sold lower than in June. New issues fell from $2,253,587,300 in 1912 to $1,-645,736,200, and fewer corporations were chartered than in any year since 1908. The copper stock market held up remarkably well, considering depression in other lines, due to heavy European demand for copper in preparation for war. Politics caused uncertainty throughout the entire year because of important legislation pending and active anti-trust investigation. During the last three months the tariff and income tax law (on October 3) and the new currency law (on December 23) were passed. Crops were about average; winter

wheat was a bumper crop, but corn did only fairly
well. To students of fundamental conditions, it
was evident that a year of depression lay ahead.

1914

By far the greatest event in this year was the
beginning of the European War. The decline of
1913 quickly developed into depression. Several
enormous failures occurred in June and July, including the Claflin catastrophe. This liquidation,
however, seemed to clear the air. There were
many indications that an improvement in business
would come with the bountiful fall harvests. Such
was the situation when on August 1 the European
War burst upon the world, bringing panic to financial circles, the closing of exchanges, and stagnation
to business. As business was well liquidated, no
serious national catastrophe occurred, and matters
soon began to adjust themselves to the new situation.

The Babsonchart area gives evidence of the
severity of the depression, which culminated
toward the end of the year. A comparison of
annual figures follows. Bank clearings for the
whole country fell to $155,000,000,000 from $169,-
800,000,000 in the previous year. Liabilities
of failures touched nearly $360,000,000, the heaviest
mortality for twenty-two years, involving over
1% of the total number of firms in business.
Immigration, however, was the heaviest since
the year of 1907. The commodity price index,
which had been declining in sympathy with

general business, shot up to $9.8495 when war was declared, by far the highest point in history, but prices soon fell off again when it was realized that imports from Europe would be resumed. Pig-iron production dropped to 23,000,000 tons, new building was very quiet, and railroad construction fell to 1,532 miles, the lowest in half a century. Railroad earnings were somewhat smaller than in 1913.

Monetary conditions during the first half of the year were distinctly easy. Commercial paper rates ruled below 4%, with surplus reserves of the New York Banks (excluding trust companies) as high as $40,000,000. The declaration of war in a moment transformed this comfortable position into a dangerous crisis. Enormous shipments of gold bullion and coin were made from New York to the Bank of England, but sterling exchange soared to $5.10. The heavy surplus in the New York Banks was soon displaced by a deficit of about $30,000,000. Money rates rose to the nominal figure of 8%, but funds could hardly be obtained at any price. Clearing house certificates amounting to $124,695,000 were issued in New York, and over $360,000,000 of emergency currency was taken out, raising the per capita circulation to $37.31. In Europe a general moratorium of debts was established. Enormous grain exports soon built up a favorable trade balance, thus stopping gold exports, and the inauguration of the Federal Reserve system on November 16 restored the monetary situation to comparative ease.

When all of the stock exchanges throughout the rest of the world closed, an avalanche of selling was turned upon the New York market. On July 30 the forty stocks dropped to 71 and the twenty bonds to 91. The New York Exchange closed, and the other United States exchanges quickly followed suit, reopening December 12. Some trading was carried on in outside markets, where prices were considerably below the closing prices of the New York Exchange. When the exchanges were finally opened, severe restrictions and minimum prices were imposed to prevent another flood of European selling, but stocks for the most part averaged above the closing prices of July 30. The twenty bonds, however, sold down to 88. The crops, especially winter wheat, were excellent, and because of " war prices " for grains were the most valuable ever grown. Wheat sold up to $1.68 a bushel. Cotton, however, was forced down to 6 cents a pound. When the war broke out anti-trust agitation by the government was dropped and the eastern railroads were allowed to increase freight rates. With these factors added to the sound fundamental condition of business, close students of the situation looked for a substantial improvement during the coming year.

1915

The year 1915 was one of phenomenal expansion, demonstrating in a most forcible way the application of the law of equal reaction to business conditions. It opened with business in the depth of depression, and ended in the midst of great expansion. The solid foundation laid in the depression of 1914 was the real basis of this tremendous expansion. War orders and continued huge grain shipments gave the first impetus to business. Gradually domestic trade began to revive, and finally, when the success of tremendous crops was assured, the boom in business broke all bounds. Although the total yearly figures show only to a limited extent the tremendous activity attained by business during the latter part of the year, they present a wonderful record. Clearings for the year increased to $188,000,000,000 compared with $155,000,000,000 the previous year. Failure liabilities dropped from $358,000,000 in 1914 to $300,-000,000, the number of small failures considerably increasing, as is usual at the close of a period of depression. Gross railroad earnings amounted to $863,000,000 compared with $837,000,000 in 1914. Commodity prices moved rapidly upward. Bradstreet's index in December was 10.6473. The iron and steel industry experienced the greatest revival in its history. Pig-iron production for the year amounted to 29,900,000 tons compared with 23,300,000 tons in 1914, while unfilled tonnage of the United States Steel Corporation nearly doubled during the year.

Monetary conditions throughout the year were extremely easy, in spite of enormous business activity. Commercial paper rates, even during the fall months, dropped to 3%, while surplus reserves of the New York Clearing House Banks (excluding trust companies) swelled to over $200,000,000, figured under the new reserve requirements. This unprecedented ease in money was due principally to the enormous importation of gold from Europe. Huge exports of merchandise from the United States to the belligerents had completely reversed the international balance of 1914, and forced European exchange rates to unheard-of low levels. Sterling exchange, which touched $5.10 in 1914, dropped to $4.50, and exchange of the other belligerent countries suffered even greater depreciation. In order to make further purchases in the United States, the European nations therefore shipped more than $400,000,000 in gold to this country. The effect of such a great increase in our money supply was immediately evident. Circulation per capita at once increased and by the end of the year had swelled from $34.55 to $38.48, while the banks, especially in New York, suddenly found themselves with more money than they could profitably employ.

The advance which took place in certain stock prices was one of the most spectacular in history. Early in the year it became evident that a number of companies were going to be greatly benefited by war orders. Bethlehem Steel, among the first of the " war stocks," in a few months' time jumped from about 46 to 600. Suddenly, late in the spring, the whole stock market began to boil, for fundamental conditions were sound and a reaction from the preceding long period of low prices was due. The greatest activity occurred in the industrials the rails being depressed by heavy foreign selling. The average of the forty stocks, which stood at about 72 at the first of the year, by December had risen to 102. A tremendous demand for funds was felt in the latter part of the year, largely for speculation in stocks. Bank loans expanded rapidly, reaching their maximum for the year $3,257,-606,000 in December. Surplus reserves showed a marked decline. Bonds were heavy throughout the year, due to the war's tremendous demand for fixed capital, although some strengthening in prices occurred during November and December. Grain prices were very high during the first of the year, wheat selling up to $1.80 per bushel. The 1915 grain crops, however, sold considerably lower. Cotton advanced to over 12 cents per pound, due to increased demand. Wage advances were evident in nearly every branch of industry and labor shared in the general prosperity to a greater extent than ever before. Domestic politics were more favorable to general business.

1916

Phenomenal expansion in United States business and finance continued throughout 1916. The Business Index remained well above "normal." Nearly every line of industry participated in the great boom and production increased far beyond all previous records. Bank clearings amounted to $262,000,000,000, a gain of more than 35% over 1915. Failures numbered 16,748 compared with 20,600 the year before, while liabilities fell off to

less than two-thirds of those in 1915. Gross railroad earnings amounted to over $1,000,000,000
compared with $860,000,000 in 1915. The Bab-
son Index of Industrial Commodities jumped from
133 to 180. Bradstreet's index rose 25%. Pig-
iron production exceeded 39,000,000 tons, 8,000,000
greater than any previous record year.

Rates for short-time money continued easy until
the last of the year, when a gradual strengthening
took place. Net gold imports of $530,000,000 kept
the banks in a fairly easy position, notwithstanding
unprecedented loan expansion. In December call
money rates at New York temporarily soared to
15%. Resumption of gold imports, however, soon
forced rates back again to low levels. The loan
item of New York Clearing House Banks averaged
$2,270,000,000 for the year, against $1,816,000,000
in 1915. The balance of foreign trade in favor of
the United States exceeded $3,000,000,000 and
about six times the average balance in peace times.
Sterling exchange was well supported by gold shipments and ruled about $4.75 throughout the year.
Exchange on the other belligerents, however, sank
to new low figures.

The average stock prices experienced a smaller
net gain than other economic subjects. This was
due to the fact that the stock market at the beginning of 1916 had already well discounted current
business conditions. Prices declined during the
summer. Early in the fall, however, when it became apparent that the war would last another
winter, great advances were scored by certain in-

dustrial stocks. United States Steel touched 129¾, Bethlehem Steel 700, Chino Copper 74¾, Utah Copper 130, Central Leather 123, etc. The whole average of 40 stocks for a few weeks in November and December held close to 110. Then came President Wilson's first peace note to the belligerents, which precipitated a drop of about ten points in the stock averages. The year closed with the 40 stocks several points lower than when it began.

Bonds gained slightly toward the last of the year, but the scarcity of funds for long time investments prevented any extended advances. During the year a great wave of industrial expansion took place. More than 30,000 new corporations were formed, among which a host of wild-cat promotions were included. Crops, on the whole, were disappointing and were inadequate to meet the foreign and domestic demand. Wheat sold up as high as $1.90 a bushel while cotton touched 21 cents per pound. Unprecedented advances in wages were obtained by labor in nearly every line of business.

1917

The year 1917 was one of radical adjustment to a war basis. Soon after declaration of war, April 6th, the Government began the task of concentrating the country's industrial power on lines essential to military needs. Business in such lines was extremely active; other branches of industry suffered from priority rulings which gave precedence to war business in matters of transportation, raw materials, etc. In both the so-called " essential " and " non-essential " lines, net profits were generally smaller than in 1916. This was due to drastic profits taxation and to price fixing. Taken as a whole, business trends were not so good in 1917 as in 1916, although the total volume of both domestic and foreign trade continued very large. The Babson Index of Industrial Commodities advanced from 194, for January 1, to 233 in July, but later dropped to 200.

With the entrance of this country into the war in April, the flow of gold to the United States ceased, causing money rates to strengthen as the year advanced. Bank loans expanded far beyond any previous record. Loans of New York Clearing House Banks jumped 85% during the year. With the heavier demand for money, Federal Reserve Banks came into active operation. By December, 1917, the amount of Federal Reserve Notes had increased to $1,251,205,000, compared with $272,873,000 the first of the year.

All prices of securities suffered a severe decline, which culminated in November. The number of shares traded dropped from 233,000,000 to 186,-000,000. The drop was the most abrupt since the panic of 1907. The bond market was monopolized by government issues, over one-half of the total transactions being in war loans. Railroads, industrial and copper stocks sold at least 30% lower than in the previous year. The price of twenty high-grade bonds dropped from 94 to 80.

Harvests were abundant, except in the case of wheat. This was a disappointment because of the needs of the Allies. The wheat crop was only a little larger than the small crop of 1916. Corn and oats, however, were the largest on record. Farmers received excellent prices and speculation in farm lands increased.

1918

On November 11, 1918, the World War came to an end. After the surrender of Bulgaria on September 30th, the break-up of the Central Powes was amazingly rapid. The closing events of the war came in such quick succession that for the most part business was caught unprepared. During November and December the majority of war orders were cancelled. As a result general business dropped off sharply from September levels.

From the time the armistice was signed to the close of the year industry simply " marked time "— awaiting developments. Cancellation of war contracts caused the temporary dislocation of many workers and some unemployment. Prices of most commodities began to decline, although not rapidly on the average. The Babson Index of Industrial Commodities declined from 235 July, 1918, to 207 April, 1919. Bradstreet's Index of 107 commodities declined from 19.1624 to 17.2244.

Statistically, 1918 was a year of highly stimulated business but profits were not as satisfactory as in 1916. Bank Clearings amounted to $332,353,-977,000 or 8% more than in 1917, largely inflated by the high prices of commodities. The volume of war business was tremendous, but production for civilian purposes was restrained to a minimum. Commercial failures were the lightest in years, an evidence of artificial stimulation and absence of competition.

The 40 stocks which had been low because of heavy taxes and government restrictions began to discount peace at the surrender of Bulgaria, and by the time of Germany's surrender had advanced about 7 points.   Money which had been fixed at 6% during the war, eased off to 5¼% when capital restrictions were removed, but money continued difficult to obtain and rates were firm for the remainder of the year.   The 20 bonds moved upward about 6 points on peace news, but the rise was based more on sentiment than on immediate improvement in financial conditions.

Taken altogether 1918 should be counted as a prosperous year.   Prosperity, however, was largely in paper profits.   Although the actual volume of business transacted was fairly large, the price inflation served to increase all business records giving too prosperous an appearance.   Certain classes had gained greatly by the war but others, principally the soldiers, were poorer because of the war.   Conditions therefore were not well balanced and business was not in a secure fundamental position.

1919

The year 1919 was one of sharp reaction from the restrictions imposed by the war.   In the early part

of the year commodity prices dropped and the
forty stocks dropped to about 80. As the year
progressed, however, a post-war boom took place.
Speculation reached fever pitch. Stock traded on
the New York Exchange averaged more than a
million shares a day. Industrial stocks rose from
83 to 119, Rails from 85 to 90. New building,
which had been confined almost entirely to industrial and war projects, during 1919 consisted of a
fair volume of residential building.

A wave of reckless extravagance swept the country. Automobile factories had orders booked six
months ahead. Bradstreet's commodity price index which had fallen to 17.2244 rose to 20.1756.
Bank clearings averaged a 26% gain over the
previous year. In May the campaign for the Victory Liberty Loan was opened and about $5,250,-
000,000 subscribed.

In spite of the apparent great prosperity, underlying conditions were becoming unsound. The
banks found themselves in an over-extended position, with loans increasing steadily. With the
ending of war-orders, overtime work at the factories
ceased and the war bonus system was abandoned.
Labor became restless and dissatisfied. Strikes
occurred in almost every line of industry. In
November the great steel strike took place involving
over 365,000 men. It was evident at this time
that although business was still showing a substantial increase over the previous year, *expressed in
dollars*, yet in *actual volume* there was a distinct
slackening. Pig-iron production for 1919 showed

a loss of 20% — U. S. Steel orders were 37% lighter.

Earnings of industrial companies showed the first break in their four year upward climb. Net earnings in 1919 were 40% less than in 1918. Students of fundamental conditions realized that a storm was ahead and began to prepare for the reaction.

1920

In 1920 the unprecedented over-expansion and inflation which had extended over a period of five years, reached its peak and practically overnight broke and turned downward. During the first months business continued at high speed. Orders were booked far ahead and many manufacturers without knowledge of fundamental conditions, felt secure. However, large stocks of goods were piling up in this country and with the re-establishment of European factories, European demand slackened. Imports of goods began to increase heavily and by March and April were more than double those of the previous year. The inevitable working of the law of action and reaction took place, starting with a sudden break in commodity prices.

Bradstreet's Index, which was 20.8690 in February, by July had dropped to 19.3528 and in December to 13.6263, showing a 35% decreas from the peak. The silk market was among the first to break, with a panic in Japan resulting in an immediate drop in raw silk in this country. Hides and wool both declined radically in the early part of the year. With the opening of the grain exchange in July, wheat sold about $2.75 and corn $1.70 a bushel. From that time, however, the trend was gradually downward and by December wheat was selling on the exchange at about $1.70 and corn at $.68. Factories stocked up with high priced material found themselves with goods worth only half as much, the market still declining and a slackening demand.

Cancellation of contracts then swept the country. Manufacturers caught unprepared found themselves in a very precarious situation. In anticipation of the orders booked far ahead, their raw material stocks were heavy. The jobbers and retailers refused to take the goods ordered, finding they could not sell at a profit. Failures, which had been during 1919 the lowest in history, began to increase. Factories closed down, resulting in a widespread increase in unemployment. Although a large amount of building was planned, rapidly increasing costs curtailed actual construction.

Money rates were very high all through the period. Commercial paper averaged 8% and call money, which had been as high as 20%, averaged about the same as commercial paper at the end of the year. Coincident with these high money rates, the twenty railroad bonds in May sold at an average of 68.5 to yield about 6.7%. They later experienced a rally in October but declined heavily again at the end of the year. The forty stocks reached their low in December, averaging about 68.28. The Federal Reserve Banks, with loans aggregating about $14,000,000,000, took a decided stand against further inflation, curbing speculation by increasing their discount rates.

The Babsonchart experienced the most severe drop of any period in its history. It crossed the X-Y Line in August, and before the end of the year an increasing area of depression was under way.

1921

The year 1921 was one of depression. The re-adjustments which began in 1921 were continued at the rapid pace which began in 1920. The precipitate fall in wholesale prices as measured by Bradstreet's Index continued until by June they were 50% below the peak in 1920.

Industrial production decreased rapidly and unemployment became general. Pig-iron production which was running close to pre-war volume at the close of 1920 declined to the lowest level experienced since the panic of 1907.

Imports felt the decrease in foreign demand in 1920, while exports did not fall off drastically until early 1921. This later situation had its greatest effect on the price of agricultural commodities; wheat, corn, oats and cotton falling to pre-war levels or below, while industrial prices in general only declined to a point 30%–40% above the 1913 level.

The heavy failures in evidence in the latter part of 1920 continued to grow in volume. Business profits measured by the returns of 100 industrial

companies were almost $500,000,000 in 1920 and
suddenly dropped to a deficit of $20,000,000.

As the banking situation strengthened, money
rates became easier. Commercial paper which had
been as high as 8% in the closing months of 1920
dropped to 6% and the year closed with money at
5%. In line with decreasing money rates, bond
prices rose from 74 at the close of 1920 to 83 in
December, 1921. Stock prices though recovering
appreciably from the low of the previous year declined again in June and August. By the end of
the year, a substantial recovery was under way.

From the low point in the spring, the Business
Index showed a considerable gain during the latter
half of the year. Nevertheless the area of readjustment which began in 1920 was rapidly
developed during 1921. Business was far from
good.

1922

The year 1922 was one of distinct improvement
in business activity. The rise in the Business Index from about 17% below normal in January
to about 5% above in December, indicated the
rapid strides in business activity as a whole during
this period and continued the recovery begun
the year before.

In almost every line production was larger than
in 1921. The building industry held first place —
there was the largest amount of new building ever
recorded in a single year. The total number of new

building projects of all kinds in the United States was estimated at 160,000 for 1922 compared with 110,000 in 1921, and 80,000 in 1920. Inasmuch as fully 30 great industries are directly related to new building, that factor had a highly important part in the improvement in general business.

Metal production increased. Pig-iron output showed more than 55% gain over the preceding year. Copper output in the latter half of the year took a phenomenal spurt. In the crops, wheat and corn yields were good, standing about the same as those of 1921, while cotton production was 20% ahead. The Babson Production Index, covering 19 principal commodities, gained about 40% over 1921. Manufacturing was also ahead, as indicated by the fact that about 14% more workers were employed.

Earning statements for 1922 were decidedly better than for 1921. A study of 100 leading companies showed that in 1921 53 companies lost money. In 1922 the number of deficits was reduced to 25. For the most part profits were only moderate, but they were much better than in 1921.

The stock market reflected better earnings. Credit conditions showed distinct improvement. Whereas in 1921 the banks were tied up with a vast number of embarrassed concerns, very few localities reported an unusual number of such cases in 1922. Failures were heavy, but in liabilities they were 25% smaller than in the preceding year. A large number of small concerns were eliminated as is always the case toward the close of a period of severe liquidation.

The condition of the banks was strong, borrowing only $705,000,000 from the Federal Reserve Banks. The year as a whole was one of relatively easy money.

1923

In 1921 and 1922 certain phases of the over-expanded condition were corrected. To a large extent commodity prices were deflated, bank loans were liquidated, and production was cut to fit a more moderate buying power.

With such a partial readjustment as a basis, business began to pick up. New building, railroad equipment and the automobile industry led the movement. From the middle of July, 1922, until March conditions improved very rapidly—in fact too rapidly. Business passed abruptly from below normal to above the X–Y Line. The process of readjustment was not completed. Those who were studying fundamentals realized that the period of expansion could not be greatly prolonged, because the foundation was not yet sound.

Building was extremely active, and in spite of a recession in the latter part of the year permits in 20 leading cities gained 30% over 1922. Contracts awarded were also well above the previous year with an estimated total close to $5,000,000,000. Public highway construction and railroad purchases each amounted to $1,000,000,000.

Production in general increased 40%. Fifty

per cent more copper was produced. Pig-iron production for the year was over 40,000,000 tons, the highest on record. There was considerable speculation in commodity prices stimulated in part by a car shortage. Crops were large but prices, though higher than in 1922, left the farmer with a low purchasing power when measured in terms of industrial commodities.

Net earnings of 100 industrial concerns which had been about $400,000,000 in 1922, increased to $540,000,000, with but 14, mainly smaller concerns, reporting deficits. Fewer failures took place in 1923, although liabilities were not correspondingly reduced.

Money rates increased somewhat as the year progressed, rising from $4\frac{1}{2}\%$ in January and reaching a maximum of $5\frac{3}{8}\%$ in the autumn. The long-swing upward movement of stock prices which began in 1921 was temporarily interrupted. The forty stocks used on Babsonchart after reaching 98 in March declined to 82 in October.

1924

The year 1924 was, in the main, one of readjustment. During much of the year business was below the X-Y Line on the Babsonchart. In the great boom from 1915 to 1920 many phases of business were thrown out of balance. A large part of the necessary readjustment took place in 1921 and 1922. In those years the banks liquidated much of their over-extended loans, industrial concerns readjusted their inventories, com-

modity prices were brought nearer to a common
level and a more even balance between supply and
demand was established. Most of the time since
the middle of 1923 the readjustment process
continued and one by one various obstacles were
eliminated.

Production in general declined about 8%.
Pig-iron production was 23% under the 1923 level.
Crops were only fair in volume but a shortage of
grains outside of the United States resulted in high
prices for agricultural products. Wheat and corn
rose from $1.00 and $.74 in the spring to $1.98 and
$1.29 respectively in December.

Building set a new high record 12% over 1923
in spite of dullness in many lines. Competition
was more pronounced than in 1923. The profits of
100 industrial concerns dropped from $540,000,000
to $500,000,000. Failures increased over 6%.

The nominations as well as uncertainty over
the elections acted as a check on forward buying.
Commodity prices as measured by Bradstreet's
Index declined 7% from January to July. Money
rates declined from 4⅞ in the spring to 3⅜ in
September. The long-swing upward in stock prices
was resumed in the summer and once the result of
the presidential election was certain, the advance
became rapid.

The best summary of the situation as a whole
may be had by tracing the outline of the area on the
Babsonchart. This shows the relative quantity of
total business. Early in 1924, the Business Activity
Index went considerably above the "normal"

line. It dropped rapidly, and by early summer
had reached the lowest level since 1922. After
the presidential nominations a steady improvement
began. From the standpoint of amount of business done, the year was unfavorable, but at the
same time certain underlying conditions were
improving.

1925

1925 was a year of expansion and general prosperity. Business as shown by the Babsonchart
was above the X-Y Line the entire year. Production in almost every line increased, and there was
at no time any industrial shortage of raw materials,
fuel, labor or transportation. Money rates were
low and aided the recovery of business. Commodity prices under the influence of hand-to-
mouth buying due to rapid transportation rose
an unusually small amount for such an active
period of business. Building construction set a
totally new record. In line with these conditions
of prosperity speculation was encouraged. The
stock average rose to the highest level ever shown
on the Babsonchart. Speculation was also ram-
pant in real estate.

The Dawes plan which laid the foundation for
loans to Europe and subsequent heavy purchases
in this country was a favorable factor. The
farmer's purchasing power helped to bring about
an equilibrium which had been unbalanced for
three years.

The profits of the larger companies excepting

textiles on the whole increased moderately. Railroad net earnings were the best in many years and many companies resumed dividends or increased the rate. The St. Paul receivership was the one discordant note in this field.

At the close of the year the Babsonchart was at the highest point on record while a study of the individual barometers indicated that fundamentally the situation was sound and a satisfactory rate of business could be expected in 1926.

1926

In 1926 business activity as shown by the Babsonchart averaged considerably higher than in 1925 and at the close of the year this chart had again reached a new record high. The Babson Commodity Price Index as well as all other general price indices averaged several points lower at the end than at the beginning of the year. Production in nearly every basic line made new records but severe competition prevailed among both manufacturers and distributors. In spite of this competition, failures both in number and percent of firms in business remained approximately the same as in 1925. This was due largely to the careful control of inventory and to continued hand-to-mouth buying. Again the value of building construction made a new high point as did the average of stocks as indicated by the Babsonchart Index.

Railroad net earnings increased slightly over

those for 1925 and profits of most of the larger
corporations attained new peaks. Profits of the
smaller and less efficient companies, particularly
during the latter half of the year, decreased.
Stock dividends were very numerous.

The very rapid and huge flow of capital to
European countries gave impetus to heavy foreign
purchases from this country, keeping our export
business on about the same level as 1925.

Towards the latter part of the year the situation
in the textile, shoe and leather industries began to
show improvement, after severe and prolonged
depression especially since 1923.

1927

There was a general sloughing off in business
activity from the early part of 1927. Prices as
shown by the Babson Index continued well into
the spring of 1927, the drop begun in 1926. A
recovery into the fall of the year followed, with
stabilization at a level considerably below 1926.
Bonds had an almost uninterrupted increase in
prices and stocks had a spectacular rise throughout
the year culminating in a peak in October. A
minor reaction in November was followed by a
partial recovery in December.

Merger movements in many industries were
begun and some important ones were consummated.
The net profits of many of the leading corporations
which were paying attention to research work
were larger in spite of severe competition and a

relatively poor year for business as a whole. Automatic machinery, efficiency of operation, and similar factors, were in evidence among successful corporations. On the other hand new incorporations fell off. The failures among smaller merchants and manufacturers were only slightly larger than the preceding year. Building activity again established a new record, but railroad earnings dropped a bit from the previous year. Retail merchants felt greater pressure than ever before from chain stores which expanded rapidly during the year.

Some bolstering was given to the general business situation during the latter part of the year by increasing exports. We closed the year by a favorable balance of trade of $580,000,000 or $200,000,000 better than the previous year. Gold, however, had commenced to leave the United States.

1928

The volume of business, as shown by the Babson-chart, recovered rapidly after the turn at the beginning of the year. After April it again declined to a low in August, but made a rapid recovery into the fall, closing the year about 5% above normal.

The balance of merchandise trade increased slightly in our favor over 1927. Increasing attention was paid to the development of foreign markets to make use of our excess capacity, to maintain large production schedules, and reduce overhead costs. Gold exports movement continued in 1928 until half a billion dollars net loss had occurred.

There was a slight improvement in the failure situation with the number of failures remaining about the same as in 1927. Liabilities, however, were lower than any year since 1925. The merger movement of 1927 continued throughout this year and industrial earnings again improved especially toward the close of the year. Displacement of labor by machinery became evident in the increase in unemployment.

The reduction of automobile output caused by the shutdown of the Ford plant in 1927 was succeeded in 1928 by the heaviest production in the history of the industry. The aeroplane industry also made rapid strides. The steel, copper and construction industries established new high records. The prosperity of these industries contributed largely to the maintenance of the general business situation on a high level. A noteworthy attempt at conservation marked the oil industry.

Bonds were generally weak though recovering somewhat toward the close of the year. Money rates increased markedly, commercial paper toward the year end averaging $5\frac{5}{8}\%$ compared with $4\frac{1}{8}\%$ twelve months before. The bull market in stocks culminated in the tremendous rise in November following the presidential election, when brokers' loans were over $6,000,000,000. Buying of stocks became the mania of all classes of people all over the country, to the detriment of their regular business. 6,000,000 share days became frequent. Radio rose to a high of 420.

1929

A most drastic decline in the stock market and a drop of more than 10% from the July peak in the physical volume of business activity marked the close of the country's record year. The principal factors contributing to the decline were the dropping off of new building and automobile sales and production. Nevertheless, both monthly and annual automobile production had reached the highest peak in history. Drastic curtailment followed.

The outstanding event of the year was the culmination of the stock market boom. Stock prices had been pushed up to absurd heights compared with existing earnings or compared with any sane estimate of future earnings. The collapse started early in September, gathered momentum until it reached panic proportions in October and November. The shrinkage was estimated at more than $30,000,000,000, the largest and most sudden drop in paper values in stock market history. Fortunes were wiped out over night and some financial houses were badly shaken.

The pyramiding of the investment trusts was one of the chief causes of the top heavy market. New security flotations for the first 10 months reached a new peak of $10,575,726,688; nearly $2,500,000,000 of which went into investment trust and holding company issues. This money was used to bid up the market leaders, and as the public began to get tired these were left in dealers' hands. Aided by undigested securities brokers loans as reported by the New York Stock Exchange rose to a peak of $8,549,000,000 in the midst of the stock market crash.

Interest rates were the highest since 1919–1920. Time money rose to $9\frac{1}{2}\%$ and commercial paper went to a daily average peak of $6\frac{3}{8}\%$. Call money on the other hand did not at any time exceed 20%, considerably below the maximum in 1919. The New York Federal Reserve discount rate rose from 5% to 6% in August but was dropped to 5% on November 1st and then later to $4\frac{1}{2}\%$. The decline in bond prices which began in 1928 was arrested in the latter part of 1929, when bonds sold at the most favorable levels since 1925.

The banking situation was uneven. The Federal Reserve Banks were in a strong position throughout the year, but the member banks were under some strain because of the large amount of loans both for business and stock market purposes. For the first time in 20 years the savings banks of the country failed to show an increase in deposits over the previous year.

International stabilization was furthered by the revision of the Dawes Plan under the committee headed by Owen D. Young, and the preliminary steps towards the establishment of an International Bank. The inflow of gold which began in the latter part of 1928 continued into 1929, but at a declining rate after the middle of the year.

Merchandise exports and imports showed a considerable increase over the year before.

Mergers in all lines featured 1929; a condition made easy by the eagerness of the public for common stocks. Some mergers were brought about by competition and some to permit capitalization of inflated book values.

The major downward trend in commodity prices continued throughout the year with but minor fluctuations on the up-side.

1930

1930 was a year of world wide depression. The decline in business activity which started in 1929 was temporarily halted during the early months of 1930, while many people stood by, wishing and hoping that a severe business depression could be averted. During these spring months the stock market had gained back about one half of its loss in the break, but on a resumption of the downward trend in business — which inevitably accompanies a depression year following a panic — stock prices continued to drop, with only slight rallies, until December 16th, when practically all "averages" made their lows for the year. Likewise the Babsonchart dropped until the lowest point for the year was registered in December.

Whereas in 1929 the stock market break was the dominating factor in the credit situation, in 1930 banking difficulties easily occupied this place. During the year there were 1,345 banks suspended, with total deposits aggregating $864,-715,000. Severe declines in stocks, commodities, real estate and second grade bonds led a frenzied public to lose confidence in the financial situation and make runs on banks.

The drop in commodity prices as registered by many current index numbers was about 20% from July, 1929, to December, 1930. Many basic commodities, such as raw sugar, rubber, silk and rayon sold at the lowest levels ever recorded up to that time. Other commodities such as copper, brass, iron, nails, tin, hides, leather, cotton, petroleum, sold down to pre-war levels. The huge world surplus of wheat sent the price of this commodity to very low levels.

An already crippled agriculture became almost paralyzed as a result of the drop in prices, numerous bank failures, and the worst drought the country had experienced since 1901.

Continued decline in the price of silver from about 52 cents an ounce in July, 1929, to the low price of 30½ cents in December, 1930, — unprecedented up to that time, — tended to unbalance international trade, particularly affecting those countries of the far east which depended upon silver as a monetary base.

Foreign trade of the United States fell off tremendously. Exports at $3,843,000,000 for 1930, compared with $5,241,000,000 in 1929. Imports at $3,061,000,000 compared with $4,399,-000,000 in 1929. The threatened dumping of products on the world markets by Soviet Russia had serious effects on international trade.

Money rates were continually reduced throughout the year. Prime commercial paper 4 to 6 months started the year at 4¾%–5% and closed at 2¾%–3%. Prime bankers' acceptances 90 days dropped from 3⅞%–4% in January to 1⅞% in December. Time loan rates dropped from 4¾%–5% to 2%–2½%. Call and renewal rates were also reduced by about one half during the year.

Gold stocks in the country increased from $4,293,000,000 in January, to $4,593,000,000 in December. However, during the year total deposits in all banks in the United States (exclusive of interbank deposits) decreased from $55,180,000,000 on October 4, 1929, to $52,784,000,000 on September 24, 1930.

Unemployment was a major problem with the total in that class variously estimated at 5,000,000 to 6,000,000 during the late fall months.

1931

A gradual recovery in volume of business took place from January, 1931, to the middle of the summer, the Babsonchart Index number of the physical volume of business increasing from 84.3 to 90.1 in April and holding at 88.2 in July.

It was only in the business elements of the economic structure, however, that this improvement took place. Commodity prices, especially those

commodities in international trade, declined rather
continuously. The Babson Industrial Commodity
Index declined from 129.7 in January to 109.7 in
December — a drop of 15%, while the Babson
Agricultural Commodity Index decreased about
37% to 65.5 in December.

Stock prices on the New York Stock Exchange
had a fair rally thru the first half of February, and
subsequently resumed their drastic decline. The
Dow-Jones average of industrials and rails stood
at 132.54 and 140.37 for the low and high respectively, in January. From this point, they declined
to a range of 52.60 to 66.33 in December. The
volume of securities in banks held as collateral for
loans by investors and speculators, who thought
that they were not margin traders if they obtained
a loan directly from the bank instead of from their
broker, was still too great. Liquidation of such
loans was attempted on every rally of substantial
proportion.

But the foreign situation, especially that of
Europe and the Far East (particularly Japan and
India) was not improving. There were tremendous American credit balances in Central European
banks arising from German and Austrian short-
term borrowings. The sudden failure of the Austrian Kredit Anstalt had startling repercussions in
Germany and in England and thence in the United
States by annihilating balances in those banks
which had been considered liquid. The sudden
withdrawal of gold from English banks, particularly by French bankers against their credit bal-

ances, resulted in a rapid depletion of English gold reserves forcing Great Britain to abandon gold redemption of its currency in September, 1931.

England's gold stocks in December totaled $587,622,000 which was a decline of 18% from the previous year. On the other hand, gold stocks in France increased 29% during this same period.

Commodity prices, therefore, in the American par currency rapidly declined as not only Great Britain but also Japan and Sweden and other lesser countries abandoned gold redemption. This rapid decline in commodity prices here resulted in a virtual world-wide panic occurring within an already severe depression.

Foreign trade of the United States continued to fall off rapidly — exports totaling but $2,424,-289,000 while imports totaled $2,090,635,000 — declines of 37% and 32% respectively.

1932

The Babson Index of the Physical Volume of Business declined almost without interruption from 88.2 in July, 1931, to 60.7 in July, 1932. The Dow-Jones Index of rail and industrial stocks declined from 120 to 27. This same index declined from 63.59 to 40.08 during 1932, the low point being reached in July.

Bond prices were affected in October, 1931, when it became evident that the physical volume of business was going to new lows, with commodity prices about 30% lower than in the plateau of the

'20's. Real estate was saleable only at absurdly low figures, in some cases foreclosure sales taking place at a small fraction of the face value of the mortgage. Thus, the margin of protection against bonds was obliterated; their values became determined by the same standards as stocks, and the entire structure of the nation was broken.

It was several months before this was appreciated by the general mass of the people; nevertheless deposits from savings banks were gradually being turned over to the government guaranteed postal savings system. One savings bank after another, and one commercial bank after another had to close its doors, currency in circulation increased tremendously as it was required by banks to stack up visibly in the cages to inspire confidence when there were rumors of a run.

In the midst of a demoralized stock and bond market in May, 1932, several industries decided to close up shop almost entirely, with the result that coal mining, the textile industry, the steel industry, and hundreds of other smaller industries were operated, for the United States as a whole, at perhaps not more than 25% of capacity. The building industry had suffered one continuous slump, all efforts at public works programs proving ineffective because that branch was a small part of the total. The average for the building industry was around 25% of the 1923-1929 levels.

Preliminary estimate of stocks of monetary gold in the U. S. on November 30 stood at $4,320,000,000.

Balance of trade of the United States was still favorable — exports exceeding imports by $295,212,000.

In June security liquidation dried up, a bond investment pool was formed under the auspices of New York banks headed by J. P. Morgan & Company, and a sharp upward movement ensued in both bonds and stocks. This soon became a terrific surge and reached a volume of trading climax in the middle of September at levels averaging 100% above the June figures. In some cases stocks were up 700% or 800%, but as a whole the levels of the spring before the decline were not reached. Business started upward for one month, but liquidation of bank loans continued; commodity prices after advancing sharply renewed their decline under the influence, at least partially, of continued depreciation of foreign currencies.

Average call money rates increased from 1.748 for 1931 to 2.056 for 1932. The Babson Industrial Commodity Index declined from 107.4 to 101.4 during 1932. The Babson Agricultural Commodity Index also decreased from 65.8 to 52.8 during the year.

1933

Serious banking disturbances gradually undermined confidence. On March 5, when the situation had reached a crisis, President Roosevelt declared a nation-wide "bank holiday." After this moratorium an increasing number of sound banks reopened; and the enactment of far-reaching emergency banking legislation revived confidence.

In April, the United States officially abandoned the gold standard. This was followed by a sharp upward surge in business and the market. Prices of many commodities soared and buying increased. In May, the Babson Index of Physical Volume not only broke through the peak of the rally of September, 1932, but also through the year-ago level. The Index rose rapidly in June and reached its high of 90 for the year in July.

Stocks participated freely in the general forward movement, the industrial averages rising from 55.40 on March 31 to a peak for the year of 108.67 on July 18; and the railroad averages from a low of 23.43 on February 25 to a high for the year of 56.53 on July 7. Bond prices also rose, although the lower grade issues were inclined to follow the more irregular movement of stocks.

The Babson Industrial Commodity Index rose from a low of 94.1 in February to a high of 138.1 in October, and finished the year at 136.0. The Babson Agricultural Commodity Index rose from a February low of 51.7 to a high of 92.7 in July, but stood in December at 83.4.

In March, employment and payrolls were at or near the lowest levels of the period thus far. During the following six months, however, the trend in both was smartly upward, until in September employment and payrolls were higher than at any time since the summer of 1931. Both showed moderate, but slightly more than seasonal, declines during the final quarter. Notwithstanding the improvement in labor conditions during the year, unemployment at the close of 1933 remained the major problem of the depression.

Money rates rose in the early months of the year, but failed to sustain the advance in subsequent months. Prime commercial paper 4 to 6 months rose from 1⅜% in January to a peak of 3% in March, but stood at 1⅜% in December. Average call money rates increased from 1% in January to 3⅜% in March, but were at or under the January level during the rest of the year.

Considerable improvement in the stability of the general business situation was indicated by the fact that failures in 1933 totaled only 20,308, or fewer than in any year since 1926, and comparing with 31,822 in 1932. Total liabilities of these defaults were $502,829,583, against $928,312,517 in 1932. Gold stocks in the country as of December 31, 1933, were $4,012,000,000, as compared with $4,045,000,000 on December 31, 1932.

1934

The Babson Index of Physical Volume advanced steadily through the year to a high of 85.0 in May. Moderate recessions occurred in the summer months. Business resumed its upward trend in the fall, but gains were moderate. The November Index stood at 72, or about 29% below normal.

The stock market during the first half-year did

little or nothing to distinguish itself. The industrial averages early in the year reached a high of 110.74, dropped in March to 98.76, but in April recovered to 106.55. In mid-July the market weakened and broke, and on July 26 the averages sagged to 85.51 — the low for the year. The performance of the market from late summer to late November was consistently good, considering the general business situation. On November 23 prices broke through their June peak to the highest level since the previous April.

Continued decline in net operating revenue of the railroads — the result largely of lower freight loadings and rising cost of transportation — naturally adversely affected railroad securities. The rail averages made their high for the year of 52.97 early in February, but by September 17 stood at 33.19, the low for the year thus far.

Heavy government expenditures on various relief and employment projects continued. As of June 15, 1934, the total public debt of the United States was a little over $27,000,000,000, or nearly half a billion dollars in excess of the former high record reached in August, 1919.

Among the outstanding features of the year were the ravages of one of the severest droughts in the history of the country. The financial status of the farmers, however, was materially improved, owing partly to farm mortgage financing and payment by the government for reduction of acreage and livestock curtailment. Farmers also received higher prices for their commodities.

The Babson Industrial Commodity Index remained at a fairly constant level during the first six months, starting the year at 136.5, and standing in June at 136.2. Moderate recessions marked the next four months, the October figure being 133.4. The Babson Agricultural Commodity Index moved up from its low of 88.1 in May to 97.4 in June, and to a peak of 114.9 in September, but dropped slightly in October to 113.2.

Money rates were extremely easy throughout the year. Prime commercial paper 4 to 6 months remained at 1¼% during January and February, at 1% for the next two months, eased to ⅞% in May, and from then on through October the rate was ¾%. Call money held at 1% through the year.

Factory employment and payrolls moved upward during the first five months of the year, but both showed moderate declines during the summer months.

The year showed marked improvement in the failure situation. Business failures for the first ten months totaled 10,299, against 17,939 for the like 1933 period. Total liabilities of these failures amounted to $150,867,954, against $450,275,000 in the corresponding 1933 period.

Two outstanding features of the year were the lagging of the capital goods industries and the continued formation of a huge base for credit expansion.

1935

After the readjustments which took place in the last half of 1934, fundamental conditions and continued large federal disbursements for relief and public projects lifted the Babsonchart Index of the Physical Volume of Business from 70 in September of 1934 to as high as 84.3 in March of 1935.

Stability marked the spring and summer of this year. This was so not only in the Babsonchart Index which held between 84.8 and 82.3 thruout the first three quarters of the year. In the final quarter, considerable impetus to business was given by an altered new model schedule in the automobile industry which made very active a period that heretofore was relatively inactive. Despite revised seasonal adjustments necessitated by this fact, business actually boomed in that industry, the output of automobiles for the year totalling 4,100,000 as against 2,800,000 in 1934.

By December the Index of the Physical Volume of Business had reached 95.6, less than 8% below the estimated position of the normal X–Y Line. This showed a recovery of 62% from the depth of the depression in March of 1933, and represented about as rapid progress as has heretofore ever been made from any of the depressions since 1870. Fundamental forces were definitely behind the revival as they had been during the rapid decline following the panic of 1929.

The Babson Industrial Commodity Price Index showed very little variation. So far, industrial and agricultural production was able to expand in sufficient proportion to counterbalance the inflationary tendencies as reflected by enormous increases in the federal deficit. By the end of 1935 the federal debt had reached $29,114,000,000 as against $26,246,000,000 at the end of 1934. Bank deposits had increased from $44,771,000,000 on December 31, 1934, to $48,950,000,000 on December 31, 1935. Most of this increase can be traced indirectly to the excess of federal expenditures over income, since the sum total of commercial and other private loans from banks, $20,327,-000,000, on December 31, 1935, showed a slight decrease from the amount of 1934.

This federal policy, coupled with the timidity of new capital to expand because of reform and interference from Washington, led to a condition of easy money in the investment markets because funds tended to concentrate into already existing securities. Thus, despite the mounting federal deficit the refunding of these federal loans, as well as the refunding of private loans was accomplished at decreasing interest rates. Consequently, stock market prices were buoyed up by a triple force:

(1) Decline in the return on other sounder investments made stocks more attractive so long as they were earning something more than 5% on cost. (2) As the year progressed, investors observed that 1935 was the first year of stable industrial and agricultural conditions, warranting higher prices because of the elimination of many old uncertainties and improving earnings. (3) The mounting federal deficits were a foreboding of the inflation-

ary developments getting out of hand.   The advantage of owning common stocks, representing property, instead of bonds representing a limited sum of money, was widely put into practice.   In fact, from a low point in March of 1935 until the recession in April of 1936, stock market averages closed higher every succeeding calendar month.

1936

The severe drought, worse than 1934's, served to strengthen agricultural prices and to raise farm income 11% over 1935.   June saw 3,000,000 World War veterans receive $1,600,000,000 in federal bonus bonds and checks.   Relief benefits continued, but as the Babson Business Index crossed the X–Y normal line reemployment permitted sharp cuts in these payments.

Despite the drought, railroads enjoyed increased traffic from other sources.   As many rail securities were still in default and reorganizations delayed, higher gross revenues flowed into urgent equipment and maintenance projects.   Caught at last by recovery forces, this major capital goods industry, with advancing building activity, became the prime spur, carrying general business across the X–Y line.

Roosevelt's landslide re-election inspired confidence in employees and consumers.   Employers aided the wave of good feeling by widespread wage advances and retail trade reached new recovery peaks.   The year closed with an unusual record of healthy progress in business and financial factors, but it also laid new labor problems at the door of 1937.

CHAPTER VIII

INVESTMENT SUPERVISION, WHAT SECURITIES
TO BUY OR SELL

YOU, as an investor, have two problems of major importance: First, *When* to buy or sell; second, *What* to buy or sell. The foregoing chapters have discussed how to obtain guidance in timing your purchases and sales from a study of fundamental conditions. Based upon the Law of Action and Reaction, the Babsonchart enables you to decide when business has turned the corner around the bottom of a period of depression and entered upon a broad trend upward. In such a buying zone, a skilfully selected and well diversified list of stocks is a favorable purchase for the long pull. Your buying of course should be outright, not on margin or borrowed money.

Likewise the Babsonchart enables you to decide when business is reaching levels of dangerous overexpansion; you are warned that eventual readjustment is inevitable. In such a selling zone, regardless of the unpredictable short swings, stocks are a sale from the long-pull viewpoint. Hence the Babsonchart, interpreted in the light of the Law of Action and Reaction with the aid of the area theory, gives you, as an investor, invaluable assistance in taking a sound long-pull position. Your judgment is fortified on the primary question of When to buy or sell.

WHAT TO BUY OR SELL

The secondary question of What to buy or sell, is the subject of this present chapter. As an introduction, it is well to glance at the progress of investment procedure during the past thirty years. The present generation of investors may not clearly recall the days when fundamental statistics were not systematically collected, compiled and interpreted. Even in those early days, however, the most successful investors contrived to gather, with much struggle and expense, a few barometric figures. These data were inadequate; and where each individual investor did his own collecting and compiling, the cost of even this fragmentary research was practically prohibitive.

The immense expansion and improvement of investment practice during the past thirty years has been mainly due to the growth of centralization and co-operation. The "clearing house idea" has been developed for the benefit of investors. This means: When fundamental statistics are centrally gathered and distributed to a group of investors, the cost to the individual is relatively nominal; and the scope and value of such work can be increased immeasurably.

Because of the extraordinary success of centralization applied to fundamental statistics, another need has been clearly indicated. This need is for some similar development in collecting and disseminating information and counsel on specific securities. For many years an approach has been made to the solution of this problem. More recently the objective has been closely reached in a plan known as the Supervised List, which we will now describe in detail.

EFFICIENCY OF SUPERVISED LIST

The Supervised List answers the investor's question, What to buy or sell, as the Babsonchart answers his question, When to buy or sell. Furthermore, the Supervised List — like the Babsonchart — is based squarely on methods of co-operation, centralization, and the clearing-house principle. The old idea was for each investor to put all his funds into some chance assortment of stocks and bonds. This hodge-podge of securities happened to catch his particular fancy. A portfolio of this personal kind might be scrutinized after a fashion; obviously, however, it could not receive fully competent supervision except at practically prohibitive cost.

On the contrary, when a group of investors decide to place at least a part of their funds in a carefully selected, well-diversified list, then here is a portfolio which can be given constant and complete supervision, — and at most reasonable cost to each investor. The fancied virtues of overloading a portfolio with "personal pets" are usually illusory and far outweighed by the solid advantages of possessing a list on which you have the protection of superior supervision.

Therefore, it can be emphasized that every person who buys, sells or exchanges stocks and bonds should consider the far-reaching merits of the principle of the Supervised List.   Regardless of whether an investor's intent is to protect his capital, enlarge his income or enhance his profit, — he needs the safeguard which is assured by this type of supervision.

ORIGINAL RESEARCH PARAMOUNT

One of the basic features of the Supervised List principle, is the assurance of original research. Only as investors pool their efforts by uniting on a Supervised List is it feasible to engage in true research and investigation.   Genuine research activities are out of the reach of the ordinary purse if each individual investor must bear the whole expense.   The kind of supervision made possible by the co-operative plan, provides originality and avoids the pitfalls of second-hand information.

From the earliest days of investment research one fundamental principle has stood out with especial clarity, namely: the soundest supervision of investments is based upon the wider viewpoint that includes not merely investments but all other economic factors.   A competent investment staff should include not alone the so-called "investment men" but a far broader personnel.   Such a staff should include groups giving their attention not alone to stocks and bonds, but also to commodity markets, labor conditions, wholesale and retail trade, industries, localities, and social trends.

BUSINESS BACKGROUND VITAL

In previous chapters it has been shown that companies can incur heavy losses by ignoring the trends of commodity prices; and can amass substantial profits by taking advantage of these tidal swings. The inventory losses caused by excessive buying on the brink of a price collapse have sometimes been severe enough to invite bankruptcy or reorganization; whereas the profits arising from inventory appreciation have sometimes equalled or exceeded the gains from the company's purely manufacturing or merchandising operations. Hence in watching a supervised list of investments, much weight must be given to commodity price tendencies from a long-pull viewpoint.

Another important guide in supervisory work is the situation and outlook in key localities throughout the country, as shaped by the locality's leading industries and activities. The rise or fall of buying power in any region, vitally affects not only local retailers but spreads back to wholesale establishments and ultimately reaches the manufacturers and the producers. It is a mistake for bondholders and stockholders to overlook what is happening in areas remote from financial centers. The purchasing power of all sections is a determinant of investment values.

Hence in supervisory studies it is most desirable to keep in touch with prospects for key localities and key industries. This requires that contacts shall be maintained with important trade associations and that diligent use should be made of trade journals. Among other nations, it is recognized and acknowledged that the trade press of America has no equal throughout the world. More real meat for investors is to be found in a good trade journal than in many a column of frothy investment chatter.

BREADTH OF VIEW ESSENTIAL

Each publication, however, specializes intensively within its own particular industry. It is professedly partisan, devoted exclusively to serving the interests of the industry which it represents. For investment purposes, therefore, it is highly important to check each industry against other industries — especially those in competition. Only by studying all industries, is it possible to make prejudices and partisanships "cancel out" and arrive at the net truth.

Trade associations and trade journals, however, tend to stress the attitude and activity of capital. For balanced investment judgment, of course, it is essential to understand also what is going on in labor circles. It is necessary to forecast the effect of labor conditions upon industries and upon individual companies and their securities. No supervision of investment holdings can be complete unless it includes intensive study of employment, payrolls, wage rates, hours of work, cost of living, strikes, and other labor conditions.

Labor tendencies are vital in two ways: (1) in effect upon corporate cost; (2) in effect upon public purchasing power. In keeping close watch of union activities and other labor elements, it is useful to obtain from news columns throughout the nation the local reports and comments on strikes and other labor troubles, wage changes, and employment trends. All such information, of course, must be verified and interpreted.

WATCH–TOWER OF THE PRESS

This same necessity of verification and interpretation applies to the use of the newspapers for keeping in touch with other tendencies. News must be not only watched but weighed. Nevertheless the press is an indispensable source of information. The investor naturally does not want to feel that "All I know is what I read in the newspapers"; but even such information would be very considerable provided it is not confined to the headlines. Particular attention should be given to the inconspicuous and buried items. Where the investor is most likely to go astray is through being over-influenced by what is headlined and played up or played down. It is not the news itself which is misleading but more frequently the angle and emphasis with which it is presented. Like the look-out men in the fire-tower in the forest, the investor should use a news story as a "sign of smoke," which should be tracked down and checked for its investment validity and significance.

There is also a wealth of information not alone in the newspapers but in magazines and periodicals, — not merely those of professedly investment or business purpose, but the general magazines as well.   Remember that if a publication continues to exist, it must maintain the interest of its readers. It must keep in tune with the times.   This means that any established and growing periodical is necessarily an indicator of the public trends which in turn are shaping investment values.   Another vast source of information — especially forward-facing facts — is the technical and scientific press.

It is true that success in investment is not learned chiefly in the volumes of a library but in the volumes of a market.   Nevertheless, it pays in investment supervision to watch continually for all new books in the fields of finance, business and economics; and to comb this material for information and ideas.   Steady consultation of current literature is very useful in developing improved supervision.   Books and periodicals offer much information, and also suggestion for independent research.   Investment supervision is immensely aided by booked shelves and filled files.   As such a collection of data grows over the years, it gathers much material that is as irreplaceable as it is indispensable.

Long before the Roosevelt administration diverted attention from Wall Street to Washington as a center of investment interest, competent investors were aware of the vast store of information in Government departments.   It is essential for thorough supervision to maintain a close examination of Government data, with systematic contacts and frequent visits to Washington.

One of the interesting developments of the past

quarter century is the growth of investment manuals and other information services in the investment field. The average investor lacks the time, as well as the inclination, to study and weigh the overwhelming masses of facts, figures and opinions that are represented by these services in the aggregate. To bring to bear upon a Supervised List this volume of data, is the function of centralized supervision.

ENDOWMENT FUNDS A FRUITFUL STUDY

An outstanding feature of the 1929–1932 collapse was the conspicuous strength of certain of the important endowment funds of churches, colleges, and other institutions. In various instances, owing to the efficiency of investment management, some of these funds exceeded by far the success of the majority of individual investors. One of the strongest elements in supervision is the contact with the managements of leading endowment funds. This does not mean any slavish patterning after their portfolios (which are a problem distinct from the requirements of individual investors), but rather intelligent co-operation. A corner stone of such work is a systematic "audit" to appraise the relative results obtained by such managements in their purchase, sales, and exchanges.

Important also is the meeting of minds among individual investors themselves for interchange of information and frank discussion of investment matters. Those who are co-operating in reducing the expense of investment supervision can profitably co-operate also in periodic discussions and informal forums. Furthermore, it is most desirable that the research workers and analysts in charge of a Supervised List meet and interchange ideas with the investors who are holding the List. When efficiently handled, national and local conferences may be made of utmost value.

Despite the great practical importance of the various points, it is impossible to over-emphasize the dollars-and-cents value of Originality. Originality is prized in literature and the arts, — but in investment information Originality is priceless! In the work of Supervision, you can put close to the head of the list of basic policies: Originality of research and providing reports with greatest speed. The world's most perishable product is not fruit or eggs, — but information. A report two weeks old may be too old: Causing losses instead of gains. That is one reason why investors should be wary of any purely synthetic service, compiled with pastepot and shears instead of first-hand originality. We reiterate the warning with which we opened this chapter: Avoid second-hand information!

CONTACT WITH FIELD

For originality of information and research it is vital of course that a supervisory staff should make systematic field studies. There is much real value to be gained from information, concerning managements for example, obtainable mainly in the field. This should be supplemented by a far-reaching network of correspondents and contacts,

— carefully chosen, effectively cultivated, and constantly used.

As an objective in such development, the purpose should be to have a representative, a correspondent, or a contact in each town of 2,500 or
more population. This would provide some form
of representation in more than 3,000 communities,
— which is approximately the number of counties
in the United States. This gives truly nation-wide
supervision.

Important also are contacts with the officials and
executives in the companies under supervision, or
under consideration for inclusion in a Supervised
List. The purpose of this, however, is to obtain
factual information rather than so-called "inside
tips" which sometimes prove to be propaganda of
doubtful value. Moreover, in all such investigations it is wise to avoid entangling alliances; these
might become a serious source of embarrassment in
event it becomes advisable to exchange out of the
companies' securities.

It is clear from the foregoing that supervision
of such scope and intensity calls for no small personnel and equipment; it needs a large plant,
elaborately outfitted and operated at heavy costs.
High-grade research and analysis are expensive
projects when performed with conscientious thor-
oughness. How can such work be made available
at reasonable expense to the individual investor?
By centralization, share-the-cost, co-operative,
"clearing house" principles. Through a Supervised List you obtain at nominal cost the benefits of

organized management applied to your personal holdings. Application of the Supervised List principles not uncommonly results in an appreciation of holdings very much greater than a neglected portfolio left to drift along without adequate supervision.

SUMMARY OF TESTS

As a summary of purposes, a Supervised List is founded upon certain vital principles, such as: (1) That a knowledge of fundamental business trends is essential to a successful list; (2) That protection comes through diversification; (3) That the greatest returns come from selecting the right groups of companies, conscientiously managed; (4) That constant vigilance by experts is absolutely essential; (5) That losses must be rigorously limited to determined proportions; (6) That the taking of profits and counterbalancing of losses should be handled systematically.

As a summary of policies: In developing, selecting and supervising a centralized list of stocks and bonds, such supervision finds guidance in the following tests of excellence.

A. Buy the securities of industries which are:
   (1) Rendering a needed service contributing to true welfare.
   (2) Not being exploited. This means you should buy before the group gets publicity and prices advance.
   (3) A "coming" rather than a "going" industry; preferring those of a "repeat" nature.

B. Invest in or loan to companies which:
   (1) Are honestly, economically, and efficiently managed, where the officers have adequate holdings and are not interested in too many outside activities.
   (2) Have either once been reorganized or been through a severe business depression.
   (3) Are reducing percentage of debt.
C. Invest in notes, bonds or stocks which:
   (1) Are well secured, both by assets and earnings.
   (2) Have reasonable market and are not handicapped by threatening maturities.
   (3) Are justified as to cost, considering what the Babsonchart indicates with respect to future prospects.

The experience of thirty years fully confirms the wisdom of the Supervised List principle. It meets most efficiently the investor's problems of what to buy and sell. We are convinced that the plan deserves the thoughtful consideration of every person who buys, sells, or exchanges stocks and bonds. It helps the investor to safeguard his capital, increase his income, enlarge his profits. Understand the principles of co-operative supervision: Such supervision, combined with its cardinal principle of diversification, brings you the most complete protection obtainable.

CHAPTER IX

CANADIAN FUNDAMENTAL CONDITIONS

IT is customary, in any broad analysis of business fundamentals, to consider the United States and Canada as a single economic entity as far as general business activity is concerned. It is, of course, true that there is a lag between any definite economic movement of general business conditions in the United States and those in the Dominion, but the indissoluble economic bond which links the two countries together prevents any long-lived prosperity north of the boundary line while depression exists on the other side.

It is an interesting fact, however, that since 1914, the average rate of increase of general business activity in Canada has been greater than in the United States. This has been particularly marked during the post-war period and the general record of Canadian business for 1928 showed the best of any year on record. Canada, with an area larger than the United States and with a population only one-tenth as great, is today standing on the threshold of tremendous possibilities. What is needed most is man power and the development of both natural resources and industries. This spells opportunities not only for Canadians, but for the people of the United States as well.

Every year sees new markets added to the trading list for Canada's exports. Approximately 20% of the net income of the Canadian people is derived from exports. The United States and Canada are each among the biggest customers of the other. The enormous wheat surplus of the Dominion alone is a tremendous factor in world commerce. The half-billion bushel wheat crop, which in 1928 marked the highest total in Canadian history, should be increased during the next few years, inasmuch as hundreds of thousands of new acres are being brought under tillage.

New inventions, chemical discoveries, mineral developments and improved facilities of transportation and communication have aided Canadian progress during the past few years. This forward looking development in the technological processes is bound to benefit new countries such as Canada far more than older nations.

We are exceedingly optimistic about the future of Canada during the next ten years. There was a short period after the war when the Dominion marked time, but she is now forging ahead under the most favorable auspices. It may be said that Canada today is no longer on the threshold of great prosperity; she has actually stepped across that threshold and is proceeding swiftly along the corridors of tremendous economic development. Her progress during the next decade is bound to attract the attention of the entire world. In order to measure accurately this economic progress research work has been going on toward a new Babsonchart of Canada.

Canadian Babsonchart.* — This new Babsonchart shows month by month in terms of the
physical volume of business activity the true
progress of Canadian business over a longer period
of time than that of any study hitherto available.
The preliminary result of this study of Canada,
which follows the same general lines as that of
the Babsonchart of the Physical Volume of the
United States Business Activity is shown on the
insert opposite page 372.

Major Groups. — In building up the Canadian
Babsonchart, business activity has been divided
into four main groups: (1), Mineral Production;
(2), Agricultural Production† as it comes into commercial channels through agricultural marketing;
(3), Manufacture; (4), Distribution. In each
group the activity in sufficient industries has been
taken to give a large percentage of the total activity
of the Dominion for that group. In each group
the more important series (listed on page 370),
have been selected, all of which, with the exception
of new building construction, can be had in terms
of physical volume rather than dollar value. To
put the series on a monthly basis however has
involved a considerable amount of original work.

The Type of Series. — Production series have
been used wherever possible, but for some impor-

* Valuable assistance in the compilation of this Babsonchart was given
by Mr. R. H. Coats, Dominion Statistician, and his associates, and by
other officials of the Dominion and of the Provinces. The more important
corporations in many fields, through the contribution of their confidential
data on production have assisted in making a more complete index than
would otherwise have been possible. The thanks of all interested in a study
of the growth and movements of Canadian business are due to those who
have so splendidly co-operated in this study.
† To prevent confusion of curves on the chart, these are not plotted.

tant industries such data are not available over the entire period, or for all branches of the industry. This necessitated the use in part of export or import series of basic materials to represent these industries. In the case of flour, newsprint, rubber and sugar the production series are available for a part of the period. A comparison of such data with imports or exports for overlapping periods has in every case shown marked parallelism. Hence, the change from one series to the other has been made by simple substitution of one series for another with an appropriate change in the weighting factors. In the case of lumber and wood pulp exports, no comparison of production and imports or exports was available, while in certain other instances such as imports of petroleum and raw cotton there is little or no domestic production.

No attempt was made to represent production by storage data, as for example in the case of milk, butter, eggs, cheese. There is little reason in theory for expecting a close similarity of movement between production and storage figures, and this has been borne out by the comparisons that have been made. Even export series, in every instance that we have studied, more nearly reflect production movement, although in some cases with a decided lag. Employment series, on the other hand, while less sensitive than production data, show a very close relationship to the latter in both cyclical and seasonal movements.

Seasonal Adjustment. — Each series is adjusted for seasonal variation determined on a changing

basis by a modification of the methods used by the
U. S. Federal Reserve Board, Prof. L. W. Hall,
and others. A seven-period moving median (arithmetic mean of the middle three items) for each
month of the year, of ratios of actuals to a 12-
months' moving average was used, both moving
means centered at the midpoints of their respective
periods. For the extreme years the curve of this
seven-period moving median was extended as
judged on the basis of the general trend of the
adjacent years. This has yielded excellent results,
and has convinced us that a constant seasonal index
is in many, probably in most, cases highly unsatisfactory. The trend line is fitted to the
data visually, pending the accumulation of more
data.

The Formula Used. — The formula used for com-
bining the individual series to obtain the index
number is the form of aggregative, $\frac{\Sigma P_0 Q_1}{\Sigma P_0 Q_0}$, that is
employed by the U. S. Bureau of Labor, the Federal
Reserve Board, Professor Fisher and others. This
formula is rated highly by Professor Fisher. It
is free of the statistical bias possessed by averages
of relatives, is easy to comprehend, simple to calculate, and makes possible a logical shift of base by
simple division.

The "ideal" formula chosen for the U. S. Babsonchart was considered less suitable in this case,
because the conditions requisite for its logical use
were not so nearly present in the Canadian data.
The use in certain cases of export or import series

Canadian Babsonchart Subjects	Average Net Value 1922-25 (In thousands)	Relative Weight % of Total	Relative Weight % of Group	Current Figures Computed By
Mineral Production	$147,911	7.5		Dominion Bureau of Statistics
Coal	60,108		40.6	Babson Statistical Organization
Gold	29,756		20.1	Department of Mines, Ontario
†Nickel	14,977		10.1	American Bureau of Metal Statistics
Silver	12,949		8.8	Babson Statistical Organization
Copper	11,880		8.0	American Bureau of Metal Statistics
Lead	12,788		8.6	Babson Statistical Organization
Zinc	5,453		3.7	
			99.9	
Agricultural Marketings	442,951	22.3		Dominion Bureau of Statistics
Cattle Sales	24,398		5.5	" "
Calves Sales	2,088		.5	" "
Hogs Sales	15,308		3.5	" "
Sheep Sales	4,069		.9	" "
Receipts of Wheat	343,376		77.5	" "
Receipts of Oats	19,710		4.4	" "
Receipts of Barley	16,213		3.7	" "
Receipts of Flaxseed	11,077		2.5	" "
Receipts of Rye	6,712		1.5	" "
			100.0	
Manufactures	1,066,306	53.8		
Wood and Paper	303,369		28.5	Newsprint Service Bureau
†Newsprint Prod. (From '15)	153,402		14.4	Dominion Bureau of Statistics
Planks and Boards Exports	111,616		10.5	" "
Woodpulp Exports	38,351		3.6	" "
Foodstuffs	186,181		17.5	" "
†Wheat Flour Prod. (From '20)	79,500		7.5	" "
Butter and Cheese Prod. ('15, '17-'26)	31,651		3.0	" "
Cheese Exports ('15, from '26)				" "
†Sugar Mfgt. (From 19)	30,347		2.8	" "
Hogs Slaughtered	17,929		1.7	" "
Cattle Slaughtered	13,070		1.2	" "

Canadian Babsonchart Subjects	Average Net Value 1922–25 (In thousands)	Relative Weight % of Total	Relative Weight % of Group	Current Figures Contributed By
Sheep Slaughtered	$2,513		.2	Dominion Bureau of Statistics
Canned Salmon Exports‡	11,171		1.0	" " " "
Building	152,542		14.3	Babson Statistical Organization
Iron and Steel Products	152,554		14.3	Dominion Bureau of Statistics
Steel Ingot Output	76,278		7.2	" " " "
Pig Iron Production	19,069		1.8	" " " "
Iron and Steel Imports	57,207		5.4	" " " "
Textiles	149,808		14.0	Dominion Bureau of Statistics
Cotton—Raw—Imports	74,904		7.0	" " " "
Cotton—Yarn—Imports	37,452		3.5	" " " "
Wool—Raw—Imports	18,726		1.8	" " " "
Wool—Yarn—Imports	18,726		1.8	" " " "
Tobacco	40,791		3.8	Dept. of National Revenue, Canada
Cigarettes	20,716		1.9	" " " " " "
Tobacco and Snuff	9,717		.9	" " " " " "
Cigars	10,358		1.0	" " " " " "
Automobiles and Accessories	35,443		3.3	Dominion Bureau of Statistics
Passenger Car Production	35,443		3.3	" " " "
Rubber Goods	32,538		3.1	Babson Statistical Organization
Petroleum Products	13,080		1.2	Dominion Bureau of Statistics
Petroleum—Crude—Imports	13,080		1.2	" " " "
Distribution	325,049	16.4	100.0	Dominion Bureau of Statistics
Net Ton Miles Freight†	325,049		100.0	Dominion Bureau of Statistics

‡Silver exports used prior to 1921.
†Exports or imports substituted prior to years indicated.

for all or part of the period to represent production; the combination of such imperfectly comparable series; and the decision to use "value added per unit of production" as a basis for weighting, made necessary the introduction of fixed weights to a much greater extent than in the case of U. S. Babsonchart, thus vitiating one of the fundamental advantages of the "ideal" formula (Fisher, No. 353).

Weighting and Base Period. — The period 1922–'25 was chosen as the base for comparison because the use of a post-war period for this purpose seems necessary in a growing country where the former levels of production are being left behind. This same period was chosen as the weighting basis as it is the latest period for which "value added" data for manufactures was then available. A longer base was not chosen because of the abnormal conditions in 1921. Finally, a recent base period for weighting is desirable to minimize error in the more recent index numbers.

In the formula used the weights are fixed nominal prices, the value added per unit of production (total value in the case of mineral production and agricultural marketings). But such nominal prices have not remained the same over the entire period, since actual prices, value added, and the representative character of series used have changed. The effects of changing base for earlier periods was investigated, using the 1910 weighting base for 1909–1912 and the 1915 base for 1913–1917, and the 1919 base for 1918–1921. The index numbers so calculated have been lower by a fairly constant amount than the index numbers for corresponding years on the 1922–25 weighting base. We have, therefore, taken the geometric average of the results obtained on the two different bases for each year and month for the above periods. This does, in fact, give a modified form of the "ideal" formula.

The Trend Line. — A tentative smooth trend line for the entire period covered by the chart, determined by the best visual approximation, shows what might be called the normal rate of growth of the physical volume of business over that period. We do not offer this as a final X–Y Line, for from some points of view it is logical to consider the years since the depression following the war as typical of the real trend, and such an X–Y Line based on that period may later be found to be a better measure for current business conditions.

FINAL WORD TO READERS

It occurs to the author that this book may possibly be the means of causing some persons who will not give the proper study to statistics and general conditions, to invest in stocks. I therefore advise every reader that, if he is unwilling to invest about one hundred dollars a year in collecting and tabulating the necessary statistical data, it is better to buy no stocks whatsoever, but to confine all investments strictly to high grade bonds such as are recommended by conservative bond dealers.

For those wanting more specific information on fundamental investment practices and procedure we have prepared the book "Investment Fundamentals," published by Harper & Brothers, New York.

Success comes not so much by *forecasting*, as by *doing* the right thing at the right time and always being willing to change one's course. For this reason much more money is made by directing one's business and investments with a purpose of *preventing* panics than by trying to *forecast* panics and then pursuing a policy based upon the belief that said forecast must prove true. With this object in view, I offer the services of my large organization that merchants, bankers and investors may always be best prepared for whatever the future is most likely to bring forth.

ROGER W. BABSON.

"No sir, ye can bet it ain't th' people that have no money that causes panics. Panics are th' result iv too manny people havin' money. Th' top iv good times is hard times an' th' bottom iv hard times is good times. Whin I see wan man with a shovel on his shouldher dodgin' eight thousand autymobills I begin to think 'tis time to put me money in me boot.

"Don't git excited about it, Hinnessy, me boy. Cher up. 'Twill be all right tomorrow, or th' next day, or sometime. 'Tis wan good thing about this here wurruld, that nawthan lasts long enough to hurt. I have been through manny a panic. I cud handle wan as well as Morgan. Panics cause thimsilves an' take care of thimsilves."

— *Dooley.*

GENERAL INDEX

INDEX

INDEX

BABSON'S REPORTS

on the

FUNDAMENTAL CONDITIONS OF BUSINESS AND FINANCE

Two basic Services (Business and Financial) designed to furnish merchants, manufacturers, investors and bankers with impartial, up-to-the-minute information on the subjects mentioned in this book.

BUSINESS SERVICE INCLUDES:

A. Barometer Letter and Babsonchart

The weekly Barometer Letter and Babsonchart analyzes the current business and financial situation; and keeps you thoroly informed on fundamental conditions.

The Barometer Letter is in no way designed to replace original thought on the part of clients, and should not be regarded as a "market letter" in any sense. It is more in the nature of an engineering report, affording a helpful check and comparison when determining what course of action and policy is the most profitable. In connection with the Barometer Letter, a summary index figure is also given which shows the changes from the normal of general business.

IMPORTANT ADDENDA

The Babsonchart, a vital part of this bulletin shows graphically the trend of this index figure during the past thirty years, brought up to date each week. It gives a comprehensive summary of the past, an exact record of the present, and the clearest possible indication of the future business of the United States. By watching from month to month the movements of the Babsonchart, one can see at a glance the trend of general business, and also the tendency of commodity and security prices. The close relation which these latter subjects bear to general business conditions is clearly indicated by the Babsonchart.

Graphic Outlook

The Barometer Letter also contains once each month the Graphic Outlook. The Graphic Outlook gives you an accurate view of the fundamental trend of the most important separate Business and Financial Barometers. Information is collected from hundreds of sources, boiled down, and furnished you on a single page. Here important statistical data are placed in graphic form where your eye can readily select that which you require. The Graphic Outlook gives you instantly the correct comparison of any of the forty-one basic Barometers of Business and Finance with the current month, a year ago, and the elapsed portion of the current year, with the same period of the preceding year.

B. Commodity Bulletin

The Commodity Bulletin gives our analysis and forecasts on the general commodity situation, and our specific advices on over 100 individual commodities. Our advice on the individual commodities is based on a close study of the general business situation as measured by the Babsonchart. Clients are thus enabled to keep their buying policies adjusted to the changing phases of the business cycle. Because of the number of commodities covered, clients are able to plug many small leaks by installing more efficient buying of secondary materials, which are used in the operation of the plant or in connection with the process of manufacturing or the conduct of the business.

C. Management Bulletin

The Management Bulletin covers matters of sales, advertising, credit, employment, etc. Wages are recognized as one of the most important factors determining purchasing power. Therefore, one of the features of this Bulletin is reports of wage changes. On the down side of the cycle it was important to know where purchasing power was shrinking because of wage cuts. On the up side of the cycle it means a reduction of selling expense to concentrate in sections where wages are being increased.

There is great flexibility in the editing of this Bulletin. Special effort is made to concentrate on those problems which are of most pressing importance at the moment. The human factor is of such great significance in our business future that in handling matters which relate to employment, wages, hours, working conditions, etc., we take into consideration the fundamental social forces which must be carefully watched by those responsible for the management of business, investments and for stable employment for workers.

Especial attention is given to changes in government and men's attitude toward government in industry. Therefore, this Bulletin immediately covered intensively the various stages of the recovery program. Changes in the worker's attitude toward his employer and in the relation between producer and consumer are also carefully followed. An effort is made to interpret current problems of management against the background of the great fundamental laws of governing human behavior.

Sales Map

Each month the Babson Sales and Credit Forecast Map portrays the sales situation thruout the United States. By means of three different colors for the states and three symbols for the cities we give our views as to the relative sales outlook. Special three months' forecasts are given for 150 leading cities each an indicator for an important trading area. As a result clients can plan their advertising and sales activities in advance and concentrate on those territories where sales, credit and collections should be best.

FINANCIAL SERVICE INCLUDES:

A. Barometer Letter and Babsonchart

As the Barometer Letter and Babsonchart, with Graphic Outlook, deal with general business conditions, they go with both our Business and our Financial Services, since it is absolutely necessary for every one, whether he be merchant, banker, or investor, to form his policies in accordance with fundamental conditions.

These bulletins give financial clients the basis for determining when to buy and when to sell securities in order to take advantage of the long swings of the stock market. Second only in importance to the knowledge of when to buy and when to sell, however, is the knowledge of how to handle funds at the buying and selling zones.

It must be remembered that these bulletins will not help the day to day trader, for no one can tell what a particular security will do. When, however, these bulletins are used in connection with the rest of the Service, they fill a very definite need of the conservative purchaser who desires all of the profit that is consistent with safety.

B. Supervised Lists of Bonds and Stocks

We constantly keep you supplied with these Lists of selected issues which we believe fulfill the requirements of a proper investment account. Most important: We endeavor to notify you of all recommended changes in the Lists to help you sell or switch before it is too late! Others get you "in"—we are equally zealous in the desire to get you "out."

Our effort is to make and to keep these Lists sound. You will receive a Supervised List every two weeks,—the bond and stock List alternating. These Lists will contain only fully seasoned issues, usually listed on the New York Stock Exchange or traded on the Curb. So far as feasible the Lists are "triply" diversified: (1) Diversified as to industries; (2) Diversified as to companies; (3) Diversified as to localities. Our conclusions are carefully compared with the portfolios of over twenty of the most ably-managed institutional funds in America.

New issues are not included in the Lists until the artificial support of the security house has ceased with the disposal of the issue, and its real level is established. Let others experiment with new, raw issues. It was these new issues which caused many banks and investors their losses. We intend that all securities admitted to our Lists shall have a sufficiently broad and active market to facilitate quick exchange when deemed desirable.

By writing or wiring us at any time, clients can obtain at once, for strictly confidential use, a copy of the Supervised List revised to date to include latest recommendations.

Confidential Releases

Specific buying, selling, or exchanging recommendations are given to you in Confidential

Special Releases. Whenever necessary (generally on a Saturday) at the close of the New York Stock Market our experts consider the whole situation and prepare appropriate recommendations. This final advice is immediately telegraphed to our territorial distributing offices from which it is mailed to our clients. This enables you to receive almost instantly by this special "telemail" system this important information. By this method the client in California gets our recommendation just as quickly as the client in Massachusetts.

Our intention that clients get the Release usually on Mondays makes this Service an instantaneous and unequalled one. All of our recommendations are given on our Special Release Cards and in our regular Bulletins. Whichever method will get the information to the client the quickest will be used. We reserve the right to omit recommendations whenever conditions do not warrant them and to make recommendations at any time if conditions indicate that this should be done.

C. Supervised List Bulletin

The Supervised List Bulletin gives you a resumé of the financial and investment situation and outlook. In this Bulletin you get our confidential discussion and forecast of the specific group of securities currently most interesting to the majority of investors. This Bulletin also gives our preliminary opinions on the most prominent of the bonds recently offered to the public. It calls attention to important bond redemptions; discusses new issues with special reference to utility franchises; and contains write-ups on industries with recommendations. It is replete with outstanding lessons and priceless investment principles.

The Supervised List Bulletin discusses the current situation of stocks and bonds and matters of specific interest to the investor. It gives information that will help our clients in the investment of their funds. A large number of the stocks and bonds in our Supervised Lists are reviewed in this Bulletin in an endeavor to keep clients posted on current high spots relative to the companies and their securities.

— ◐ ◑ —

The bulletins described are the basis for our Financial and Business Services. They are available to business men and investors in various combinations and at different prices. Our aim for the past thirty years has been to supply through these bulletins authoritative information on fundamental business and financial conditions, the sound foundation upon which concrete plans can be based. By shaping your business and investment policies to meet changing conditions — in accordance with the law of action and reaction — you can make far more satisfactory progress and profits.

BOOKS BY ROGER W. BABSON

1907 INVESTMENT STOCKS. WHAT AND WHEN TO BUY—Roger W. Babson.

1909 BUSINESS BAROMETERS—Roger W. Babson.

1912 STOCKS AND BONDS—Babson Statistical Organization, Incorporated.

1912 COMMERCIAL PAPER.

1913 THE FUTURE OF THE WORKING CLASS—Babson's Statistical Organization, Incorporated.

1914 THE FUTURE OF THE CHURCHES—Babson's Statistical Organization, Incorporated.

1914 THE FUTURE OF THE NATIONS—Babson's Statistical Organization, Incorporated.

1914 THE FUTURE METHOD OF INVESTING MONEY—Babson's Statistical Organization, Incorporated.

1914 THE FUTURE OF THE RAILROADS—Babson's Statistical Organization, Incorporated.

1914 PROSPERITY AND HOW IT MUST COME—Babson's Statistical Organization, Incorporated.

1915 THE FUTURE OF US BOYS—Babson's Statistical Organization, Incorporated.

1915 THE FUTURE OF SOUTH AMERICA—Little, Brown & Co.

1915 THE FUTURE OF WORLD PEACE—Babson's Statistical Organization, Incorporated.

1919 W. B. WILSON AND THE DEPARTMENT OF LABOR—Brentano's.

1920 A CENTRAL AMERICAN JOURNEY—World Book Co.

1920 COX THE MAN—Brentano's.

1920 FUNDAMENTALS OF PROSPERITY—Fleming H. Revell Co.

1920 RELIGION AND BUSINESS—Macmillan Co.

1921 MAKING GOOD IN BUSINESS—Fleming H. Revell Co.

1922 NEW TASKS FOR OLD CHURCHES—Fleming H. Revell Co.

1923 BUSINESS FUNDAMENTALS—B. C. Forbes Publishing Co.

1923 ENDURING INVESTMENTS—Macmillan Co.

1923 WHAT IS SUCCESS?—Fleming H. Revell Co.

1924 RECENT LABOR PROGRESS—Fleming H. Revell Co.

1927 A CONTINUOUS WORKING PLAN FOR YOUR MONEY—Babson's Statistical Organization, Incorporated.

1927 INSTINCTS AND EMOTIONS—Fleming H. Revell Co.

1928 A BUSINESS MAN'S CREED—Fleming H. Revell Co.

1929 STORING UP TRIPLE RESERVES—Macmillan Co.

1930 EASY STREET—Fleming H. Revell Co.

1930 NEW WAYS TO MAKE MONEY—Harper & Bros.

1930 INVESTMENT FUNDAMENTALS—Harper & Bros.

1932 CHEER UP—Fleming H. Revell Co.

1932 FIGHTING BUSINESS DEPRESSIONS—Harper & Bros.

1932 WASHINGTON AND THE DEPRESSION—Harper & Bros.

1933 FINDING A JOB—Fleming H. Revell Co.

1934 WASHINGTON AND THE REVOLUTIONISTS—Harper & Bros.

1934 THE NEW DILEMMA—Fleming H. Revell Co.

1935 WHAT ABOUT GOD?—Fleming H. Revell Co.

1935 ACTIONS AND REACTIONS—Harper & Bros.

1936 CHURCH ATTENDANCE—Fleming H. Revell Co.

1936 THE COMING REVIVAL—Fleming H. Revell Co.

BABSON INSTITUTE

The complexity of modern business calls for special training for those who would attain the highest success with the least waste and loss of time, energy and money. The Babson Institute was organized to give this training in a business environment and by the use of business methods.

Babson Institute is operated by trustees under the educational and charitable laws of Massachusetts. It aims to give its students a thorough understanding of the fundamental principles involved in Production, Finance, Distribution and Management. The work covers these four branches of business activity:

1. Practical Economics and the Handling of Commodities.
2. Financial Management and the Care of Property.
3. Distribution and the Control of Markets.
4. Management and the Handling of Men.

THE THREE DIVISIONS

The work of the Babson Institute is carried on under the three following divisions:

DIVISION ONE is known as the *Resident Division* and comprises an intensive one to two years' course at Babson Park. This course is designed for men who are likely to come into responsibility or property. No formal examinations are required, but men must be sufficiently mature and seriously interested.

DIVISION TWO is our *Extension Division* prepared for those who wish additional training in the fundamentals of Finance, Economics and Psychology, but who are unable to come to Babson Park for personal work. In so far as is possible it covers, through printed Lesson Bulletins, the same subjects taken up at our Resident School. *There is also a special correspondence course for Bond Salesmen.*

DIVISION THREE is our *Personnel Service Division*, the purpose of which is to build up the goodwill of employees and help direct their thoughts along constructive lines.

This service consists of two parts — "Stories" which are distributed through Pay Envelopes (or other convenient means) every two weeks, and "Posters" which are put up in a conspicuous place weekly.

DIVISION FOUR is the School For Positions. This pioneer work begins with analyzing the person to decide upon a suitable vocation. He is then given appropriate training. Finally he is provided with contacts to help him secure employment in some field for which he is best fitted.

Further information regarding any of these Divisions will be sent upon request.

BABSON INSTITUTE
BABSON PARK, MASS.

DATE DUE

	261-2500		Printed in USA